For Eddik

REBELL

END OF THE BE

At last!
Doug McArthur

Douglas McArthur

www.douglasmcarthurauthor.com

All characters in this publication are fictitious
and any resemblance to real persons, living or
dead is purely coincidental.

ISBN 978 1 8382 1802 7

Printed and bound by CPI Group (UK) Ltd
Croydon, CR0 4XY

Published by
Douglas McArthur Media
Abergavenny, Wales

www.douglasmcarthurauthor.com

Grateful thanks to my long-suffering wife Lu, who has supported my quest for Romans in far-flung fields up and down the country.

Thanks also to editor and proof-reader Sandra Dronfield and cover designer Ken Dawson.

Thanks also to my beta readers whose fresh eyes made me re-think certain passages.

PLACE NAMES

Aqua Arnemetiae	Buxton
Brigantia	Land of the Brigantes
Burrium	Usk
Caletum	Calais
Camulodunum	Colchester
Deva	Chester
Durobrivae	Water Newton, Cambridgeshire
Eboracum	York
Gobannion	Abergavenny (pre-Roman name)
Isca	Caerleon
Isurion	Aldborough, West Riding
Isurium Brigantum	Roman name of Isurion
Levobrinta	Forden Gaer, Montgomery
Lindum	Lincoln
Londinium	London
Mamucium	Manchester
Mediolanum	Whitchurch, Shropshire
Melandra	Nr Glossop, Derbyshire
Portus Dubris	Dover
Rigodunum	Brigantium settlement Castleshaw
Segontium	Nr Caernarfon
Seteia Astuarium	Nr mouth of river Dee
Verulamium	St Albans
Ynys Gybi/Caergybi	Holyhead (Holy Island)
Yr Wyddfa	Mount Snowden

Rivers

Sabrina (Roman)	Severn
Hafren (Celt)	Severn
Tamesis	Thames
Wysg	Usk

(Isle of) Mona	Anglesey

BRIGANTIA
ISURION
EBORACUM
RIGODUNUM
MAMUCIUM
YNYS GYBI
MONA
SETEIA
MELANDRA
SEGONTIUM
ASTUARIUM
DEVA
AQUA ARNEMETIAE
MEDIOLANUM
LINDUM
YR WYDDFA
LEVOBRINTA
R Hafren
R Sabrina
DUROBRIVAE
GOBANNION
R Wysg
BURRIUM
VENTA SILURUM
ISCA
CAMULODUNUM
R Tamesis
VERULAMIUM
LONDINIUM
PORTUS
DUBRIS
CALETUM

Rebellion is the second book in a trilogy about the invasion of Britannia by the Roman legions. The first book, The Red Mountain, starts off with preparation for the invasion of the west, a wild mountainous region we now know as Wales, peopled by fiercely protective tribes prepared to fight to the death to keep their freedom.

Unfortunately their tactics were non existent. They traditionally worked themselves into a frenzy then rushed madly at the enemy, engaging him with swords, clubs and spears. That may work against another hill tribe but against the martial skill, discipline and training of the Legions it was a recipe for disaster.

I enjoyed writing Red Mountain and Rebellion and look forward to starting on the third, yet to be named, because they are based on the slim but tantalisingly few facts that have come down the ages to us.

I used these facts to make my stories and colour my characters. I hope you enjoy them and will stay with me for the third book in the series. This inevitably raises the question, what happens next?

The answer? I don't know. We'll all have to wait and see.

REBELLION
THE END OF THE BEGINNING

Waiting to go into battle is never easy. From the hardened veteran to the newest fresh-faced recruit, there are always demons. The nerve-jangling doubts as the battle draws ever nearer, sheer naked terror, anger, don't let me disgrace myself and let me come back alive and in one piece, all race round the mind.

The young soldier looks to his older colleagues and envies their seeming lack of nerves, but it's all a charade. The veterans have seen it all before - the broken bodies, the dead comrades - but by the grace of their gods, so far anyway, they have been lucky. Will this battle be the one? Will they be carried from the field - blind, maimed, dead? Try not to think about it, they say quietly but fiercely to themselves. Surrender to the discipline and get stuck in, that's the way to stay alive, they say to each other. Just get it done, then thank the gods and laugh about it afterwards. As it has been through the ages. Just get it done.

This time, the prize was a big one. On one side, the two biggest and most warlike tribes in what would become Cambria, a mountainous land-mass on the western side of Britannia, defending a seemingly unassailable ridge. On the other, two battle-hardened legions of Rome. The tribes were feeling confident. They had already seen off one suicidal frontal assault ordered by a Roman commander quite capable of sacrificing the lives of his men if it meant personal glory for him. What they didn't know was that a spy in their midst, Lenculus of Alesia, a

Roman auxiliary, had found the back door to their position and he was just about to turn the key.

Silence dampened the first cohort of crack Roman legionaries shuffling warily across a makeshift bridge, giving safe passage through the swamp that was the Celtic first line of defence. Weapons were covered in sacking and they wore more dark sacking over booted feet, helmets, body armour and shields. As well as effective camouflage, the sacking's main job was to deaden any noise from the column.

This was the witching hour, just before dawn, the infantryman's favourite time to move into attack formation, when hopefully the enemy's concentration was at its lowest ebb.

The night was pitch-black, the moon blanketed by a low cloud base, helped by an icy mist rising from the dank, murky swamp.

At the other side of the swamp, they cautiously stepped off the makeshift bridge of planks lashed together over bundles of tree branches, feeling their way onto unknown land. Waiting for them, crouched in bushes, was a pathfinder, one of the legion's special forces, dressed like a local in a rough wool tunic smeared in animal grease to keep the elements out. He silently pointed to another pathfinder, crouching by a single track which disappeared up into the dense forest. In single file they stealthily followed him through the trees covering a steep rocky hill, cursing under their breath, to be stopped before they breasted the top.

Each soldier firmly grasped the trailing cloak of the man in front of him. None of them knew where they were going, trusting completely that their guide knew the route. And no one wanted to lose the column in the dark.

Just before the top of the hill, the guide pathfinder crouched and stretched his arms out, the signal for the cohort to spread out in a line following the contour of the hill and then lie down on the dewy grass.

These were the most experienced eight hundred fighting men of the First Cohort, XX Valeria Victrix Legion. They had been specially tasked, said their centurion, to spearhead the attack by no less a personage than Publius Ostorius Scapula, second governor of Britannia. Their job was to lead the surprise attack on the Celtic army waiting for them on the front edge of a sheer ridge.

The Celts, believing their rear to be protected by natural obstacles, would pay a shattering price for ignoring the danger of leaving their flanks and rear exposed.

They confidently expected the next attack to be a repeat of the debacle when so many Roman lives had been lost in a disastrous frontal assault. But they were wrong; there was an alternative, found by Lenc the spy, which his commander seized on. Thanks to Roman engineering ingenuity, a specially selected band of the most experienced men in the legion forded a seemingly impregnable swamp at the rear of the Celtic camp. They then silently climbed up a forested hill to a position above and behind the camp to wait for dawn. When they went to ground, they were just below the brow of the hill, with the tented camp one hundred paces below them. The ranks of Celtic warriors waited in the trees another three hundred paces beyond that, on the murderous sheer ridge, looking in the wrong direction, watching for an attack that was not going to happen.

The Celts were facing the wrong way, expecting the Romans to repeat their earlier mistake and attack up the suicidal sheer ridge, whereas the legion veterans were safe and undetected on the back of the hill. The cohort lay quietly, ignoring the cold and damp, waiting for dawn, when they would sweep down on the unprotected Celtic rear with as much aggression and fury as possible.

These men were proud of being the chosen men of their supreme leader, but tried not to show it, merely shrugging off the governor's testimonial to their fighting spirit. But they were quietly pleased with his encouragement and every man was determined to put on a good show. After all, the governor wanted them in the front line because they were the best. And that was the end of it.

As they lay on the damp grass, they were aware of more of the legion quietly filing in behind them and lying down.

The legionaries could only move into position in single file and in strict silence, so when dawn came up, whoever was on the hill would make up the attack shield wall and the rest of the legion would just have to catch up as quickly as possible.

"We don't need that lot," was the confident whisper, "We can crack this ourselves."

Some of the men managed to sleep as they lay on the wet ground then, as dawn almost reluctantly changed the landscape from blackness to a murky grey, the signal was whispered from man to man to stand by.

At the end of the attack line, kneeling with them, was a man dressed in tribal clothing of homespun wool and a long cloak, but carrying a Roman cavalry sword. His head was shaved but his beard was full and clipped under his chin.

"Pathfinder," one of the soldiers whispered confidently.

As the forest behind them started to take shape in the lightening sky, the pathfinder Agrippa, commanding the legion's special forces, motioned to the senior centurion. The centurion nodded, and at his signal every man knelt, careful not to show themselves above the hill ridge-line. Sacking covers were cast aside, swords unsheathed carefully with a soft metallic scrape, and shields braced on left arms.

They cautiously crept forward to the breast of the hill, swords ready, then crouched again, waiting for the signal to unleash death and destruction, which was not long in coming.

"If I hear a sound from any of you lot, I will personally rip your throat out," growled the centurion.

"Lord, I'm desperate for a fart - is that allowed?" whispered one wag to the delight of his mates in earshot and took away some of their tension.

"Fart now and I'll jam my sword so far up your arse you'll never fart again," the centurion furiously hissed.

They were fired up now, ready to go, all eyes on their centurion, who finally raised his sword, then swung it, pointing over the rise of the hill. "Right lads, let's show them why we're the best," he growled.

As one, they stood and stepped off, quickly breasting the top of the hill and starting down the other side. Silently, their pace increased until they were jogging steadily downhill, careful not to skid on the damp grass. They ran, shields up, swords out, towards the still silent, tented camp of the Ordovices and Silures, the two Celtic tribes they had come to fight. Their orders were simple. Don't stop, do maximum damage to the camp, kill anyone in the way, but above all, fight through the camp and form a shield wall beyond. Retaliation was certain to come from the warriors on the ridge waiting in vain for another frontal assault. Which wasn't going to happen.

The centurion raised his sword. "Twentieth," he roared, leading the grim march towards the camp. Only then did a puzzled Ordovician sentry turn to look uphill. His eyes widened at the sight of two hundred legionaries running straight at him, shields up, armour shining and pointing their swords forward. He gulped, swallowed, then at last shouted the alarm, but too late. He was the first casualty of the Roman assault, cut down by a sword slash which almost took his head off, as he tried to run to the tents for protection.

With an exultant shout, the spearhead soldiers thundered after their centurion, all wanting to be first to charge through the Celtic tents. Their bloodlust was up as puzzled tribespeople emerged from shelter, rubbing their eyes, then seeing the approaching wall of armour, turned and ran, anywhere away from men hell-bent on extracting revenge for their dead comrades on the ridge.

One old man, hair wild, still half asleep, stood by himself, unafraid and hefting his sword as the enemy bore down on him. Almost contemptuously he was swept aside and trampled before he could swing his longsword. The cohort did not even break step.

The thought of plunder in the tents did not stop the avenging Romans, who only paused to throw burning embers onto the tents or kill anyone in their path. They knew their mission, plunder was something to look forward to when the battle was won. At the lower end of the camp, the centurion stood in the open, facing his oncoming troops with his arms extended outwards. "Shield wall," he bellowed. "Shield wall."

With precision discipline the ranks skidded to a halt on the dewy grass and immediately jostled into their lines, shields interlocking at the front, three deep. So far it was not an impressively long shield wall, but already auxiliary archers were speeding to the two ends of the wall to dissuade any attackers from trying to turn the edges. As the wall formed, the next legion wave, with heavier armour and carrying spears to hurl over the shield wall at the attackers, reached the brow of the hill and without pausing, hurried through the burning tented camp to form the second rank of the shield wall. Then finally the wall was completed by the Hestati, the youngest and fittest of the legion, but also the least experienced.

As they shuffled in their ranks in anticipation of the Celtic assault, a grizzled veteran on the end of his line welcomed the newcomers as they pressed into position. "Stay with me, kid. Watch and learn, and I'll show you how to stick a Celt."

The youngster swallowed and gripped his shield in front of him, with his gladius short sword ready to flick out at the side of the shield just as he had been taught in his long hours of training. "Never mind the barbarian in front of you," was the constant mantra, "leave him to your mate, you go for the one on your right."

As the sun rose sullenly over the distant mountains, the improving light revealed the Celts massing above the treeline below and in front of the lines of Romans, eyes narrowed, swords gripped, waiting patiently to sate their blood lust. Almost as one, the front rank started a menacing drum roll of noise by hammering with sword hilts on their shields, daring and defying their opponents to meet them in battle.

At the tree line, the Celts seemed to be having some sort of conference, with shouts and gesticulations aimed at the growing shield wall. More and more of the warriors arrived from the ridge, alerted to the new danger, grouping together, then, with a wild yell, the whole mob ran at the shield wall, at least two hundred paces away.

"I make it about four hundred of them," said the centurion dispassionately to Agrippa. "They'll be fucked by the time they get to us."

Agrippa nodded. "How many men in the wall?"

The centurion grimaced. "We've got a full cohort in the line, thus far, with more coming up all the time. We'll be all right," he said confidently.

Agrippa, who could hardly remember the last time he had stood in a shield wall, was more sceptical, but held his counsel. The attackers wavered as a shower of spears fell on them from the rear of the wall. They rallied as their leader, a long-haired, striking young woman, her face contorted in rage, ran on in defiance of the lethal spears to be the first to strike the shield wall. She was helped or hindered by a broad-shouldered man with hair down past his shoulders who appeared to be trying to strike the wall, while at the same time protecting her. If the legionaries were surprised that the first strike from the enemy was from a woman, it made no difference: the enemy was the enemy. More of the Celts battered into the wall, but despite being outnumbered, Roman discipline was maintained as instinct and training took over. The shield wall stood confidently firm as the attackers visibly wilted after their long run up the hill. Bravely they hacked furiously at the wall of Roman shields, but frustration grew as they realised how ineffectual their efforts were.

Both sides took casualties, but it was the attackers who fared the worst. If the Celts managed to strike a Roman hard enough for him to fall, the man behind would step up and take his place.

At the front of the wall, the attackers had no protection. They tried to bludgeon their way through, maddened by the Roman short swords flicking out from the side of shields to strike unprotected bodies.

The long-haired woman was hacking and thrusting at the wall with a determination matched by the man who stood at her side, until, at last, she took a vicious slash on her sword forearm. She staggered back, glanced at the wound and was shaping up to rejoin the fight when she was dragged away by two tribesmen.

Sensing that the tide had turned against the tribes, the centurion bellowed: "Twentieth, one pace forward, MARCH!" As one, the grim-faced soldiers crashed forward. The bewildered tribal warriors had no choice; they had to step back or be crushed. Once they went onto the back foot they were lost. Again, the centurion roared out: "Twentieth, one pace forward, MARCH!" Again, the warriors had no choice but to take another step back as the Roman machine took another irresistible step.

Agrippa registered the protesting woman being led from the battlefield, and surprised himself by feeling relieved that she had been spared. She fought well, he thought.

Caratacus and his tribe, the Catuvellauni, fought at the battles of Medway and Tamesis, where they were soundly beaten. Afterwards Caratacus raised small bands of warriors to raid and harass the Romans, to the extent that some of his family feared crushing revenge by Rome. The tribe agreed to announce that Caratacus, his household and a small party of warriors would be banished allowing him to try and unite the tribes of the west. Leading the Silures and Ordovices, he had some success but once again failed when he attempted to take on the legions in a set-piece battle.

When the fateful battle on the seemingly impregnable ridge ended, and Lenc the spy heard about Caratacus's flight from the field, kidnapping the only woman he ever cared about, he left his post in pursuit. This would certainly mean he would be branded a deserter and if caught would be crucified. To the fierce tribesmen of this wild country, he was also a traitor and would be run through without a second's thought, if he was lucky - the tribes had just as many imaginative methods of torture as his own Roman army.

He sat dejectedly on his horse, carefully plodding along the mountain path in the wind blasted central uplands, his head dropping momentarily in despair at his predicament. He had deserted the legion after a monumental fight, sworn to rescue the Silurian Princess Veldicca from a barbarian he had dared to call friend, and betrayed the tribes in their hour of need. He was friendless in a hostile world. Could things get any worse?

Yes, they could.

He was an auxiliary, attached to the XX Valeria Victrix, and had volunteered to spy on the Silures, in anticipation of the legion's campaign to subdue the west of Britannia. How could he know this would generate confusing loyalties with the very people he was supposed to betray?

He was a Gaul and had the look of a Celt, with dark, curly hair, although cropped short in the manner of the legion, and a slightly swarthy complexion, which not even the seemingly constant, insidious rain on this island could wash away. His arms carried several tattoos. The running boar of the XX Valeria Victrix and the spread-winged stork of the III Gallorum, his auxiliary cohort, which he had joined as a boy soldier. There was a message to Antenociticus, the patron god of his auxiliary regiment, and as if keeping his options open, the crossed hammer and axe of Toutatis, an older god of war. His body carried several scars, souvenirs of his service, in various dangerous outposts of the empire. In truth he had been delighted when he was posted to Britannia as an engineer, building forts and roads as the island was occupied. It never occurred to him that one day he would be on his own, a deserter and spy, pursuing a man who dreamed of being the first king of Britannia.

He tried to ignore the cold wind slicing through his waxed

woollen cloak as dark thoughts seethed round his mind. His horse picked her way along the path, jumbled with rocks sheered from the high hills either side. He had a burning need to find that bastard Caratacus whose ambition to be King of Britannia had decimated two tribes and allowed Rome to continue its subjugation of this wild country. And then kill him.

With two of the four legions in Britannia closing in on him, Caratacus had agreed to make a stand, on a long ridge with a dank swamp front and rear. The terrain should have been enough to protect the Silurian and Ordovician tribes which made up Caratacus's army and, thanks to the impetuous thirst for glory of a commander of one of the legions very nearly succeeded. Sabinianus, Legate of the XIV Gemina Martia Victrix, caught up with the Celts, safe on their ridge, and despite specific orders to the contrary, decided on a frontal attack losing the best part of a cohort – eight hundred men – to the rocks rained down on them from the heights above.

The battle was eventually won thanks to the "back door," found by Lenc, which allowed the pathfinders, the legion's special forces to lead the Twentieth into a successful surprise attack.

When his planned triumphant stand against Rome failed, Caratacus murdered the war leader of the Silures and kidnapped their princess. Caratacus had lost his own wife, captured by the Romans, so needed another to bear him fine sons in his quest for the throne of Britannia, and who better than a warrior princess? Such was his logic.

CHAPTER I

A weak sun rose over the battlefield as a melancholy keening and wailing gave a bleak background accompaniment to a scene of death and war spoil. It was the combined sound of women crying for their dead, mixed with the groans of those who would soon die.

Thick smoke defying the cold rain still belched from the few burnt-out tents after the legion had swept through, taking anything of value they fancied. Bodies lay everywhere, and soldiers moved among them, checking the dead and despatching the wounded. As the sun came up the captured warriors submitted to shackles and with heads bowed, tried to resign themselves to a life of slavery, living under the crushing might of Rome. At least with the back-breaking work they would have to endure, it would not be for long.

Publius Ostorius Scapula, the second governor of Britannia had given the order and by subterfuge had surprised the Celtic army in its seemingly impregnable position and taken it with gratifyingly small loss of Roman life. Ostorius Scapula was not a well man; it was an open secret that he had some fatal illness which he took great pains to try and conceal. Every man under his command knew that the governor would not recover while attempting to subjugate a turbulent country like Britannia with only four legions.

The considered opinion of the rank-and-file soldiers, gossiping quietly round the camp fires, was that at least another four legions would be needed to tame the wild and warlike

Britons. They took satisfaction from knowing they had done an incredible job so far, not by luck, but by discipline and bravery. They also knew that could only take them so far. The legions had paid a price in men for their victories, and replacements took a long time to filter through. Scrimping bean counters responsible for the resupply of Britannia took their lead from the parsimonious Senate far away in Rome, happy to revel in the victories of their diminished army in Britannia, but highly reluctant to pay for it, both in men and equipment. The front-line soldiers' lament down the ages.

Scapula was not a big man, but he had an aura of competence and command. Men followed him for no reason they could articulate, simply that he was a good, thinking soldier, and importantly they trusted him.

But at the end of a great victory over the Celts, he was angry and looked round at the scene of devastation with an unmatched fury in his eyes. He could not forgive the naked ambition of one of his commanders, Sabinianus, Legate of the XIV Gemina Martia Victrix, who had been specifically ordered not to make a frontal assault on the Celts. The enemy was safe, high on a ridge with a never-ending supply of rocks to rain down on the hapless legionaries, tired after wading a deceptive swamp.

The loss of nearly eight hundred men in a suicidal attack by a commander so desperate for glory was difficult for the Governor to swallow. His first thought was to send Sabinianus back to Rome in disgrace, but beyond his fury he knew he had to tread carefully as the fool could be a potent enemy. By the time he arrived in front of the Senate, he would have prepared a story reflecting only his glory, acceptable to senators with no qualms about throwing away eight hundred fighting men.

No, there must be a better way. But for the actions of one man, thought Scapula, we may well have had to fight our way up that ridge. Then the butcher's bill for the Valeria Victrix would have been similar to the Gemina Martia: unacceptably high. It wasn't that the governor had a sentimental streak -

pure economics drove his fury. The Roman army, the alleged garrison of Britannia, was woefully under-manned and to lose so many of the fighting men of the Gemina Martia to satisfy their commander's lust for glory was a price too steep to pay.

Deep in thought, Scapula ducked under the flap of the tent hurriedly erected for his use on the edge of the battlefield and looked round for his orderly. He half-smiled as he registered the small academic-looking man, on the edge of the command group, dwarfed by the governor's bodyguard and personal entourage, all competent-looking burly soldiers. He gestured to the orderly, who quickly and silently slipped past the armour-clad men to the side of his writing table and stood expectantly, his tablet poised for messages.

"Take ten men of my escort and lead Vellibia, the wife of Caratacus, and her party of children, personal bodyguard and slaves, to my headquarters below the ridge. Separate Vellibia from them all and keep them under cover till I can return.

"Then bring me Agrippa the pathfinder chief, and Legate of the Fourteenth, Sabinianus. Keep them separate and under cover."

He nodded brusquely to acknowledge the orderly's deep bow.

As the orderly hurried away, Scapula clasped his hands behind his back, and walked slowly out onto the battlefield so he could take in again the scene of sorrow and destruction. Smoke from a dozen fires drifted across the jumble of bodies, swords and shields, some Roman, but mostly tribal. A few women were moving slowly through, lifting heads, trying to identify loved ones. Ignoring them, a group of tired soldiers stretched out on the grass, taking their ease as they exchanged stories quietly relieved they were still alive, after a short but vicious exchange on that cold, damp hill. Scapula recognised them as the spearhead of his assault group.

"Well done, men, you fought well," he said, forcing a smile onto his face as he pushed his fury to the back of his mind.

His legionaries struggled to get up in his august presence, but he motioned them to stay still on the ground.

"Stay there, stay there - you deserve a rest after that great victory."

They sank back with satisfied smiles on their faces as Scapula squatted down among them. A soldier with a blackened face and a ragged bandage round his forearm ventured: "How long do we stay here, sir? Are we going to chase that bastard Caratacus?"

Scapula reflected on his answer. "I would very much like to carry on northwards and destroy the Druids, that nest of religious vipers on Mona," he said. "And at the same time send men after Caratacus, but I fear we are too few on the ground to do much more with winter coming on. I think we will winter at Deva, send the pathfinders in pursuit of Caratacus and in the spring make Mona a wasteland. With a bit of luck, you lot should have a deservedly easy winter before campaigning again from Deva."

"Sorry, sir what about the Fourteenth? They were stationed at Deva."

"So they were, but unfortunately they were so badly mauled in their ill-timed frontal assault, they don't have the strength to maintain the Deva garrison. I shall leave that honour to the Twentieth and the Gemina Martia will go east to strengthen the garrison at Lindum."

The chosen men of the spearhead glanced quickly at each other, then gazed down at the grass. They knew what those casual words meant to the honour of the Fourteenth, but no one was going to mention it, at least not in front of the governor.

With that the great man stood and brushed down his uniform. "It's been nice talking to you men. You can take pride in a good job well done. Rome is proud of you."

With that the soldiers all struggled to their feet and snapped to attention.

Scapula nodded and smiled again, and strode from the killing field. He had other battles to fight.

He climbed down the sheer cliff face and used the secret ford to cross the swamp, then veered right to his command group camp. After giving the password to the sentry on the perimeter, he headed straight for his own sparse quarters in the centre of the camp and once inside the main headquarters settled wearily at his table with a beaker of warmed wine.

His orderly came in almost immediately and explained that he had put Vellibia in one tent, the pathfinder Agrippa in another, Sabinianus in yet another, and the Caratacus household in a bigger tent close by. All were guarded.

"Good," said Scapula thoughtfully. He was about to give out his orders when he was consumed by a massive coughing fit. Taken by surprise, he hurriedly pulled a piece of linen from beneath his chest armour to cover the spots of bright red blood brought up from his lungs.

The orderly looked on anxiously, not knowing what to do. "Can I get you some more wine, sir?" he asked.

Scapula waved his hand to indicate no and added, "Give me a little time to compose myself, then bring the barbarian princess to me. You can bring some wine for us both then."

The orderly bowed and backed out of the large tent.

Scapula wiped his mouth and grimaced at the sight of the bubbly bright red blood, then when he heard people approaching, hurriedly stuffed the linen back under his armour. He stood as his unwelcome guest Vellibia, wife of Caratacus was shown in. By, she is a beauty thought Scapula appreciatively.

Long red hair, thick and uncombed, hung over her shoulders. She was half-dressed in riding gear and a long cloak, after being disturbed from sleep when the attack went in and captured shortly after that. She was wearing heavy slave shackles on her wrists.

"I am sorry we have to meet under these circumstances," said Scapula eventually in Latin. "Let me have those shackles removed."

"Have you news of my husband?" Vellibia asked defiantly. She was terrified, and struggled to keep her fear under control. Her fists were clenched in their manacles and the colour had drained from her face.

Scapula shrugged his shoulders and opened his palms. "He got away with his bodyguard shortly after the camp was taken. I have scouts out and we think we know where he is going because the priest Cainos was with him. More than that, we shall have to hope we get more information as the day goes on."

Scapula offered his guest a beaker of wine. She hurriedly shook her head then relented, took the wine and drank it gratefully.

"One small mystery," Scapula continued, "he had the Princess Veldicca of the Silures in his escaping party - can you explain that?"

Vellibia shook her head. "I have no idea, except perhaps he was helping her to get safely away from the battlefield." She looked down at her wine.

"Well yes," agreed Scapula, "it's just that we found the body of Trenos, her future husband, who, although wounded trying to break the shield wall, died from a dagger thrust. I doubt very much that it was a Roman who killed him."

"What are you trying to suggest?" demanded Vellibia angrily. "Are you trying to say that my husband killed him?"

Scapula studied her haughty face and added softly, "I have no idea. I also have no idea why he would do such a thing."

Vellibia looked down again, then back at Scapula. "What do you intend to do with me and my household? We are nothing to you without my husband."

A weary Scapula sat back down at his table and gestured the princess to a chair near a burning brazier.

"To be honest, I don't really know," he said as he passed a hand over his brow. "I suppose that I shall have to keep you in captivity until we find your husband, and for your sake, I hope we catch him alive. He, you, and the rest of the family will probably be transported to Rome where he will be tried. What happens to him, and of course you and your children, will be in another's hands. In the meantime, your children can stay with you and you can keep one maidservant. I am afraid the rest of your retinue will go into slavery.

"I shall take you back to Camulodunum and there we will await the fate of your husband. Unsatisfactory I know, but it's the best I can do. In the meantime, you will be treated as befits your rank, unless you give me cause to think otherwise."

She bowed her head and softly said, "For the sake of my children we will cause no trouble."

"Good, good," replied Scapula as he gestured one of his guards forward with a hammer to knock out the pins holding the chains.

With her hands free, Vellibia massaged her wrists. She bit her lip and hesitated, then asked: "Have you no idea where he has gone?"

"As I said, I have men out looking for his party but it's difficult, over four thousand men took flight and are running all over these hills. To find one party of twenty-odd is therefore even more of a challenge. But we are patient and we are pretty sure where he is going to find a bolt-hole."

"And where is that?" asked a clearly puzzled Vellibia.

Scapula poured some more wine. "I think I mentioned that the conniving priest Cainos was with them. Everything points to him being a self-appointed guide and that he will take them to the Isle of Mona. It is the stronghold of the Druids, a devious bunch that I would very much like to destroy. And Mona is also the last hiding place for a lot of the tribesmen hiding from the legions so we can solve a lot of problems by clearing out the whole nest. All I can promise is that I will try to see that you are kept fully aware of what is happening."

With that Scapula stood. "Lady, I am afraid you must excuse me, I have a lot to get on with." She nodded as the guard came back.

"Put her in her own tent, and get her children and one servant to join her. She will let you know which one."

He walked with Vellibia to the flap of the tent and bowed as she left. "Bring Legate Sabinianus to me," he ordered the guard.

Legate Sabinianus could be forgiven for being apprehensive about his interview with the governor. Through his vaulting ambition, he had ordered a frontal attack on the Celtic stronghold, losing a significant percentage of his legion in the process. He had managed to justify the loss to himself, but he wondered whether the supreme commander of all Roman forces in Britannia would see it the same way. He wondered what his blond Germanic slave boy was doing now. He would give anything to be curled up in bed with him.

"Ah, Sabinianus, come in," said Scapula when the commander of the Fourteenth finally plucked up courage to announce himself. Warily he entered the tent, not sure whether this pleasant Scapula was a good thing or not.

"Now, come and sit here at the table, there's some wine for you."

Sabinianus uneasily sat down at the table and put his fingers round the metal beaker. Scapula sat back in his chair and looked at the legate thoughtfully. 'God's blood,' he thought, 'I can smell the fear leaking out of him.'

He smiled. "Now, Sabinianus, as you can imagine I have heard all sorts of stories about your legion and the assault on the ridge, so I felt it only fair to hear the story directly from you. You may also wish to explain why you decided to attack despite my explicit orders not to."

Sabinianus was transfixed with terror. He opened his mouth a couple of times but nothing came out.

"Perhaps you did not get my order?" probed Scapula gently, leaning forward in his chair. "Perhaps you thought that a quick direct assault would settle the matter and perhaps the barbarians would run from the might of the Fourteenth?"

Sabinianus looked across the table at Scapula. He seemed to be genuine, and there was a strange smile of sympathy about his mouth.

"Yes, yes, that's exactly it," gabbled Sabinianus quickly. "We arrived at the ridge without orders and it seemed logical to me to act in the best traditions of the legion and attack straight away. Show these bastards the might of Rome."

Scapula sat back again and smiled. The smile was more wolfish now. "Of course you did, which is what any commander would do. Unfortunately, it went wrong and the barbarians won a great victory."

Sabinianus hung his head. In a small voice he added: "My men were afraid; the officers did not want to attack. I had to show them the Celts were beatable. We had to beat them. It is the duty of every Roman soldier - prevail, or die."

By this stage he was close to tears. He looked round the tent as if searching for something, anything that would release him from this torment. If the governor had shouted and raged at him it would probably be better. Probably.

"Of course," soothed Scapula. "Of course it wasn't your fault, could have happened to any officer scenting victory and all that it brings. If you had brought it off, you would have been the toast of Rome. It may even have bought you my job."

Slowly, what Scapula had casually dropped into the conversation sank in. Sabinianus jerked his head up. "No sir, no. What I did was for the good of the army in Britannia and of course the Senate. I had no thought of personal gain at all."

"Of course, of course," soothed Scapula, still with a small smile diluting his words. "But now I have to decide how to redeploy my army. With the barbarians dispersed, campaigning is over till the spring. I shall send a small force in pursuit of Caratacus and in the spring we shall return and burn the Isle of Mona to the ground. In the meantime, the Fourteenth and Twentieth will march to Deva. The Twentieth will winter there, and you will carry on over the Penninus to Lindum, where your legion will be on wall-building and defensive duties until your numbers are made up. After all, you are hardly a fighting force right now."

Sabinianus was bewildered. "But, sir, that will be seen as a punishment. I…" he hesitated and licked his lips, "…I mean, the legion, may never recover."

Scapula raised his hand placatingly. "Yes, that is a possibility, but don't you see, it is also an opportunity for you to regain the trust of your men, rest them, then harden them up for next year's campaign. I am sure you and they will win great victories."

With that, he smiled again and stood. The interview was over. Sabinianus was still bewildered but could think of no other protest or argument. Gently Scapula took him by the elbow and steered him to the tent flap.

"Now get some rest," - a tone of concern still in his voice - "then tomorrow brief your officers. I need you to be on the march before the mid-morning."

As the desolate officer shambled out, feet dragging, Scapula grimaced. What a stupid, unfeeling, selfish bastard, he thought grimly. I could cheerfully run a sword though him myself and save us all a lot of bother.

He shouted to his orderly to fetch Agrippa of the Pathfinders and failed to choke off a desperate bleeding cough into his now bright-red piece of linen. By the time Agrippa arrived and threw up a passable salute, Scapula was again composed and sitting at his table.

Scapula poured a beaker of wine and pushed it across the table to Agrippa. "Sit down, please," He looked at the pathfinder steadily.

"What of young Lenculus? I never got a chance to thank him for his work. Where is he now?"

Agrippa sipped his wine. "Sir, it's a bit complicated. Lenc took a bang on the head, but as soon as he recovered and heard the news that Caratacus had kidnapped the princess, he decided to set off after them straight away. Right now, he is the best chance we have of finding the bastard."

He felt it probably wise not to add that Lenc could not know that his pursuit of Caratacus would have his governor's approval albeit in hindsight. That didn't help Lenc, he thought, who would probably be thinking the whole Roman army would be chasing him as a deserter, thirsting to nail him to a cross.

"As soon as the present task you have for me is complete," he added, "I propose to find Lenc and by so doing, find Caratacus."

"Good, good," approved Scapula, who saw no need to ask his special forces officer why he thought there was a present task for him.

"The person I was talking to in this tent before you were summoned, did you by any chance hear any of our conversation?" asked Scapula, seemingly unconcerned.

"I felt it my duty to listen in, sir," said Agrippa staring over his commander's head at a small patched tear in the tent.

"Good, good," he said distractedly. "I imagine you understand why I was so decent to him?"

"I can make a very good guess, Lord."

"Enlighten me."

"Lord, you are in a difficult position. You cannot crucify Sabinianus even for gross dereliction of duty, he is a Legate, appointed by the Senate. His men would probably love you even more because the stain of their disgrace, although not removed, would be lessened. And they would know that you knew where the blame lay. But you can never lose sight of the man's influence in the Senate. If you spared his life but relieved him of command and sent him home, by the time he got there, he would have worked up a great story of his martial prowess. In the eyes of the Senate, spurred on by the support of the great and the good prepared to take his gold, he would be the tactical hero, thwarted only by the jealousy of his commander who wanted to take all the glory for himself. Is that about it, sir?"

"Pretty accurate," conceded Scapula. "You should have been

a lawyer, not a fucking soldier."

"No sir, I am quite happy as a simple fucking soldier."

Scapula smiled and rubbed his chest. The wine made the pain bearable, which in the past few days had flared up badly. His personal doctor was no help at all, just shook his head ruefully and administered opium as strongly as he dared.

"So can you see what's coming next?" he asked carefully.

Agrippa took a sip of wine. "Judging by the way you have taken me into your confidence, I imagine that you're expecting that when the Gemina Martia parts company with us at Deva and starts the long trail over the Penninus, that somewhere along the way Sabinianus will probably have a nasty and hopefully degrading fatal accident which will show him up as the selfish fool his men think he is."

Scapula nodded. "Exactly that. It will probably take place on the road to Lindum, a good way from Deva, so that no one in my command can be accused of anything, but I imagine it will look very much like a tragic accident and the officers of the Fourteenth will not want to look too closely."

"I think you can be assured of that sir, and when the news gets back to the Senate, there won't be many who would want to honour a man who lost so many men so wantonly and also openly flaunted his sexuality in front of his legion. I understand that has been more than a bone of contention within the ranks, sir."

Homosexuality, while accepted both within the ranks and officer class, was generally considered not something to be openly on show. A tussle in the barrack block perhaps, but not made obvious by a man with absolute power of life and death over the six thousand soldiers under his command.

CHAPTER II

Perhaps it was the jolting of her horse threatening to throw her onto the mountain pass, which finally pulled Veldicca back to consciousness. Her ankles had been tied with rope strung under the belly of the horse, and her hands tied to the pommel of the saddle. A horseman either side kept pushing her upright in the saddle as she swayed uncontrollably.

Veldicca was in her late teens and a princess of the war-like Silures of west Britannia. With the death of her father during the Roman assault, she was nominally Queen of the Silures, but whether she would ever be able to claim that title remained to be seen. She looked down at the bonds that tied her to the saddle and tried to remember how she came to be in this predicament.

Despite the red weal on her face, where Caratacus had hit her, she was still a beauty with a young girl's lithe body, used to the outdoor life, with - until these last few days - always a ready smile and eager for the next adventure.

As the mists of darkness gradually cleared, she made a conscious effort to take control of her senses. Blearily she looked up and round and registered the warriors flanking her and holding her on her mount. She could see she was in a column of about twenty riders, all Caratacus's sworn men, on a craggy hillside. It was difficult to see very much as scrubby rowan, growing out of cracks in the rocks brushed against them either side of the stony track on the side of the steep hill.

Suddenly, with a sickening certainty, the memories started to come back to her - the death of her father, the suicidally brave attack on the Roman shield wall, the murder of her betrothed Trenos and then Caratacus intending to take her for his bride. That's when, still almost unconscious from a swinging blow from Caratacus, she had been tied onto a horse and the group fled the battlefield.

She looked down at the painful sword slash on her forearm. It had been hurriedly dressed after the abortive attack on the hated Romans but was weeping blood, the bandage an ugly dark brown colour.

Momentarily, Veldicca gave way to despair. What on earth had she done to deserve this? Fleeing from the Romans was one thing, but why had she been kidnapped and tied to a horse, especially by tribesmen who were supposed to be allies? Surely he can't be serious about me being his bride? He would wake up with my dagger in his heart if he so much as touched me, she thought. She looked ahead and there towards the front of the column she could make out the blond head of Caratacus. I will kill him one day, she promised herself venomously.

Two days before, Caratacus had been in charge of an impressive army of Celtic tribesmen: the Silures and Ordovices. They had a seemingly impregnable position on a sheer ridge and initially repelled a frontal assault from a legion cohort, inflicting a crushing victory. So sure that their back was protected by the swift-flowing Sabrina river, a swamp and a sheer cliff face, they felt no need to waste men on defending their rear, but somehow the Romans found a way to penetrate the natural defences and by the next morning had an overwhelming body of men on the top of the hill. With their possession of the high ground, the Roman soldiers swept through the small camp set up behind the line of defenders, killing Veldicca's father and capturing Caratacus's family, before forming an impregnable shield wall.

Caratacus ordered the Ordovices to stand fast on the ridge and the Silures to attack the shield wall. In vain, despite their superior numbers, the Silures battered themselves against the wall, and with more enemy reinforcements sweeping down the hill, eventually broke and ran, scattering over the countryside to escape the vengeance of the victorious Romans.

As the tribes' resolution dripped away in the face of implacable legion discipline, Trenos the warrior betrothed to the Princess Veldicca, raged at Caratacus, that it was all his fault, that they should never have attempted to take on the might of the Roman army in a set-piece battle. This personal attack on his leadership qualities was too much for Caratacus who smiled as he stabbed Trenos through his chain mail and into his heart in front of the horrified Veldicca. Instinctively Caratacus saw in Veldicca a solution to some of his problems. With his family killed or captured, he needed a queen. Veldicca was of high birth, albeit from an insignificant coarse tribe in western Britannia, but she was attractive and young. She would do, he thought. She would be made to come round and accept her lot; after all, how many women would turn down the throne of Britannia? Which is why, when the warband fled the hill, they took an unconscious Veldicca with them, tied to her saddle.

That's the trouble with women, he thought, too damned sentimental.

He hadn't been thinking straight, he accepted that. Punching the princess was probably a mistake, but his world was crumbling and his dream falling away before his eyes as the Romans advanced. Trenos and his angry denunciation of his carefully thought-out master plan to defeat the Romans became the focus of all his frustration. Pushing his knife into the young warrior, the hesitation of the blade as it stalled on chain mail, then the extra push that sent it up into the heart, made him feel vindicated. The look of surprise and rage in the eyes of the young Trenos was something he would savour for a long time.

Me, he thought, the future King of Britannia! No, he conceded, he wasn't functioning right at all, but didn't he have the right to take spontaneous action? He was after all going to be king, maybe not immediately, but soon. Dark clouds gathered in his mind as he tried to push the consequences of his actions out of his fevered brain while sitting in the dark and damp coldness of the forest.

Kidnapping the princess was an impulsive spur of the moment action which he now thought he may have cause to regret. Maybe the best bet would be to have a bit of fun with her then give her to his bodyguards with strict instructions to dispose of her afterwards.

With that comforting thought he felt a bit better, and started to wonder if anyone had any food.

The Druid Cainos became their guide. Night had fallen but he led the group unerringly off the sheer hill, and through the swamp river to the safer higher ground on the other side.

After wading and swimming the swirling Sabrina River, their perilous flight in the darkness took them through a range of hills with unseen obstacles at every step. With Cainos in the lead, their horses took them over rocks, big and small, around fallen trees in the pitch-black, dead of night. The only consolation: if it was dangerous for them, it would be doubly dangerous for the pursuing Romans.

Caratacus and his small band fled through the dense forest from the vengeance of not only the Romans, but the tribes who were betrayed. Branches whipped his face, and with all manner of obstacles unseen under foot, his sense of impending danger became even more acute. In his mounting panic, he was starting to convince himself they were never going to get out of this evil forest, never see the light of day again.

Then just ahead, as Cainos rode slowly into a clearing and reined in, he raised an arm and the half-asleep warriors behind bumped into each other as they stumbled to a halt.

Caratacus swallowed and fought to control himself as Cainos tethered his horse and walked back down to the middle of the column towards him. "Lord, we should stop here to rest. I am pretty sure we have shaken off any pursuit, but we should stay here till daylight, then we can move much faster."

Caratacus nodded his agreement, and thankfully sank to

the leafy forest floor. All he could say when Cainos diffidently suggested that guards should be posted at both ends of the track was, "Yes, yes, if you think it necessary," before rolling himself in his cloak and pulling the hood over his eyes.

Veldicca was half-helped, half-pulled from her horse, and with her hands untied, sank to the ground, rubbing her swollen wrists. Her captors also slumped down, a discreet distance away, rolled themselves in their cloaks and tried to sleep.

Some managed a few hours' fitfull shuteye, but even exhausted, most just lay on the ground willing dawn to come. Which it eventually did as the sun reluctantly probed through the canopy. There was little talking as they chewed on the last of their stale bread before readying their horses once again.

Veldicca was once again unceremoniously dumped on her horse and despite her protestations, her hands tied to the pommel. Caratacus didn't seem to be taking much interest in the day's march, so it was Cainos who once again led the way along the rocky path through the mountain pass.

All that day they rode hard, only slowing when darkness made their progress too dangerous, but it was still several hours into the night before Cainos judged they were safe from pursuit. He called a halt in a clearing beside a chuckling brook allowing the riders to gratefully dismount and stretch their aching limbs in the moonlight. Veldicca had her bonds untied and was unsympathetically pulled from her horse. She slumped as her guards let her go, and almost fell. Despite her pains, she rallied and pulled herself upright, determined not to show weakness in front of her captors.

Cainos hurried to her side and pulled her long cloak over her shoulders, fastening it carefully at the front. "I am sorry we don't have any food or shelter, my lady. We left in rather a hurry, but I am sure this will only be a temporary setback. We will have you back with our own people very soon, I am sure."

Veldicca looked at the priest quizzically. Whose side was he on? He had condoned, even taken part in her kidnap, and seemed hell-bent on keeping her captive. Until she got some answers, she decided that the best course of action was to stay aloof and wait for an opportunity to escape.

Slowly she turned to face him. She was at least half a head taller, which for some reason pleased her. She took a pace forward, forcing him to look up at her as she spoke quietly but strongly, so only he could hear.

"I don't know why I am here, and why I am being treated in this way, but I will find out, and if I have anything to do with it, the people who have abused me will suffer. Do I make myself clear?" Cainos could only gulp, bow gracefully, and mumble softly, "Yes my lady."

That night they camped under the tree canopy at the top of a valley which gave them some protection from the wind, but not the cold. A fire would have been too dangerous - a beacon for vengeful pursuing Romans - so they shivered through the night, neither sleeping nor waking until thankfully a weak sun finally heralded daylight.

Caratacus woke with a start. He was freezing and looked round, not sure what he was doing, lying on the cold, lumpy ground under his cloak in the middle of a dank forest. He knew it was dawn because he could at last make out the trees and figures around him, but there was no warmth to the sun and a pervading mist seemed to seep into his bones.

Around him, his men were beginning to stir, sitting up, scratching and yawning; a couple were even running on the spot to try and get some warmth into their bodies.

He looked round and saw with rising anger that Veldicca, the Silurian princess and the only woman in the party, was also stirring and looking round with a bemused expression on her face. Well may you look surprised, you bitch, he thought vindictively. I offer to make you the Queen of Britannia and you throw it in my face – well, we'll see about that. Before I'm finished, you'll be begging me to marry you.

Veldicca saw him looking and quickly turned away, then

stood and pulled her cloak tightly round her shoulders. Cainos, hurried to her with a concerned look on his face as he reached out to touch her elbow. Caratacus watched and listened as the priest gently walked her out of the ring of his bodyguards and further into the trees.

"I will stay here, lady, while you go a little further to do what you need to do. I will make sure no one comes near." He was pleased to see a small smile of gratitude from her, which he thought was a step in the right direction. Perhaps she is coming to terms with her situation he thought.

"We are going downhill, which is a good sign," Cainos said loudly to Caratacus, making sure that the nearest warriors could also hear him. "That's good, because the going will become easier, but as we come out onto a plain, we will have to take even more care because we will be visible, not only to the Romans, but to the tribesmen who managed to escape as well."

Caratacus nodded at this news. "Are there homesteads on this plain? Somewhere we can get food?"

Cainos gave this some thought. "Lord, perhaps we should accept that we are going to go hungry all day. We must tighten our belts until further north, away from the battleground. Don't forget, it's not only the Romans who would wish us harm but renegade tribesmen and they could be in large enough bands to overwhelm us. If we approach farmsteads, we might well find we are very unwelcome. I fear the best thing to do is to pass them by and look for food and shelter tomorrow when we have covered more distance."

Reluctantly Caratacus agreed with this advice, but he didn't like it. "Comes to something, when you try and unite the country, do your best without thought for yourself and all you get is ill-washed peasants wanting to run you through. Don't know why I bother, I really don't."

Tactfully, Cainos dropped back, leaving the would-be king to his petulant mutterings. With a half-smile he fell in beside Veldicca, tied once again on her horse. The track was wider and could easily take two horses riding side by side and he wished her the best of the morning. "I am afraid our future king is not feeling his best. Being cold and hungry with half the Roman army looking for him is not conducive to his good cheer."

For the first time in days Veldicca cheered up. "Serves the poor mite right," she said with satisfaction. "Maybe now he will decide to go back to an easier life and leave us alone. There is only one reason, well two really, why I would regret his riding away from us, and that is that I have promised myself I am going to kill him at the first opportunity. I will have revenge for my father and Trenos."

Cainos fell silent. He had his own thoughts on the tribal betrayal but felt it best to keep his own counsel.

"That's as maybe," he ventured. "In a day or so we will be on Mona, and I dearly hope that we will be able to resolve this mess. I am sure that the Arch Druid will send you home with an escort, but how he will react to Caratacus I have no idea. We shall just have to wait and see, but in the meantime, it would greatly help your cause if you could at least be civil to Caratacus. He is used to getting his own way, and we know he is impetuous with an evil temper. While you are his prisoner, as it were, it will help if you don't antagonise him."

Veldicca pondered this then nodded. "I can see the sense of your advice. I will be civil but nothing more. If he puts a hand on me, I will have his eyes out and enjoy doing it."

"My lady," Cainos bowed in acquiescence. He couldn't think of anything else to say.

All that day the war band rode north. They were aware of small bands of men, running or on horseback in the distance, but none came close. As night started to fall, they once again found themselves in an outcrop of large rocks, studded with trees. Cainos called a halt and declared the spot as good as any for their night stop. "There is water here, and enough wood for a fire. It would be nice to have a haunch of deer to put on the fire, but you can't have everything. I am sure we will find food tomorrow."

Gratefully the party hobbled their horses to allow them to graze and then spread out to look for wood to make a fire. With nothing better to do, they sat round the blazing fire for warmth, then rolled out their blankets while trying to ignore their rumbling stomachs. Thankfully they were spared rain that moonless night, and the wind was lessened by their rocky shelter. The warriors woke with the coming of the dawn and immediately packed their kit away and strapped it to their saddles. Cainos once again escorted Veldicca into the trees to ensure her privacy. She also managed to splash some water on her face and the ugly gash on her arm. She wrapped the wound in her last strip of linen and hoped that she would get some more that day. The wound needed stitches, but all she could do was bind it tight and hope the day's riding wouldn't be too painful.

Caratacus snored on, oblivious to the activity around him, until his senior guard, Aeron, shook his shoulder, and leaning in said, "Come lord, time to go."

Caratacus stirred and looked round blearily. At first, he had no idea where he was, then it all came back to him. His doubts of the night before vanished with the dark and he felt more optimistic that the God's ambitions for him would be fulfilled. He felt better, and nodded.

"Give me a minute and we can mount up."

Aeron was heartened to see that his Lord was returning to his old self and offered him some ice-cold water from the nearby stream.

"The horses have all been watered lord, but we have no fodder for them," he continued. "We will have to find some on the march today, because right now the horses are as valuable as the men."

Caratacus nodded. "We will find them, and us, some food for the journey. We're sure to find some today."

He looked reflectively at his seasoned second in command. "I have decided that we shall leave these tribes to their own stew.

They lack the finesse to take the fight to the Romans, I realise that now. They may fight well, but they fight as individuals, at worst as tribesmen and care not for the bigger picture.

"If we head for Brigantia and persuade them to join with the Catuvellauni, we will still have a far bigger army than the Romans and can sweep down the country, dealing with them as we find them. The legions have split their forces and are too busy taking on the western tribes, so it will be easy for us to fall on Camulodunum, then Verulamium and Londinium. After we sack their towns, we can turn our attention to whatever Romans the westerners have left us and deal with them accordingly.

He nodded appreciatively, "Don't know why I didn't think of that before I put my trust in those damned lazy thieves in the west."

Aeron tactfully stayed quiet as his leader outlined his new master plan. He had his own thoughts about how to defeat the Romans, even whether it was possible, but he kept them to himself. As long as there were some spoils, he was happy to go along with the plan.

Before they set off, Caratacus held a council of war. His men gathered round and on the outside of the circle stood Veldicca with Cainos.

"After being let down so badly by the Silurians and Ordovices, a shifty, cowardly lot, I have decided to cut my losses and raise my army in central Britannia," he started. "Looking back, that's the direction I should have taken in the first place, but I was swayed by the westerners' reputation as warriors. Clearly I was mistaken."

He ignored the gasp of indignation from Veldicca, who was being shushed by the priest.

"I think we should head for Brigantia. Cartimandua, the queen there can call on one of the biggest bodies of men in all of Britannia, and if I can persuade her to take arms against the invaders, we can sweep south, pick up with our own tribe, the Catuvellauni and between us we will be more than a match for the Romans."

As Caratacus was coming to an end, Cainos whispered to Veldicca: "You have to trust me, I will get you out of this and back to your people, just follow my lead."

He turned to Caratacus: "Lord, may I make a suggestion? It's about your betrothal to Veldicca."

In truth Caratacus now realized he had made a hasty mistake in bringing the Silurian princess with him. She was a firebrand and would be difficult to tame, and there was also the little stumbling block of his own family, who could still be alive.

But Cainos was talking. "Lord, your plan to involve the Brigantes is a good one, but may I suggest that first you should consider petitioning the Arch Druid on Mona about your proposed marriage. If we can persuade him that it would be a good thing for the tribes, for the Druids and for Britannia, it would give you a solid base for your aim to unite the country."

Caratacus reflected. "Do you think he could be persuaded?"

"Lord, if we present our case properly, I see no reason why we can't persuade him that it would be a good thing all round."

Caratacus smiled. "In that case, I think Cartimandua can wait while we go and see this priest of yours."

As the warriors bustled about, preparing their horses and snatching a mouthful of anything edible that could be found in the bottom of saddlebags, Cainos steered Veldicca away from them, and down the track a short way.

"I expect you are wondering why I made that suggestion," he started.

Veldicca was fuming. "To say I was shocked is a huge understatement," she hissed. "Do you really think I would even consider marrying that murderer, even for the throne of Britannia? I would rather have the pleasure of sticking my knife in his guts."

"Yes, yes, I fully understand, but you must appreciate that you are in a very tricky position here. If Caratacus decides that he doesn't want to marry you, or he can't because he is already married, then you become a liability and will be dealt with. Once we are on Mona, you will be under the protection of the Arch Druid and if he can be persuaded that you are under duress, he will probably send you home with an armed escort. But we have to get you there in one piece first."

Veldicca reluctantly saw the sense in the priest's words and nodded her acceptance. "Do you think you can persuade him to let me ride without being tied to the saddle?" she whispered.

"I'm sure that can be managed," the priest suavely agreed.

Once in the saddle, Cainos rode next to Caratacus. "Lord, in front of us is a range of mountains, which, at this time of year, is usually impassable, because of snow. We will need to skirt round them, and when we hit the coast, turn left to find the ferry over to the island. Veldicca has indicated that she will not hinder you or attempt to escape if you release her from her bonds. We are travelling over some rough country which must be quite difficult, tethered the way she is."

Caratacus thought for a second, "All right, no need to tie her on her horse, but if she gets up to any nonsense, tell her she won't get a second chance."

Now that a decision had been made, Caratacus was in expansive mood. "I must say, I'm looking forward to meeting this head priest of yours. Sounds like a pretty impressive type. If we get him on our side it should help with the big job ahead."

Cainos agreed. "As well as ministering to our people's spiritual needs and advising them on a host of things, the Druids also run an intelligence system throughout the whole of the land. If the Arch Druid decides to let you have access to that it will be a fantastic boost for you. Imagine knowing where the legions are, their strengths and what they are planning."

Caratacus leaned back in his saddle. "Maybe there is more than one reason for meeting this priest," he said reflectively.

CHAPTER III

Lenc couldn't be sure where his quarry was heading, but he had a shrewd idea that Cainos the Druid priest would lead the fleeing war band to the Isle of Mona to seek sanctuary. However, right at that moment, his priority was shelter. He had been riding all day over an increasingly mountainous terrain and he could sense that daylight would soon be slipping away. He had seen few people or signs of habitation, but then who would live in this barren wilderness, he thought morosely.

Since leaving the carnage of the battlefield he had not taken too much account of his surroundings although he knew he was riding roughly northwards, which should eventually bring him to the sea. How far away that might be, he only had a hazy idea.

At last, his tired horse stumbled out of a narrow valley onto a wider trail that wound downhill. Around him, the hills swept away, ever upwards, with silver flashes of cascading water running down to the valley floor. Underfoot, rocks loomed out of the marsh grass, and every indentation in the ground was filled with ponds of an oddly red-coloured water.

Then through gaps in the wet mist, and torn by the icy wind, a relieved Lenc glimpsed a tantalisingly small light, which meant habitation and hopefully friendly shelter. As he approached the roundhouse, he could see it was quite big with a dry-stone wall to about shoulder height, then thatch above, rising to a point. The light he had seen came from one small opening. He realised he had been lucky to see it, as it only showed when a gust of wind blew a covering blanket to one side.

He wondered what his reception would be from whoever was in the farmhouse. They won't see many strangers here, he thought, and those that do happen by might well not be the friendliest. He searched for the words in the local dialect and shouted, "Hello in the house, I'm looking for shelter."

This failed to get a response, so Lenc dismounted stiffly and banged on the rudimentary door, then stood back in an attempt to look less threatening. At last, he heard the squeal of an iron bar being lifted, and the door creaked slowly open. A white-haired old man timidly poked his head round the door and looked out, blinking fearfully. His hair and beard were thick and straggly and there was a sheen of grease on his homespun tunic.

Lenc stitched a big smile on his face as he spoke. "I need shelter," he said. "I have some food which I can share with you, but I don't think I will last the night if I have to stay out here."

The old man seemed to consider and cocked his head to listen to a female voice inside the room who was shouting at him to let the stranger in. Finally, the old man jerked his head and held the door open. "I will find shelter for your animal," he said.

Lenc nodded his thanks and gratefully stepped into the farmhouse. It was dimly lit, but there was a roaring fire in the centre and various animals in pens either side of the door. Lenc could make out some cows and sheep, and wrinkled his nose at the smell but at the same time was grateful for the warmth they gave off.

He looked round and could just make out an old woman with a scarf tied round her lank hair stirring something in a pot suspended over the fire, and four men - who with their swords close to hand obviously warriors - sitting on stools near the fire.

One smiled at him and cautiously reached for the knife strapped to his waist. "Well Roman I'm surprised to see you here, I thought your job was done."

Lenc felt a sinking feeling as he recognised the man as Alun Anarawd who led the Ordovices on the ridge and an enemy of old.

Alun struggled to sit up, wincing as he gave up trying to draw his knife. Only then, Lenc noticed the blood-soaked bandages around the chieftain's arm and torso. His face was white and drained, stark against the beard clipped below the chin. His three companions, as one, put their hands on their swords. Each of the three carried swirling tattoos on their faces, disappearing into their long hair and beards.

Alun looked down ruefully and just said, "One of your Roman mates stuck me after we left the hill. They killed my father and brother and many of our men. Bastards."

Lenc nodded. "I don't suppose you believe me, but I am sorry for your loss. I was on the top of the hill where Caratacus betrayed the Silures. Princess Veldicca was kidnapped and her betrothed, Trenos, the Silurian chieftain, murdered."

"What - but why?" asked a bemused Alun. "The fight was over. The Romans tricked us somehow and came at us from the rear. I know the Silures tried to stop them, but who could stand up to a Roman shield wall attacking downhill? I never saw Caratacus again and thought he would have been captured."

"No such luck," grated Lenc. "He got Trenos to lead the Silures against the shield wall. Veldicca had just seen her father cut down and wouldn't stay out of the attack. She and Trenos fought hard but eventually she took a bad gash on her sword arm. Caratacus, of course, took great care not to get too close himself, then when Trenos called off the assault, Caratacus stabbed him to death and kidnapped the princess. I think, thanks to Cainos, that bastard priest, Caratacus and his men got off the hill and away. Now it's for me to find and kill him and rescue the princess."

"Revenge is sweet," agreed Alun. Then he paused, looking searchingly at Lenc. "So how did you get off the hill when there were Romans everywhere?"

Lenc had been waiting for that question, relieved that the Ordovician had not realised that he had been absent for two days, guiding the legion across the river from the rear.

"If you must know, I was on the right of Trenos and Veldicca's line and took a whack on the back of my head. When I came to, the legion was marching on towards your positions. Everything was pretty chaotic, but with the legion in control I made myself scarce and found a stray horse, which was a godsend. If they'd caught me, I would have been executed as a deserter.

"I was pretty certain the Druid Cainos would still be with Caratacus, and he would suggest the island of Mona as a likely bolthole."

Alun conceded the point but warned: "I can see why he would want to hide on Mona, but it could be a very effective trap. Being on an island means you've got nowhere to run."

"Agreed," said Lenc. "I wouldn't expect him to stay there long. Just enough to draw breath and decide what he is going to do next. He still thinks he is going to be the first King of Britannia and will be as intent as ever on raising an army. It's just that he has to go somewhere where they don't know of his present defeat. From Mona he could take ship to Hibernia, or land anywhere along the coast right up as far as Caledonia. It would also be a big help if he had the blessing of the Arch Druid when he starts trying to raise the tribes again."

"If I catch him, he will be a short-lived king," growled Alun. "Our tribal lands run right up to the coast, but the people of Mona only give allegiance to the Druids. If Caratacus makes it to the island, I will help you find him and then you or I will kill him. But I make you a promise, Roman, once that bastard is dead, you will be next."

For what seemed like an eternity Alun's baleful gaze was fixed on Lenc's face. Then he shook himself and allowed himself a short coughing laugh, which ended in a wince as a jolt of pain coursed from his body wound.

"Ha, that's in the future. For now, warm yourself by the fire, have some food, and you can tell me more of why Veldicca was kidnapped."

Once more comfortably replete after a meal of gruel and hard brown bread, and warm from the fire, even the smell in the byre was becoming more tolerable. The old couple had gone to their bed on a platform above the cows, and Alun's three warriors lay stretched out to the side of the fire, fast asleep, their weapons by their sides.

"The Romans attacked from behind, from the top of the hill," explained Lenc. "They must have found a way to cross the swamp and come at us from the rear. They got into position in the dark and at sunrise hammered through the camp, then formed a shield wall to carry on the attack. It was a total surprise. While your tribe took over guarding the whole ridge, Caratacus ordered the Silures to attack the first wave of Romans before more could arrive. They did their best but it was hopeless. They kept fighting until they were exhausted, wasting themselves on the shield wall. Veldicca and Trenos were in the thick of it, but Caratacus never so much as drew his sword. He took good care not to get near the Roman blades."

Alun nodded. "I saw him some time around then and told him what I thought of him and to never come near the Ordovices again. Then I went back to my men to defend the top of the ridge. When it became clear that although there was a whole legion on the other side of the river just waiting for us, the danger was now at our rear, so I gave the order to retreat. I led my men along the top of the ridge, then we struck off to the river, which we managed to cross, then headed for the mountains, chased by Roman cavalry. That was when my father and brother were cut down. After that skirmish, we buried our dead, then my band dispersed to their homes to hide their weapons until needed again."

Alun looked down, then back at Lenc. "With the death of my father I became the leader of the Ordovices, so I thought I would make myself scarce for a while till things blow over - I didn't fancy gracing a Roman crucifixion. But I still don't see why Caratacus kidnapped Veldicca. What happened to his wife?"

"As I said, the camp was overrun first and the Romans were

looking for Caratacus, but all they found was his wife and household who were immediately taken prisoner," explained Lenc bitterly. "Caratacus must have thought that because he is to be king, then he needs a queen. If his wife was captured, then he needs another wife. Veldicca is of royal blood and no doubt will bear fine boys to carry on that bastard's glory."

"I take it as a personal insult that he is on Ordovician territory," replied Alun. "And for that reason alone, I will help you find him. Whether you kill him, or I do, will depend on who catches him first."

"Fair enough," conceded Lenc. "Your help will be much appreciated, especially as I don't know the territory. How long will it take us to get to Mona?"

Alun pushed another log onto the fire and thought about his response. "We either go over the mountains or round them. Cainos will know the mountain paths and how treacherous they are, especially as it could be snowing hard there any time soon. The snow has not yet started, so we might be lucky, but we have to be prepared for anything. The weather up there can change in minutes. I expect Cainos will recommend going north-east round the mountain range, then when he hits the sea, turn west again until he reaches the crossing place to Mona. If they do make it to Mona, they will cross the strait on the ferry. As a Druid, he knows that his problems will be over once they are on the island.

"If the pass is clear and we go straight over the mountain and don't go waist-deep in drifting snow and don't die of exposure, we should catch up with them, perhaps even before they leave the mainland. If they do make it to Mona they will cross the strait on the ferry. Our problems will really start on the other side as it is very much a Druid island. They won't take kindly to us threatening one of their own.

"It's a risk because it means going through the pass below Yr Wyddfa the highest peak. The mountain is too sheer to ride straight up it, so the track takes its own path; it's longer but surer. The danger comes from the weather, which is changing daily. We can hope for light winds but must expect snow, sleet - everything the gods can throw at us."

Lenc shrugged. "How easy will it be to get on the island undetected?"

Alun thought for a moment. "They keep a good lookout on the Mona side of the ferry crossing, so the chances are we would be identified as people worth investigating. They don't like strangers on Mona, but there will be a lot of tribesmen fleeing from the Romans looking for sanctuary, which will be a good cover for us. On the other hand, if we were to sneak ashore from a fishing boat, the island is so small we would soon be found out, and that would be even more damning. I think the best thing is to stick to our story and take the ferry just like everyone else."

"Put like that, I think you're right," agreed Lenc.

As dawn struggled to break, Lenc woke as the farmer and his wife climbed stiffly from their bed space above the animals. She leaned down and carefully passed a pot to her husband, who took it outside. This reminded Lenc that his own bladder was bursting, hurriedly he pulled on the leather riding boots liberated on the battlefield and wrapped himself in his long wool cloak. The other men were also raising their bleary heads, scratching and looking round. Lenc went outside, turning his head away from the keen wind that howled against the hovel. His cloak was smeared with animal fat, to deter both wind and rain, he could only hope it would keep the snow out as well.

Quickly, with his head down, he hurried round the side of the low building to get out of the wind then over a short stone wall where he found the old man intent on the same business. He nodded agreeably as he finished his morning waterworks and Lenc started his.

At the side of the stable byre was a horse trough fed by a diverted stream. The icy water was running fine into and out of the trough, but covered in ice where it was still. Lenc grimaced and, using his elbow, tried to smash through the ice, but all he managed to do was hurt himself. Looking round, he picked up a rock and bashed the ice hard enough to crack and break it, then tapped it until he had enough space to get his hands into the freezing water. After an initial hesitation he reached in and cupped a palmful of water which he splashed on his face. The shock was expected, but even so, the water was bitter cold. He gasped and repeated the process, shaking his head to get rid of the already freezing drops.

"You have some strange habits, you Romans," said Alun grudgingly as he crossed the stone wall and lifted his tunic.

"Never mind, Ordovice, after a few years under the Romans you will wonder at anyone going out in the morning without washing his face."

Alun laughed at the response. "And that is one good reason for us to fight to the death to keep you bastards out. I shall stay dirty, thank you. Dirty and warm."

As they were saddling and loading up the horses, Alun sidled up and looked reflectively at Lenc. "Have you ever been in the mountains in winter?" he asked.

Lenc nodded. "I have experienced cold, if that's what you mean. I know what it is to march in the snow. In the forests of Germania, the weather took almost as many of us as the barbarians."

"Good," conceded Alun, "because where we are going is as bad as anything you have experienced so far. The wind and snow can be straight in your face at a speed and intensity that can knock you over if you're not careful. The track is ill-defined, and if you step off it, and lose contact, you likely won't be found until the spring. Yr Wyddfa, the biggest and most unforgiving, is where we're going. There's a pass in a break in the mountains, but if you make a mistake, it will be your last. We set off now, and if the gods are willing, we should be through the pass and on our way down to the coast before sunset. I certainly don't intend to camp on the side of the mountain."

Lenc cinched his horse's saddle tightly. "Don't worry about me, I'll get there all right."

Alun grunted and swung stiffly into the saddle, grimacing in pain as he tried to protect his wounded side. His three warriors were already mounted and waiting patiently for the sign to move. Not wanting to be the reason for a hold-up, Lenc hurriedly made his last preparations and climbed onto his horse. They moved off in single file along the rutted track as the old farmer went back inside to the warmth and fug of his fireside.

As they moved onto the track, Alun swung his horse round to face Lenc. "Roman, I fear my manners are wanting. I have explained to my men who you are and why - for the time being anyway, you must live - but I haven't introduced you. The one nearest to you is Madawc, behind him is Iestyn, and at the back is Darren. They have agreed to ride with you as comrades, but if I fall, they will take my oath to kill you when Caratacus is dead. Just so you know."

Lenc nodded to the three, who looked back at him implacably, their facial tattoos adding an air of menace. All three had straggly hair down past their shoulders, and although their winter furs were wrapped tight around their bodies, sword hilts were easily accessible.

Alun led the small column out onto the track, allowing a first look at the forbidding mountains pressing in on them. They rode in single file, climbing steadily along a northern slope with a series of lakes beneath them. To their left, above the lakes, the grey and forbidding Yr Wyddfa rose sharply to disappear into the mist. No trees, but bracken dying off and jumbles of fallen rocks, looking like petrified river beds as they tumbled down to the valley floor. The only living thing on the slope seemed to be cascades of mountain streams falling in straight lines from above the mist.

Lenc shivered. He imagined the snow and wind waiting for them higher up.

"Won't be for long though," he said to himself. "It's just a day, then we'll be at the coast."

Sure enough, as they ascended, so the wind rose, buffeting them and their horses as they plodded along, men and beasts with their heads down trying to keep out of the worst of the weather. Least it's not snowing, thought Lenc hopefully. Oh shit, he thought minutes later, as first rain then sleet hit them with tiny needles of ice.

All that morning they followed the track, catching occasional glimpses of the baleful Yr Wyddfa to their left as the mist swirled above them. The weather kept changing dramatically, as rain turned to sleet, then snow started to fall, followed amazingly by patches of sunlight.

What a place, thought Lenc. All four seasons in one morning. Then, coming out of an oak forest and through a momentary break in the mist, Yr Wyddfa was exposed in all its glowering beauty.

"You see to the right," Alun shouted, "where the mountain drops quite steeply, then rises again - that's the pass."

The track they were following seemed to be running parallel with Yr Wyddfa, showing off its sheer rock-strewn sides. Below them, the mountain side dropped steeply to the valley floor, with twinkles of light reflecting on a series of small lakes. Alun explained they were riding on what was probably an old sheep track, which was why it meandered slowly upwards, finding the easiest route, closely following the contours of the mountain. It was still a stiff climb, and looked even higher, steeper and more forbidding closer up. It was going to be a close-run thing, thought Lenc, whether they could get to the pass and down the other side before night-fall.

The small column of riders, heads and bodies wrapped in their cloaks, hunched against the cold, plodded steadily up the windswept track. There was no sky, no sun, just the shrieking head-wind blowing straight at them. To their right the rock of the mountain rose almost vertically until it disappeared into the mist. To their left the land fell away to lakes which collected the ice-cold water from the surrounding hills in the valley bottom.

Their last sight of the lakes had been earlier that morning, as they climbed until the mist clamped in, restricting their world to the horse in front and the steady clomping of the horse behind.

Lenc rode behind front man Alun, but after several miles, he was so cold he could barely concentrate on keeping just behind the rump of Alun's horse. Thankfully his own beast seemed to know what to do and kept just within distance. Lenc was under no illusions - to lose the group now would result in a cold and lonely death.

Alun roused and looked back at the column. "You all right?" he shouted at Lenc, who waved back then quickly pulled his hand back inside his cloak. Alun grinned, his eyebrows coated with hoar frost. "We're doing well, really, we should get over the pass well before dark."

Lenc nodded. He was superstitious enough to wonder whether the gods would take that optimistic forecast as a challenge. Since that first flurry of sleet and snow when they set off, the weather had been relatively kind. By midday, the sky was still dull grey and the wind howled manically. Up to then, they had stayed dry, but it was not to last. In came the rain, almost sideways, stinging exposed faces and hands in its ferocity. As their heads bowed, thinking things could get no worse, the rain changed to sleet and hail, then finally snow, which at first seemed like a relief - at least it didn't sting.

Despite the wind, the snow was sticking on the ground, making the path difficult to follow. Alun slid from his horse and holding the reins, motioned the rest of the band to dismount. They gathered round him as he crouched behind his horse so his voice could be heard. His face was pallid, with frozen snow sticking to his eyebrows and beard.

"It will be safer to walk from here," he struggled to shout against the wind. "The path is getting obscured, but we've gone too far to turn back. Our safest plan is to keep going and hope the snow doesn't settle too much between here and the pass."

He looked round at his tribesmen and Lenc. "All agreed?" he croaked.

The four nodded without speaking. "Good, the quicker we get going the quicker we get there. All we can do is keep our heads down and keep going. Don't stop and don't lose sight of each other. If you sit to rest, you'll never get up again."

Once again, he took up the lead position and with head bowed led the small party upwards into the teeth of the shrieking gale, dragging his reluctant horse by the reins.

Afterwards Lenc could not say how long they climbed in the numbing cold. A small part of his mind stayed alert, watching his feet, making sure he stayed with the others, while the rest of it strayed off to warmer, sunnier climes, where the thought of his nose and ears turning to ice and dropping off would have provoked incredulous laughter. His little farm back in Gaul was arid and rocky; there was snow there in the hills in winter but never seemingly as bitter and intense as this. He shut the image out as he conjured up the warmth of the Mediterranean and a bright golden sun in a clear blue sky. I'll get back to that someday, he promised himself.

Finally, as they stumbled on, Lenc was aware of Alun just ahead, capering like a madman. "The pass is just ahead," he shouted excitedly. "We've made it. Once we're through, the going should be easier."

Shaken out of his daydream, Lenc could only nod and plod on. There was no celebration in him. He did manage a look round and registered that for the first time he could see the rock wall either side, rather than just climbing upwards on one side and a sheer drop the other, but his fuddled brain could not work out what that meant. According to Alun, it was a good thing.

The wind still howled, tearing at their cloaks and the snow was by now thigh-deep. He was too tired to register that underfoot the path for a short distance was level, then almost imperceptibly was definitely going down. Eventually he dared to hope that the worst was over, then firmly shut that thought from his mind. If this was a false summit and we still have more to go, I'll just curl up in a ball and be found in the spring, he thought.

Alun was waiting for them, sheltering behind a big rock. He motioned them to stop and they all crowded thankfully out of the wind. He pulled his cloak hood back so they could all hear him, his beard and eyelashes still coated in ice.

"We made it," he said flatly. "Only the gods know how, but we did. We are on the downward slope which means we have to take just as much care where we put our feet, but the quicker we get down the quicker we'll find shelter. One last push and we'll soon be warming ourselves in front of a roaring fire."

His delighted grin seemed unreal, but the slap on Lenc's arm was real enough and roused him from the torpor he was falling into. Lenc shook himself, and said: "Let's get on with it then, no point standing about here enjoying ourselves."

Alun nodded, turned his horse and started walking. Lenc, then the other three fell into their positions, but at least there was the semblance of a spring in their step, knowing the worst was over.

Even so, it seemed a mind-numbing eternity to walk off the mountain. The weather eased slightly on the way down but was still dangerous. Lenc had fallen into a trance-like state, plodding along, when he stumbled into the rear of Alun's horse. Befuddled, he looked up and registered a friendly light at the open entrance to a walled compound, and Alun gesturing to them.

In the dim light, Lenc could see that the spoil from a ditch, dug round the compound provided the earth to form a rampart. Tree trunks with sharpened tops were rammed into the earth to take the rampart up even higher.

Alun led the way, clattering over a wooden bridge into the compound where a night-watchman pointed out the stable before disappearing back into his shelter behind the entrance.

Quickly they stumbled into the stable, immediately feeling the relief of shelter from the icy gale. The stable was round and stone built, to shoulder height, under a thatched relatively watertight roof.

Light wooden walls separated the horses in one half of the building, and two large pens taking up the rest of the space held cattle and sheep.

For his part Lenc had never been so glad to step into the stench and fug of a stable.

"We must dry the horses down, get them fed, then we can go next door where food and ale is waiting. The sooner the better," said Alun with a grin.

With limbs aching Lenc wearily dragged the saddle and travelling gear from his horse and found some dry straw to rub his horse down. She snorted impatiently as if she also knew the ordeal was over. Lenc stroked her ears and steered her to a feeding trough, where she whickered and plunged her nose into the oats and bran.

His last act was to drape a blanket over his horse and pat her affectionately on the rump before joining the others waiting to go next door.

"Gods, I'm glad that's over with," he exclaimed. "Let me get to that fire."

CHAPTER IV

The war band of twenty warriors, led by Caratacus and guided by the Druid Cainos, rode north along the ridgeline of a range of steep-sided hills. The intention was to avoid both the Romans and other fleeing tribesmen. The terrain was studded with cold streams which were fairly easy to ford but a spectacular waterfall proved an insurmountable obstacle. They dismounted and walked their horses down a precipitous slope alongside the cliff face which the torrent of water tumbled and crashed down. Cainos led Veldicca's horse as they slipped and slid down the slope until they could find a spot where they could safely cross. All that day they rode hard, always north towards the long blue stain of mountains on the horizon.

With dark fast approaching Cainos pointed to some lights twinkling ahead. "It's an Ordovician farmstead," he shouted to Caratacus. "There will be shelter there and hopefully some food. Best, I think, not to mention who you are. May I suggest we are merely fleeing from the battle?"

Caratacus could see the sense in this, if they were being pursued, either by the legion or the tribe, it made sense not to give their escape direction away.

"What about the girl?" asked Caratacus, who not for the first time, was beginning to regret kidnapping her to be his future bride.

"I will speak to her, and try and persuade her that it is in her own interests to keep her head down and not try to escape. I think she still trusts me and will do as I say."

Caratacus grudgingly nodded. "Do your best," he added.

Their approach to the farmstead, flanked on three sides by wooded hills, was heralded by a furious barking from a pack of brindled deer hounds, restrained by three older men. Standing to one side was a man with an air of authority who watched the riders approaching. Cainos rode forward and greeted him respectfully, explaining they had ridden hard from the battle site and would be grateful for shelter for the night before moving on north.

"You were at the battle with the Romans?" queried the farmer.

"Aye," said Cainos, "we thought we had the taking of them but they were too clever for us. We escaped and will fight again."

"You are not the first through here from the battle," said the farmer, "and probably not the last. You can bed down in the stable as my house is not big enough for you all, but we can find food for you, and I can at least find a bed in the house for the lady and yourself, priest."

Cainos was startled at this offer, annoyed at himself for not anticipating it. "That is most kind. I am sure we are all grateful for your hospitality."

"My people will show your men where to put their horses and bed down. When they are ready, they can join us in the hall." With that the farmer stood back, and his men, who had dragged the dogs back into their pen, pulled back the doors of a barn for the war band.

"Have I to sleep in a barn?" hissed Caratacus to Cainos incredulously. He clearly chose not to remember that he had spent the last two nights shivering under his cloak on damp grass.

"Lord, it is better that we keep your presence a secret," replied Cainos in a whisper. "Before long the countryside will be alive with Romans looking for you, so I think it best if you act as a simple warrior. Leave Veldicca to me. I will persuade her it is in her best interests to keep up the pretence, at least until you decide what you are going to do. Besides, dare I say, sleeping in a barn is a marked improvement on last night."

Caratacus shrugged, then nodded his agreement. "Keep a good watch on her, because by the gods, if she endangers me, I shall dispose of her as I did her intended." He paused. "Might have a bit of sport first, of course. It would probably be a comfort to her in her last hours that she was deflowered by the future King of Britannia."

Cainos bowed and murmured, "I am sure that will be a great comfort to her, lord."

As Caratacus led his horse into the barn, Cainos caught the bridle of Veldicca's horse and helped her dismount. He looked round and saw that no one was watching and pulled a small knife from his robes and cut the bonds tying her hands. She nodded her thanks and rubbed her chafed wrists, then slumped as if fainting before collecting herself and standing upright, regaining some of her colour, her eyes blazing.

"Well priest, my father and my intended are dead, the tribe is decimated - probably most of them dead or slaves - while that bastard Caratacus is free to spin his web with unsuspecting tribes once again, and I am a prisoner apparently to be his bride, and you, a priest, are doing his bidding. What am I to make of all this?"

Cainos took an alarmed step backwards. "You are quite right, my lady. But please believe me that everything I have done has been to try and keep you alive. The Romans out-thought us and beat us with guile. Then Caratacus showed his true colours, but I was not in a position to challenge him; I had to go along with him for your sake.

"He wants me to guide the war party to Mona and an audience with the Arch Druid. He wants his marriage to you blessed, despite already being married, and with that blessing carry on his quest to be King of Britannia. The man is mad and obsessed with his own destiny. Nothing will stand in his way, which is why we have to fight him like the Romans did, with cunning and guile.

"Veldicca, please believe me, I am on your side, and I want nothing more than to see you reunited with your people as their rightful leader. How we achieve this I don't know, but I promise you, when we are on Mona and Caratacus is pressing his petition to the Arch Druid, I will find a way, and if that means that Caratacus will be sacrificed in the holy fires then his death will do more good than his living.

"In the meantime, can I tell Caratacus that you will make no attempt to escape or to betray him, and that you don't need to be tied? In particular, it is important that while speaking to our hosts, you say nothing about your predicament. I can promise you that if Caratacus feels he is about to be betrayed, he won't hesitate to have you killed. If you can just stay away from the subject, we will get through this and I am sure that all will be resolved in your favour when we go to Mona."

Veldicca was relieved that the priest seemed to be on her side, maybe she could escape this depth of despair and get back to her people after all.

"Cainos, I agree. I hope I am right in entrusting my life to you. As you say, I am supposedly the leader of the Silures tribe, but I can only take my rightful place if I remain a virgin. If I choose a man as my husband who is acceptable to the tribe that's one thing, but if Caratacus violates me, even if I bear his children, I can no longer lead the Silures. You understand that?"

Cainos was momentarily distracted by the statesmanlike calm of the young princess. "Lady, I do understand and I am your man. I will direct you as best I can and will lead you out of this darkness. We have to be clever, calm and patient, and we will prevail. You are showing that you are a leader and I applaud that. We will prevail."

Despite herself, Veldicca giggled. Suddenly she was a queen, even if she was a queen to just one man. She had to assume the airs of a queen and fool all these other men. Well, she thought, that won't be too difficult; she and her girlfriends had made an art of winding men round their fingers - as a queen that should be a lot easier.

Veldicca felt much better now she knew she had an ally, albeit one she did not entirely trust, but still wondered if there was a search party looking for her. Probably not, she decided, as the tribe would have scattered after the defeat by the legion. And that led to another thought. When the tribe's warriors finally returned home with the news that her father and Trenos were dead and she was missing, probably kidnapped and possibly also dead, there would be a period of mourning and after a suitable time, if she did not make an appearance, then the tribal elders would pick a new leader. The sooner she got back to her tribal lands the better.

Would Lenc follow her, she wondered. He had shown a disregard for his own safety when he made that crazy bid to carry her off before the battle - would he do it again? Not if he got another bang on the head from a cooking pot, she remembered, smiling.

In the meantime, she had better start practising her airs and graces as a fine lady. With that new and interesting thought in her mind, she tilted her chin imperiously and walked across the farmyard to the big house. Waiting for her in the doorway was the farmer, who was by now reconciled to feeding so many people.

Veldicca smiled as the farmer saw her approach and gave her a bow. "You are very welcome in my house, lady. I am Geraint of the Ordovices and I am looking forward to hearing of the battle. I have two sons who joined the fight and would have news of them. Do you think they will be home soon?"

Geraint led Veldicca into the large hall, where extra places had been laid to feed the warriors. Inside, by a large fire, stood a beaming lady, who walked forward to receive Veldicca.

"Lady, let me introduce my wife, Gwenffrewi," smiled Geraint. "She is also desperate for news of our boys."

"I am afraid I can't tell you very much," said a saddened

Veldicca. "When we arrived at Levobrinta, which is where your fellow tribesmen said we would have the best chance of defeating the Romans, our forces split in two, either side of a chasm which split the ridge. Ordovices on one side, Silures on the other. There was one attack by the legion which we repulsed quite easily, then that night the Romans somehow managed to cross a swamp at our backs and at dawn attacked from the rear. My father, the leader of the Silures, was one of the first to fall. After that, it was hopeless - the Romans cut us to pieces. If I can give you any comfort, Levobrinta is in Ordovician country so your lads would know the terrain better than my people, so will probably have a better chance of escaping.

"The responsibility for taking on the Roman shield wall fell to the Silures, while the Ordovice stayed on the ridge. We lost a lot of men to the Roman assault, but your tribesmen, I understand, had not yet fought and had the opportunity to escape when they saw they were almost surrounded, so I do believe there is hope for your sons."

Geraint's head dropped and he nodded soundlessly, squeezing his wife's arm.

It was quite lame, she thought, but better to give these people hope rather than the probability that their sons would have been hunted down mercilessly and either killed as they ran, or sold into slavery.

Only then did Gwenffrewi see the crude bandage on Veldicca's arm where a Roman sword had sliced her. Apparently pleased to have something to do, she took hold of Veldicca's other arm and led her towards the fire. "Sit here my dear, and we'll clean and dress that wound properly."

Gratefully Veldicca sat by the warming fire and allowed her eyes to close as the older woman scurried about, finding warm water and fresh linen to dress the wound. Carefully she peeled the blood-soaked bandage from Veldicca's arm; she drew in her breath and her eyes widened when she saw the extent of the wound. It was about a hand-span long in a right-angle shape and still weeping blood. It was deep.

"This needs stitches," said Gwenffrewi emphatically.

Cainos, who had sidled closer to the fire when he saw the farmer's wife and Veldicca talking, took a closer look at the wound and agreed it needed stitches.

"In the absence of anyone else, I can stitch it up. I've had some experience of patching people up before."

Gwenffrewi was clearly relieved that the priest would take responsibility and stood back as he carefully wiped the excess blood away. "I will need a needle and your strongest thread," he said.

Cainos carefully opened a small leather pouch hanging from his rope belt and poured a powder into a horn beaker, then added some warm water. He indicated that Veldicca should drink the draught.

"This is belinuntia, a special potion which will help with the pain." He smiled as she drank it down, then gravely rolled up the sleeves of his robe and washed his hands in the warm water. He dropped the needle into a separate cup of boiling water straight from the fire, then carefully bathed the open wound in another water-based mixture smelling of foxglove, which also came from his pouch. "This potion to clean the wound was taught to me by apothecaries from far beyond Rome. They taught that everything must be as clean as possible."

He retrieved the needle from the boiling water, and with his tongue sticking out of his mouth in concentration, carefully passed the thread through the eye of the needle. "My lady," he added gravely, "this is going to hurt. I will be as quick as I can, but this must be done."

Veldicca wiped her sweating brow and smiled at Cainos. "You must do your best. I will try to bear it."

She looked away from him, and with her good hand, grasped the arm of her wooden chair. Cainos swallowed and bent over his patient. He tentatively took hold of her arm, then gripped harder and quickly stabbed into the skin. He was quick, but even so, Veldicca sucked in her breath in pain. She kept still and was determined not to cry out. The pain was excruciating but she kept silent.

I am the leader of my tribe, she told herself. I will not show pain. She gripped the chair arm fiercely as the waves of agony coursed through her, and then after what seemed a lifetime, the pain eased. Cainos stood and looked at his handiwork. "You did well, lady. I have seen hardy warriors incapable of taking such pain."

Veldicca opened her eyes and looked down at the stitched wound and smiled. "When I need some embroidery doing on my favourite gown, I know who to come to."

Cainos smiled back and carried on carefully binding the wound.

By now Caratacus and his bodyguard had been welcomed into the hall by Geraint who offered ale which they gladly accepted.

Caratacus took in the makeshift surgery at a glance. He smiled, "I am pleased to see your wound has been dressed, my dear, I hope it is not too painful?"

Despite her fury, Veldicca smiled back. "I gained my wound fighting the Roman shield wall. There were a lot of deaths and injuries inflicted on my people in that hopeless battle, yet were you not in it as well? You and your men must have been nimble indeed as there does not seem to have been any injury to any of you."

"When you are as experienced in the arts of war as I and my men, you learn very quickly how to inflict the most damage without receiving any in return," replied Caratacus smoothly.

Veldicca seethed; she wanted to denounce Caratacus for hanging back, letting others do the dangerous work, but with a warning look from Cainos she focussed on the fire and took no further part in the conversation.

"Perhaps we should be thinking of the future rather than the past," interjected Cainos hurriedly. "We took a beating on that hill, but we can learn from it, one good thing that we can build on is that for once Ordovice and Silure fought together. If we can maintain that good feeling, I feel sure that it will bode well for the future."

Gwenffrewi looked worriedly at her husband, feeling the atmosphere crackling, and was relieved when her steward announced their meal was ready. She linked arms with her husband and led the way into the dining hall, where a blazing fire cast a warmth over a frosty atmosphere.

After an otherwise uneventful night, the sun rose over an easterly mountain as the travellers mounted up. Veldicca, her arm strapped under her cloak, thanked the elderly couple for their hospitality, and hoped that their sons would ride home to them soon.

"You are very kind, lady," murmured Geraint. "I cannot guess at your current tribulations but I hope that they are resolved in your favour very soon."

Cainos, who was listening, added: "Sir, your words are wise and we thank you for them. One day we will raise an army which will drive the Romans back across the sea. Until then we must keep ahead of them."

Geraint nodded. "I wish you both well and should you return this way, our house is open to you."

The warriors were already mounted as Cainos helped Veldicca into her saddle then hauled himself onto his own horse. Caratacus eased over to the old couple and leaned down towards them. "May I add my thanks for your hospitality, it was much appreciated on a cold night."

Geraint stiffened. "We would never turn anyone away and I can only wish you god speed for the rest of your journey, wherever you end up."

Caratacus smiled; he wasn't sure whether there was a veiled insult there somewhere but let it go. "Farewell, and thank you again. I hope your sons get home soon."

With that, he touched his forelock and pulled his mount round and motioned to the war party to follow. With a final wave Cainos and Veldicca followed. As Geraint watched, half of the war party fell behind, forcing Cainos and Veldicca to move up to the middle of the column, forming an escort front and back.

There's little love lost there, thought Geraint grimly.

The journey from the hospitable farm to the coast was uneventful except for the jarring pain to Veldicca's wound. Cainos had fashioned a sling which kept her arm tight to her body and mitigated the bumping of the wound somewhat, but even so the pain was constant. Cainos had given her a draught containing more belinuntia which eased the pain, but he explained he could not give her too strong a dose otherwise she would be in danger of falling from her horse.

"I am sorry, my lady, you are just going to have to live with this until you heal. I daren't administer too strong a dose of painkiller."

"No matter Cainos," said Veldicca steadily. "Thanks to you the pain is manageable and it also helps me to stay focussed on what I must do. I have to be true to my mission which is to return and lead my people. In that, I am in your hands."

"Believe me, lady, nothing is closer to my thoughts than that you are reunited with your people. I will kill Caratacus myself before that happens."

"Thank you, Cainos, you give me heart that you will find a way out of this mess."

They rode all day, trying to stay in the valleys, but sometimes had no choice other than to climb up onto the windswept moor. The view from the top was spectacular with the glowering range of mountains and the might of Yr Wyddfa to their front, and all around, the land, covered in red bracken, falling away to dark forests. Eventually after several ascents they descended into a wider valley with a small stream trickling through it.

"What now priest?" said Caratacus, who could hardly bring

himself to look at Veldicca. "Where do we go from here?"

Cainos leaned back in the saddle. "This stream falls from here to the sea getting bigger and stronger all the time, and marks the edge of the mountain range. We will follow it all the way to the coast, then turn and head for the ferry to Mona. Once on the island we will finally be safe from the legion. It will take a full invasion before they dare to cross to the island." He pointed to the west. "There is the Isle of Mona, and there on the mainland the range of mountains which we are going round. Look at the snow on the tops - we would surely have perished trying to go the straight route over the top. All we have to do now is ride down to the coast and keep going until we get to the ferry. It will be two journeys across because of our numbers but we will soon be on the island which will be safe from Roman patrols." Then quietly. "And even Ordovician war bands."

For the first time in two days Caratacus smiled at Veldicca. "Well, my dear, have you thought any more about being married to the future King of Britannia? My dear wife is surely dead, killed by the Romans, so there is no impediment to my marrying again."

Veldicca composed herself as Cainos gripped her hand. "For the life of me, I cannot understand the advantage you think you will get by forcibly abducting me and thinking that I will happily comply with your wishes, even lose my virginity to you in your desire for royal children and respectability."

Cainos squeezed her hand even harder.

Caratacus leaned over to Veldicca, and said in a low voice, "It doesn't matter whether you understand or even like it. If I can arrange a marriage and I get you pregnant, I will keep you until you give birth to at least one boy and after that you can do whatever you wish. Go back to that Silurian hovel if you want."

Caratacus smiled but they all knew he was talking nonsense. If Veldicca failed to produce boys, or once she did, her life would be forfeit.

Abruptly Caratacus switched on his most winning smile.

"Let's not talk of such sombre subjects. You will make a great queen. Can you not imagine being on the throne of Britannia? Why, your tribespeople will make a pilgrimage to our palace to see you, the greatest lady in the land. Does that not sound like something to strive for?"

By now Cainos was almost paralysing her good arm with the pressure he was putting on her hand. She smiled at him and turned to Caratacus. "Lord what you are offering is so far out of my understanding, I fear I can hardly take it in. Perhaps when I have had a chance to digest it properly, I may be more inclined to accept it."

"Good, good," said Caratacus. "We will be going before the Arch Druid, seeking his blessing. Will you be agreeable and persuade him that this is the path you want to go down?"

Veldicca bowed her head. "Lord I will think on this deeply. I think perhaps I have little choice."

CHAPTER V

Somewhere in the northern wilds of the Penninus, the mountainous backbone of Britannia, Agrippa and his small band of pathfinders set up camp to await the arrival of the XIV Gemina Martia Victrix. They had ridden hard to get into position ahead of the demoralised legion which had taken such a battering before the tribes were eventually defeated. The night before, they broke their journey in the wooden fort at Mamucium, the most far-flung outpost of the empire. The fort was garrisoned by a cohort of Spanish auxiliaries from the Ala II Asturum, trying to keep warm and out of the biting wind straight off the sea.

The Fourteenth were on the march to bolster the Lindum garrison one of the Legion's few well-established stone forts in the province.

Agrippa had called an orders meeting for his band to brief them on the task ahead. They were camped in a sheltered spot in a clearing just off one of the several drover's tracks across the lower Penninus and were comfortably lying on their blankets round the camp fire.

"Gents, I think I should tell you the plan, such as it is. And if anyone has any objections or qualms about it, say so now." Solemnly he looked round at his men, all of whom seemed interested in what was going to be said next.

"The Fourteenth will be making their way past us here on their march to Lindum. At their next marching camp, we will be in position to fulfil our mission, which is to kill their legate,

Sabinianus in a way which cannot reflect back on either the Twentieth, the Fourteenth, the governor, or ourselves. In short, it either has to look like an accident, or if it's a murder we will have to provide a killer who will be found dead beside his victim. I suspect that one of Sabinianus's pretty young male friends would fit this category."

Again, Agrippa looked round carefully at his men. None seemed shocked that he proposed murdering a high-ranking officer, second only to the governor himself. They had all seen the wanton waste of life at the battle with the tribes, and through soldiers' gossip, knew how Sabinianus was thought of within his own legion.

"Tomorrow, we leave the horses in the forest with one man, and join the column as stragglers catching up. When we get to the marching camp, the armour you have been carrying that I scrounged at Deva, will be enough to make us look authentic, especially as we won't be alone among the lads in missing some kit. As long as we don't get into gossiping with the soldiers, they'll just think we're reinforcements, or dropped behind and are catching the column up.

"We need to find out the disposition of the guards round the command tent, and we need to know exactly who is inside. When the camp has settled down for the night, we can sneak into the tent and in a very short time come up with and execute a plan. Be left in no doubt, if we fuck this up, we will all be crucified instead of earning the gratitude of every man left standing in the Fourteenth."

It was late morning before the battered remnants of the Fourteenth eventually trudged past the pathfinders, hidden in trees on high ground overlooking the track. Agrippa frowned in disapproval as he noted the way the men were marching, their lack of column discipline and the slovenly way their kit was worn. To a man they would rather be anywhere else than trudging on that road with only wall-building to look forward to. 'Maybe we can change that,' he thought.

He let the straggling column file past and after a short pause, climbed from the saddle, tossing the reins to the pathfinder who drew the short straw and would remain by the road with the horses.

"Caius, follow us at a discreet distance and use your judgement about where you are going to hole up for the night. If all goes well, we should be back down the track after first light. Look out for us because we may need to leave in a hurry. If we don't get back by sunrise, ride to Deva and seek out the governor and tell him we failed." And with a grin, added: "I don't suppose I'll be minding too much what the governor thinks if I'm hanging up on a cross."

Caius watched as his comrades shook out on the road in column order with Agrippa at the head of the small band.

"Remember, you are back as foot soldiers now, just remember how to march. By the way you start out on the left foot, everybody got that? Good, quick march."

There were some ribald comments from the middle of his column which Agrippa affected not to hear, but grinned anyway. They had an afternoon's marching to do, although Agrippa did not want to catch the column too soon. His fear was some inquisitive soldier would realise they were not of the Fourteenth and raise the alarm, but at the same time did not want to leave it too late so they were still behind the column when it arrived at the marching camp.

That evening the pathfinder group found itself safely inside the marching camp being thrown up on a windswept site high in the Penninus.

The marching camp was a ritual well known to the legions. They marched all day, then dropped their packs and picked up entrenching tools to dig a trench to completely encompass the camp. The spoil was stacked on the inside of the square, to give at least a semblance of defence. Then the following morning the last task before resuming the march was to fill the trench in again.

Agrippa was aware that his men should be helping to dig the trench. He was concerned that his group looked a bit suspicious, mainly because no officer could bear to see soldiers lying about idle. He quietly told his men to split up into pairs and walk about, looking as if they had a pressing task to complete. "Keep your eyes open and try not to draw attention to yourself. Meet back here before dark."

The group moved out and Agrippa walked purposefully to the centre of the camp where the command centre would be. A collection of tents surrounded by carts was obviously the centre, but Agrippa dared not stop. He kept going, walking past orderlies and slaves busily setting up the creature comforts for the exalted ranks inside. By risking a sneaking glance whenever possible, he thought he had identified Sabinianus's personal quarters and command tent at the centre of the complex. But which were the sleeping quarters, he had no idea. He kept walking then turned and circled round to come back on the other side of the command tent. Amid the frantic activity of setting up the camp there were still guards wandering round keeping an eye on proceedings. Agrippa counted four pairs of men carrying full weapons, who seemed to be making a casual circuit of the command area which would probably be maintained all night until the camp was broken in the morning. Then the guards would revert to their roles as bodyguards for Sabinianus and the senior officers in the command group.

Once back at their camp area, Agrippa tried to draw a plan of the command post on a wax tablet. He knew that the public area, where conferences were held and the orderlies worked, would be at the front, and Sabinianus would have a connected private area of a living room, kitchen and dining area, and of course, the bedroom. Some leaders had done away with this ostentatious display, it was all kit that had to be transported, but he felt that Sabinianus would not be that sort of officer. He would not sacrifice his lifestyle whatever his soldiers thought of him.

As he sketched out his plan, his men gradually drifted in and sat on the grass around him. "Anyone got any ideas about which tent he may be in?"

"Well boss, I was three years a young soldier working in this sort of environment and they don't change very much from one camp to another," offered one of his men. "To the rear there will be a line of small tents, attached to the big one. These are a meeting tent and dining area only accessible from the main tent, and the other two will be a galley and sleeping area. The legate will receive guests in the meeting area, who would only come from the conference area, but the galley and his bedchamber would need external entrances to bring food in and for the sleeping area, a way for any guests to discreetly come and go."

Agrippa supposed that made sense. "How the other half live, eh?"

He made some adjustments to his wax drawing and looked at it. "We don't have enough information," he said ruefully. "We can't proceed until we get a clearer picture of what's happening inside these damned tents, and at least confirm which one he will be sleeping in."

One of the pathfinders stretched out on the ground with his ankles crossed, put up his hand. "Why don't a couple of us just wander over and offer to cart some furniture around? From what I saw they were frantic to get the camp set up. Surely they'll be glad of some extra hands, besides who would question us?"

Agrippa thought quickly. It would be a risk but the operation depended on better intelligence.

"Yes," he decided swiftly. "Two volunteers for furniture moving duties."

Two men quickly raised their hands and wasted no time in buckling their equipment on and headed for the command tent.

From then until dark, when the two pathfinders returned was a nerve-wracking time for Agrippa. The operation depended on this information, but if his men were found out, they would all discover how sharp the interrogator's knives could be.

Eventually, to his immense relief, the two came back, one carrying a leather flask of wine which he handed round. "Our reward for being good little soldiers and helping out. They were very grateful," he said.

The other soldier sat next to Agrippa and took the wax tablet. "This one is the sleeping tent," he said, pointing to one of the three smaller tents. "It's the last in line and next to it is the meeting tent where the legate can sit and take his ease in private and next to that isn't a galley, but a dining area where the top knobs will eat. The galley is another tent on the other side of the pathway so food has to be brought in, which means there's quite a lot of traffic around there. That would go on until the meal has been served then cleared away. It will then depend on whether Sabinianus wants to sit with his seniors or curl up in bed. Given the distance they have travelled today, I don't think they will be late to bed."

Agrippa agreed. "Right, Flavius and Ignatius, you will be with me. The rest of you spread yourselves out round the tent but stay out of sight. I don't fancy our chances much if we have to fight our way out, and that option isn't something I want to think about. There will be a guard on all entrances to the tents, so we're going to have to find a place to get under the wall of the main tent. From there, there should be no guards on the inside, but there will be sleeping servants, so it will just be a matter of finding the bedroom. We three will creep into the tent, and if the bastard is on his own, we kill him and if his playmate is with him, which I am sure he will be, we kill him as well. Smothering should do the trick. Keep them quiet as well.

"Order of march, first Flavius, then me, then Ignatius. We will set off at the third watch of the night, which should give us plenty of time before dawn and the rest of you follow on in pairs and take up positions where you can see the tent but still stay hidden. We need to keep a sharp eye out for roaming sentries but try to keep out of their way. The order of the day is stealth and speed, because if we get involved in a fight, it's fair to say we'll be fucked. Now get your heads down and at least look as if you are sleeping."

The camp was dark and still when Agrippa cautiously pulled aside his cloak. He was frozen, but his only thought was on the mission ahead. He shook the men either side of him who stirred and in turn shook their neighbours. Without a word, Flavius stood and stealthily moved out, followed by Agrippa and Ignatius. The rest would follow at intervals. Security would be tight round the command post, but at this time in the morning its guards would feel fairly secure. Any attackers would have to deal with the sentries on the hastily dug perimeter ditch, then take on half a cohort of Rome's finest before getting anywhere near the command post. An attack from within was too fanciful to contemplate.

Cautiously Flavius led the way, keeping to the side of the path, walking on the balls of his feet. The camp was quiet with only the odd snore from a closed-up tent to break the silence. Suddenly Flavius stopped, crouched, and raised an arm, the signal for the other two to melt into the dark off the path. Up ahead was a moving light, which gradually disappeared. After a minute Flavius waved them forward and grabbed Agrippa by the arm. He moved in close to whisper: "We've reached the command area. That was the two-man guard randomly circling the inner compound. We should come on the legate's command centre about half-way down, where we should be able to slip under the tent wall."

Agrippa nodded his assent and Flavius looked round in the dark before carefully stepping back out onto the track, creeping along the path as stealthily as possible. Unknowns were whether there would be guards outside the sleeping area and the servants sleeping on the ground at the entrance to the private area. Flavius stealthily tiptoed forward and crouched down when he reached the tent wall.

"Well done so far," whispered Agrippa, "Can you raise the wall?"

Flavius felt along the leather binding where the tent met the ground and grunted when he found a large wooden tent peg holding the side down. He took hold of it with both hands and tried to pull it out of the ground. At first it wouldn't budge. "Come on, you bastard," he whispered frantically and rocked it from side to side, then with a sigh of satisfaction, slowly drew it from the ground.

"We must remember to put it back when we leave," whispered Agrippa. "Let's go."

Flavius held the tent wall up and quickly Agrippa squirmed under, followed by Ignatius who held the wall up for Flavius. There was a night light of sorts in the gloom, giving enough light for Agrippa to make out the curtain drawn across the legate's private quarters.

"Watch where you put your feet," he hissed.

Carefully they crept forward and past the curtain. Agrippa checked. There were two bodies fast asleep near the internal entrance to the sleeping chamber. He pointed the two out and carefully stepped over one into the entrance. The others followed. Inside they could just make out a large double bed covered in furs in the centre of the tent. Agrippa crouched and quietly crept round to the head of the bed then cautiously raised himself so he could see the occupants. His eyes narrowed as he took in the heads on the pillows. The light was poor, but he could make out two sleeping figures, one man, obviously the legate and a blonde, curly haired boy. Both fast asleep.

Agrippa sank back to the carpet again and rejoined his men. They moved away from the bed to a corner and huddled together. He silently raised two fingers.

He leaned in closer. "Judging by the hair length, Sabinianus is in the middle with a lad on the right. If we all move to the top of the bed, I will knife Sabinianus, and one of you smother the boy. He won't be a problem, but Sabinianus might take two of us. No matter how much they struggle, they mustn't make a noise. All right?"

Both men nodded and bunched up their cloaks, while Agrippa carefully drew his dagger. Back at the top of the bed, each man took his position while Agrippa slipped forward, finding Sabinianus's hair. He slept peacefully on his side, with an arm round the young boy, while Agrippa held the knife in both hands pointing towards him and carefully placed it just under the legate's chin. The other two waited, poised, at the bed head for Agrippa to strike.

Suddenly the silence was split by a hoarse shout outside. They froze in near-panic but the feared retribution and armed men bursting in failed to appear. As silence returned, Flavius let go his breath in a sigh. Agrippa nodded, and with his free hand, squeezed Flavius's arm. When he turned back to his task Sabinianus had unconsciously been disturbed and was now lying flat on his back. Agrippa let out a long breath and once again steadied his knife. He looked fleetingly left and right, licked his lips then plunged the blade in under the legate's chin, pulling it savagely towards him through the mouth and straight into the brain. Quickly he pulled the knife out and slashed across the neck ensuring that his victim could not utter a sound and was dead immediately.

The blond boy's eyes opened in alarm as he woke from deep sleep. His lips moved as he struggled to comprehend what was going on, then, as he was about to let out a scream, Flavius pushed his bunched cloak down over the boy's face with all his strength. His terrified shout was smothered in the folds of the heavy cloth as at first he struggled desperately, pulling at his assailant's arms, but gradually subsided and lay still. Carefully Flavius lifted the smothering cloak and felt for a pulse.

"Right, that's it," said Agrippa quietly. Sabinianus's dagger, found in his belt on a chair was smeared in blood and wrapped in the boy's right hand. Then he carefully lifted the boy's left hand and cupped it round the right hand and the dagger.

"Sorry, boy," he whispered quietly as he firmly grasped both the lad's hands and without hesitating drove the knife into the boy's dead heart. Agrippa sighed and for a second hung his head, then looked up at his men, who both nodded in understanding.

"Time to go, boss," whispered Flavius, "you had no choice, it has to look like the boy did it."

By dawn the small party was out of the marching camp and swinging back down the road to their horses and then the road to Deva. There was a tense moment as the outer sentries made to challenge them as they were marching back the way they had come, but they lost interest when they saw Agrippa at the front with his trademark vine stick marking him as a centurion.

Caius was waiting for them in a stand of beech trees and whistled as they approached. They quickly discarded their soldier's armour and dressed once more in the way of the local population and rode hard for Deva.

"What they'll make of that lot is anyone's guess" said Agrippa, "but I fancy they won't be looking for conclusions for a while. They'll be more interested in hushing it all up."

Flavius nodded. "Trouble is, you know how soldiers gossip - it will be right round the camp in minutes."

Agrippa agreed. "Not our problem. Let's get out of here and get on with some proper soldiering."

Deva was built on a sandstone bluff and stood out for miles on the horizon, overlooking a bridge crossing the River Dee and close to a natural harbour. It was still a mud earthwork topped by tall tree trunks making the first crude walls. Agrippa and his men approached the north gate - even this was a rudimentary earthwork, protected by timbers.

As they rode nearer, Agrippa held his arm up to his eyes to examine the fort more carefully.

"There's funeral cloth across the gate," he said. "Don't tell me they already know of Sabinianus. If that's the case we'd better push on."

Flavius came up and studied the fort.

"Can't be, boss. We travelled on the main road, and if a courier had passed us, we would have seen him. Must be something else."

Agrippa grunted. "I hope you're right. We would look a bit silly wandering into a trap. I think I'll go forward by myself and ask the guards who they're mourning."

Agrippa motioned to his men to dismount when they were in proper sight of the fort and trotted on alone. When he arrived at the massive gate, he shouted to the guards: "Centurion Agrippa of the Twentieth Pathfinders. What's the black banner for?"

A disembodied voice replied from the castle: "Advance and be recognised. We are in mourning for Governor Scapula. He died on his way here."

Agrippa reeled at the news, the more so because it was completely unexpected. He knew that his supreme commander was not a well man but this was a shocking blow.

"I will fetch my men," he shouted and wheeled his horse, thinking furiously.

When he came up with his men, resting in a small copse of trees, he blurted out: "Scapula is dead. And as you can imagine this gives us a few more problems."

Agrippa tried to weigh the pros and cons as he tethered his horse.

"First thing, if you thought we were in a difficult place before, we could really be in the shit now. I would bet that Scapula never mentioned our mission to anyone, so if our involvement is going to get out, it's going to come from one of you." He looked round solemnly. "If anyone blabs about this, whatever the circumstances, we will all end up on the cross. Do I make myself clear?"

They all nodded acceptance. "Good," said Agrippa. "This is our secret and we will keep it to the grave. Scapula was a good man and cared for his troops - that's why the legate had to go. In time he would have risen to the highest offices in the Senate, and those arse-licking bastards would believe him a great officer.

"Instead, his reputation will be torn to shreds, which the army hierarchy will try to hush up but it will very soon be an open secret throughout the legions. We did a great thing when we sent him to his gods; let's not fuck it up with loose talk.

"Having said that I think we should find somewhere to sleep then have a bit of a celebration. We've had a hard time of it of late, and I fancy there is more to come."

CHAPTER VI

Once fed and thawed out, Lenc and the Ordovicians spent a dreamless night by the fireside of the mountain tavern and in good spirits, resumed their journey to the coast.

"We'll soon find out if we've arrived before them," said Alun while they were on the trail. "There's only one ferry, and Caratacus and his party do stand out a bit."

The ferry boat had seen better days. She was drawn up against the shore in a narrow creek, the bow pointing out to sea. She was built rather like a barge with only a simple structure at the stern to house the tiller and keep the elements off the skipper. A single mast was stepped in the centre of the vessel, surrounded by pens to corral any animals transported to and from the island.

This was a wild part of the coast with the towering hills of Yr Wyddfa providing a backdrop to the narrow strip of land along the coast. One of the few collections of homesteads was the small fishing village of Segontium, further along the strait, separating Mona from the mainland. Life in this isolated outpost was harsh, probably why it had attracted an unsavoury reputation as a haven for pirates.

The morning was clear and crisp, under a bright blue sky and an autumn sun. Below them they could make out in detail the land falling away to the strait between the mainland and Mona beyond, which Lenc studied with interest. The land rose easily from the strait and seemed to stay flat long into the distance. A forest, punctuated by clearings with a few dwellings, seemed to span the entire coastline, and beyond, far in the distance he could just make out a low line of hills.

"An interesting looking place," he observed.

"Aye, it is that all right," agreed Alun. "It's a small island but pretty much self-contained. They grow and rear everything they need, so don't tend to want anything from the mainland. Visitors are tolerated but are treated with suspicion, especially as they suffer from raiders from Hibernia, Caledonia, even further afield. The Druids have helped, mind - they have their own town and seat of learning which they built themselves, and they have their own security, which has defended the island pretty well. Raiders tend to avoid the place and go where there are easier pickings."

That's something to think about, reflected Lenc. From what I've heard, these druids may have something to share with us. Perhaps we should be befriending them instead of thinking of them as enemies.

His train of thought was destroyed when Alun pointed down the track to some nondescript buildings on the seashore. "Here we are at last," he yelled.

The clattering of hooves, as Lenc and the Ordovicians rode onto the small jetty, roused a farmer and his boy tending a small flock of sheep. They stared at the riders without expression as they waited patiently to board the vessel.

The five horsemen dismounted and tethered their animals to a fence, as a dispiriting light drizzle started, then looked round for signs of activity. Their arrival seemed to be a signal for a broad-shouldered woman wearing oiled sacking to defy the rain and sea-spray, to appear from a nondescript hut made of driftwood. She was strong-looking, with wild hair down her back, but with a friendly enough red-cheeked face.

"Five of you, is it? And horses?" she asked.

Alun answered with a nod.

"Half a silver coin should do it. We sail shortly on the tide; I'll tell you when to board." She nodded and was about to disappear back into the dubious warmth of her hut when Alun called her back.

"Have you seen a party of horsemen, maybe about twenty of them, with a blond-haired, big fellow, a priest and a black-haired woman recently?" he asked.

The ferry woman put her hands on her heavy hips and laughed. "I remember that lot for sure – they arrived yesterday mid-morning, it took two journeys to get them across. Why, are they friends of yours?"

"Not exactly," said Alun hesitantly, "but we do need to talk to them."

"You'll get every chance to do that," she replied. "My ferry is the only way on and off this island, so there is nowhere else they can go. Just rest awhile and when the tide turns, we'll be over there before you know it."

Alun looked round uncertainly. "Suppose we just have to wait, then," he replied.

Other than the ferry woman's hovel, there was no shelter on the creek, so the five stood with their backs to the wind, hunched against the strengthening rain. Then, after what seemed a soaked eternity the ferry woman once again appeared and a teenage boy led a draught horse down to the creek. The woman shouted to the farmer to keep his sheep back; she would load the horses first. The teenage boy jumped aboard and with the help of two smaller urchins, re-arranged the trestles to corral the horses in one pen. The lad signalled to the woman who gestured to Alun to walk the horses on board. She removed a length of the side of the ship and laid it down onto the bank as a platform for the horses.

"Bring them on, slowly now," she ordered.

Alun whispered soothing words to his horse as he led her down onto the makeshift gangplank, onto the deck of the old boat. She was nervous and her eyes rolled in fear, but she did not hold back as Alun stroked her and gently led her down onto the boat. When fully on board, the boy took her bridle and led her into the pen, then signalled for the others to follow. Once one horse was on board, the others followed docilely. Lenc came last and steered his horse into the pen and the boy pulled the gate shut. The horses had some room to move, but were effectively caged so could not thrash about if panicked.

After the horses, the sheep were driven into their own pen, and the gangplank pulled up. Lenc and his companions leaned on the side as the boy harnessed the draught horse to the prow of the ship; ropes were cast off on the ferry woman's command, and the horse put his head down and slowly walked along the bank as his harness took the strain. As the rope tightened, the horse plodded steadily as gradually the boat slipped away from the rough quayside. Slowly the ferry turned its head towards the open sea and just before it cleared the narrow creek, the boy freed the rope from the horse as the ferry slipped out into the strait and the running tide.

Alun nudged Lenc, "According to the ferry woman, they're just a day ahead, so we are catching up with them, but I reckon they still have enough distance on us to make the Druid town before we sight them."

The ferry woman sat on a stool, her right arm guiding the tiller to steer out into the centre of the channel. She had discarded her oiled sacks, and sat astride her stool in a thick black wool dress down to her feet. A once-white shawl kept the wind off her neck, covering her shoulders and resting on a more than ample bosom. She smiled happily at Lenc as she noticed him looking.

Alun leaned over to Lenc who had hastily torn his fascinated gaze from the woman who made steering the boat look so easy. "This can be a dangerous place," Alun confided. "The tide comes from both directions and changes four times a day. Drovers have been known to swim their cattle across at low tide, but I wouldn't recommend it. The water level can go down to just knee-deep, but there are sandbanks you can sink into, and when the tide turns it can come in faster than a man can run. Not a place to be if you don't know what you're doing."

Lenc nodded; he could see by the action of the sea that the

current was strong, with spray whipping off the top of rippling waves, caught by the offshore wind. Ahead was their destination, which he studied with interest. The island seemed quite low - although in the distance there were those hills, he had seen from the mainland being buffeted by the Oceanus Hibernicus. In the incessant rain it seemed a dreary place. Turning, he looked back at the mainland and the snow-capped line of mountains looming out of the mist. By Mithras, did we truly walk over that? he thought incredulously. Yr Wyddfa was further back and shrouded in mist but the lower slopes were dark and brooding. He shivered involuntarily.

The ferry woman leaned hard on her tiller, sending the boat across the tide as the island drew nearer. Lenc could see their destination, a small jetty surrounded by low buildings, sheltered from the northern winds by a thick semi-circle of trees. The two urchins moved to the bow of the boat and waved to another lad standing on the jetty. This one had a rope coiled in his hands, and as the boat moved slowly towards the jetty he threw the rope, which was deftly caught, pulled in and tied off on the prow. When the rope took up the slack, the tethered prow stayed still, forcing the rear of the boat to swing round until facing completely the opposite direction, nudging gently against the wooden jetty. Quickly the boys made the rear fast, and the ferry woman grunted approval.

Quite a neat trick, thought Lenc as he stood idly in the freshening wind. He turned away as the two boys untied the ropes holding the horse pen and coaxed their horses down the ramp to dry land. When the horses were led away, the boys released the sheep, who surged down the ramp, relieved to be back on solid ground.

He jerked back to watchfulness as he registered two men on the jetty dressed as priests. They were standing aimlessly, but taking an interest in the passengers on the ferry. Nothing wrong with that, thought Lenc. Maybe the arrival of new people to a small island would be the most exciting thing that happened all day. But there was something odd about these priests. They looked fit and somehow did not stand like priests. They had close-cropped hair and full woollen gowns but stood easy and alert in a state of readiness. The giveaway was the longsword each man had strapped to his waist.

Lenc frowned as his gaze moved on to Alun and his three tribesmen who were walking their horses along the jetty, getting them used to being back on land. He risked a look back at the priests. Who were walking towards him.

The taller of the two priests stood in front of Lenc and looked him up and down. "What is your business here?" he finally demanded.

"What's it to you?" returned Lenc.

The second priest put his hand on his colleague's arm and tried for a smile, not very successfully. "You are obviously a stranger to Mona," he said. "Otherwise you would know who we are. We are the Arch Druid's guard, known as Druidae, and it is our responsibility to ensure that visitors are here for legitimate reasons."

Lenc thought about that for a few seconds. "I could ask you what you consider legitimate reasons, but instead I will just say that I am not interested in you or your Arch Druid, and that I have a reason for being here and it is nothing at all to do with you or your religion."

The exchange of veiled threats was likely to escalate but then Alun, who was securing his horse to a rail, hurried over, anxious to calm the air of rising tension which looked likely to end in iron being drawn.

"Gentlemen, please, there is no reason for suspicion. My friend here is a Gaul and knows nothing of the vital work you do. He was also wrong that his and our business do not concern you, because we will be looking to seek an audience with the Arch Druid as soon as possible."

Alun quickly explained that he and his men were Ordovician and were familiar with the island, but Lenc, the Gaul, had never set foot here before. "It's a complicated story, but we're looking for a war party of about twenty Catuvellaunians led by a big blond-haired man. They will have a priest, Cainos and a young woman with them. Like us they fought against the Romans, but now we need to find them. We know they arrived yesterday, but did they give any clue what their destination was?"

The two priests glanced at each other, seemingly unsure how much to divulge. "This band is on the island and yes, they arrived just yesterday," confirmed one eventually, "but it's not a war party. The leader is looking for our Arch Druid's blessing to be married. Not only that, but the Catuvellaunian is to marry the lady you mention, who is a Silurian princess. It should be quite a celebration."

Both Alun and Lenc fought to control their surprise at this revelation. "Well, that's wonderful news, eh Lenc?" stammered Alun. "Let's hope we'll be in time for the celebrations."

We need these people on our side, thought Lenc swiftly. Time to eat some shit. "Gentlemen, please accept my apologies for my earlier behaviour. I had no idea of your important duties. Now that you know of our plans, perhaps you could give some directions to where we would find your leader and meet up with our friends and join them in what, I am sure, will be a most memorable occasion."

With the air cleared and everyone smiling, the priests were happy to give directions to the Druids' stronghold. "Take the track north, and you will come across the main roadway on the island. Go north-west, you won't miss it - it is the biggest and most imposing town you will ever have seen. You have plenty of time. Cainos is a well-known and devout Bard, and with his support, I see no reason why the Arch Druid would not give his wholehearted recommendation, but we have about ten days till the next full moon, which will be the most auspicious occasion."

"Good news indeed," agreed Lenc, who looked round for an excuse to cut the conversation short. He smiled. "Please excuse us, but we need to get on the road."

The priests silently nodded as Lenc turned and joined the Ordovicians, saddling the horses by the side of the ferry.

"They were just about the scariest priests I've ever come across," said Lenc. "They may have been dressed as priests, but they look and act more like soldiers, just like the Vigiles, the legion's police."

Alun looked at him carefully before throwing the saddle on his horse, then stepped back and looked round. "Druidae," he said carefully.

Lenc looked puzzled. "Yes, one mentioned Drudae, who or what are they? Are they priests?"

Alun gripped him by the arm and moved in close. "Get your horse saddled and let's get out of here. I'll explain later." He gestured to his three men to get a move on, and with the horses safely saddled, they lost no time in mounting and cantering off the quayside. Lenc risked a look as they went past the priests, then hurriedly looked away as he saw them staring fixedly at him.

Once on the trail, Alun set a brisk pace, uphill, through a beech forest, hugging the coastline. The track meandered through the trees, then as the terrain started to level out, burst into the open, alongside small fields separated by low walls of stone. When they had put in some distance from the jetty, Alun paused, looking back to make sure they were not being followed, then stopped at a stream to let the horses drink.

The riders climbed down and gratefully stretched their legs before Lenc raised the subject on all their minds. "What do we do now?" he asked. "Looks like we're going to kill someone who is probably the esteemed guest of the most important person on the island. And if those two pretend priests were anything to go by, we won't just be able to wander in and stick a sword into him."

Alun paused in rubbing his horse down with snatched up grass. "We could wait for them to leave the island, but they probably won't do that until they feel safe. In the meantime, it looks as though Caratacus is going to work on the Arch Druid to get agreement to marry Veldicca. That way he can not only say he is in union with the Silures but he has the backing of the Druids, before going on to try and get support from other tribes. Either way he has to be stopped - the man is a walking disaster area, all he seems to be good for is getting fighting men killed."

Lenc thought a moment. "What about Cainos? I've never held the ethics of the priesthood very highly, but I took him for a reasonable man who had the best interests of the tribes at heart."

"That's a good thought," pondered Alun carefully. "The other problem is Veldicca. From what I know of her, she is not very likely to just walk meekly into a marriage she doesn't want. Surely all she would have to say is that Caratacus is already married, and no priest could bless their union. Unless they have her drugged of course. Which means we are back to Cainos."

The small group fell silent, each man digesting the dilemma they were about to ride into.

Lenc broke the silence: "There is so much we don't know. The first priority is to get more information, so I think we are going to have to get into the Druid town and see what we can find. We need to know where Caratacus and his men – and of course Veldicca and Cainos - are staying. A word with Cainos could be very useful."

That night, they stayed in a deserted stone shepherd hut with a thatched roof that had seen better days. They were grateful that the rain stayed away, and there was enough dry wood nearby to build a warming fire. They ate the last of their food, then rolled up in their blankets and cloaks to try and snatch some fitful sleep.

The next morning saw the small band saddled up and on the road early. They were travelling on fairly flat land and judging by the lush colours of the meadows, prime growing country.

After some hours on the road, Alun eased back on his saddle and pointed ahead. "Do you see those hills in the distance?"

Lenc could see a blue hazy shape rising above low cloud and nodded. "That's our destination," he added. "Beyond that is the sea; north and west is bog. The Druids have their town on the higher ground in a vast forest of oaks which they consider to be sacred. If anyone asks, we should stick to our story and say we are seeking sanctuary after the defeat by the Romans. Close enough to be the truth."

Gradually, as they drew nearer to the hills, they could see that the whole hill range was swathed in verdant, fully mature trees, which Alun confirmed were oaks. As they rode closer still, they could pick out wooden buildings, each in its own clearing among the trees. At the top of one hill rising through the forest, was a stone-built tower, which seemed to be the most prominent building of the town. Next to the tower was another stone building with a flat roof, just clearing the surrounding woodland.

"The Druids' town is an unusual settlement," explained Alun. "It's called Caergybi and is built on what they call a holy island, and the whole town is laid out to reflect their religion and centres of learning. At the centre is that stone tower, which is the Arch Druid's mansion, with the Great Temple and Supreme Tribunal. Radiating out from that are the three disciplines of the religion, each in their own forest groves. According to the ancient sources, the priests are divided into three orders, Bards who are poets, singers and historians; Ovates interpret sacrifices and omens in order to tell the future; and the Druids who observe natural phenomena are the philosophers, teachers and diplomats. Each have their own colleges and accommodation among the trees and both men and women from all over the world come to study, sometimes for up to eighteen years.

"We will find a bed in Coleg Derwyddon, I have stayed there before, and as long as you don't mind lots of novice monks being droned at by their tutors, it's not a bad place to stay and we will be central.

"At the furthest extremities are the underlings, the servants, and slave barracks - all the people who make the whole place function. It's a thriving metropolis but well disguised in the woods."

Lenc realised he was keen to see this strange seat of learning; certainly it seemed like nothing he had experienced before. "What about those warrior priests, where do they fit in?"

"They have their own barracks close to the Arch Druid's mansion at the highest point of the hills," replied Alun, "which is where we should find Caratacus and his party. Cainos will have made much of Caratacus as the future King of Britannia and they will have been received as honoured guests. We, on the other hand, will be lucky to find a bed in the travellers' hostel."

"I must say I've never heard of militant priests before," said Lenc thoughtfully. "My experience has always been they were more interested in god bothering rather than waving swords about."

"You don't know the half of it yet," laughed Alun. "We are about to enter the centre of one of the greatest religions of all time. Over the years the Druids have spread out all over the known world. They have formed alliances with other religious groups much further afield than the Roman Empire spreads. They study here for many years then go out into the world, spreading the word of their religion and their knowledge of law, philosophy, magic, the future as well as the past and their word is law. And that's their strength; they have a network of priests which extends into every town and country which also gives them an intelligence network second to none. I would be willing to bet you that the Arch Druid knew of the defeat of Caratacus before the would-be king had ridden off that ridge."

As the line of hills came closer, Lenc started to pick out the shapes of the buildings among the trees. "Wouldn't it have been easier to cut all the trees down, then use the wood to build with?" he asked Alun.

"The oak is a sacred tree to the Druids," explained Alun, "and they are very sparing of how many they chop down. They would far rather cut just enough to make the space for a building, then drag cut timber from elsewhere to make up what they need. It gives them seclusion and privacy and yet the space to hold their classes."

That evening after claiming their beds in a dormitory in the priests' hostel, the five walked further into the town in search of a tavern. After being in the saddle all day, food, drink, and perhaps some local knowledge was in order.

"This looks all right," said Lenc as they came across a substantial roundhouse with a swinging sign above the door. Like the other buildings, this one was made of wooden planks under a thatched roof. Painted on the sign was a jolly priest about to drink from a foaming mug.

"Looks promising," agreed Alun.

Inside, they found an empty table against the rough whitewashed wall and gratefully sat down. Strangers were obviously common in the bar because none of the other patrons even bothered to pause in their conversations as the five pulled off their heavy cloaks and looked round expectantly. There was a warm fug in the room and a big log fire in a brazier in the centre. Almost immediately a young serving girl, her apron stained a variety of dull colours, tried a small smile on the five newcomers as she put a large brown earthenware pot on the table and a matching mug in front of each of them.

"What's this?" asked Iestyn suspiciously.

"It's our local beer," she replied defensively.

"What if I want something else?" he countered.

The girl shrugged. "You can please yourself - there is nothing else. It's beer or nothing."

"We'll take the beer," said Alun, smiling, and then added, "Is there any food on offer?"

The girl nodded.

After a short pause, Alun followed up his question. "Can you tell us what the choice is? We are rather hungry as we have been travelling all day."

"Stew," she replied, then added, "mutton."

"I expect it's stew or nothing, is it?" he countered, and then added: "No, let's have five bowls of stew - I am sure it will be delicious."

She nodded and went through an opening at the back into what must be the kitchen and beer store.

Lenc looked round and registered that several of the other customers were spooning down the stew, which gave him some encouragement. It probably won't kill us, he thought reassuringly.

Madawc poured the beer into their mugs and tentatively tried a sip, then a large glug. "It's not bad," he said with some surprise.

As they each sampled their beer, the serving girl reappeared balancing a tray with their bowls of stew and hunks of bread. She dealt the food out as her new customers fished in their clothes for their wooden spoons. Dirks were drawn to spear the bread.

"I don't know whether it's because I'm starving, but this is pretty good," said Alun between mouthfuls. All he got in return was appreciative nods from the others between slurps.

After scraping every last morsel from their bowls, they sat back regretfully. A little more would have been very acceptable.

Lenc took a draught of his beer, then looked round at his companions and spoke in a low voice. "With all the problems that we had before we started, I can see we have a few more now. Neither Alun nor I can be seen by Caratacus, or his bodyguard, or even Cainos, but we have to know where they are staying and what they are saying to the Arch Druid. It's pretty obvious that Caratacus wants the blessing of the top man, both in raising the tribes and marrying Veldicca, so I think that just coming up with a plan to catch Caratacus on his own and kill him isn't going to work. We have to discredit him with the Druids and get them to kick him out, then we can kill him. Somehow or other we are going to have to get Cainos on his own without Caratacus knowing we are here."

Lenc sat back and looked at his companions.

Iestyn took a slug of beer from his mug and said slowly, "Us three could go for a sight-seeing wander and see what we can find out. When we have a better idea of the lie of the land, a plan may come to us."

Lenc didn't like the idea of the three warriors acting like tourists, although their gawking at the Druid architecture would probably seem genuine enough. But in the absence of anything better, it was probably a good start.

Alun nodded his head in agreement. "Probably the best we can do as a beginning," he said thoughtfully. "If you can get an idea of the layout of the Arch Druid's mansion, the barracks, and where favoured guests are likely to be put up, that will all be helpful. Then we're going to have to find a way to contact Cainos. That's not going to be easy."

CHAPTER VII

The hostel was clean, but spartan, so the next day, when the three Ordovices wandered off on their intelligence gathering mission, Lenc and Alun were left with little to do. Sitting at a table outside facing the street, and watching the locals going about their business soon began to pall.

"I don't think I can stand this excitement all day," Lenc eventually confessed.

Alun nodded agreement. "Trouble is, I think we're stuck with it. We can't go up to the town till the others return, and I can't think of anything I want to do to pass the time. We could take a ride to the coast, I suppose."

"And why not?" said Lenc. "Bit of sea air won't do us any harm, and it might pay us to see if there are any boats available. It's possible we may have to leave this place in a hurry."

With a decision made, they collected their horses from the paddock at the rear of the hostel, saddled up and rode out the way they had come, before turning west to skirt the Druid town on its hill.

"The coast should be straight down this path," said Alun.

Once off the hill, the land smoothed out to low-lying grassland stretching to the sea in the near distance and as far as the eye could see to the south. The clumps of marsh grass and reed beds indicated that sea water was just below the surface, although their track seemed firm enough.

"This must flood regularly," observed Lenc. "It would take some draining to make it worthwhile farmland."

"Why bother," laughed Alun. "The island is rich in farmland further inland; there is plenty of good soil for the farmers there. I think they are pretty well self-sufficient, even with hungry priests and the warriors who have fled the Romans all demanding food and drink."

They rode on, skirting a dark-watered lake, with the cries of wading birds to keep them company, eventually coming to the shingle beach. The sea was calm and lapped up against the stony beach which stretched away in both directions until disappearing into the low mist. Behind them, the marshland marched away to infinity with no barrier to stop the chilly wind straight off the sea. Lenc looked round carefully but failed see another soul. They could be the only people in the world, he thought as he wrapped his cloak tighter.

"We're going to have to go further afield to find a boat," said Alun thoughtfully. "Maybe we should be thinking of the other side of the island which faces the mainland. We're much more likely to find a fishing boat there, although we would probably have to leave the horses behind."

"It's something to think about," agreed Lenc, "but until we can come up with a plan, we should keep all our options open."

The two dismounted and walked their horses along the shore, their cloaks gathered round them to keep out the cold wind. A weak sun glimmered through a low mist in an otherwise clear blue sky.

"What say we ride along the beach and see if we can circle the town?" suggested Lenc. "I'd like to see the port - that's where there might be a boat."

Alun nodded in agreement. "That's a good idea, always best to know the lie of the land, but we'll have to watch our time; we should be back for the others before dark. The other snag is that the town is on a smaller island and I'm not sure how wide the channel is between it and Mona."

They steered their horses down to the high tide mark, where the shingle turned to hard, damp sand. The horses seemed to enjoy the change underfoot, and Lenc and Alun let them have their heads increasing their speed, splashing through puddles and jumping the small streams coming off the land, cutting their path through the sand.

After an exhilarating ride, they eventually reined in as the seashore turned towards the headland, and there ahead of them was the sea channel, separating the island from the rest of Mona. It wasn't very wide, maybe forty or fifty paces, but its depth was unknown. Judging by the water stains up the bank, they had arrived at low tide.

They looked at the seemingly placid stretch of water doubtfully, then looked at each other.

"What do you think?" Alun casually asked.

Lenc looked at the stretch of water. "Doesn't look too bad," he replied cautiously. "We could try it, see how far across we can get, then if it looks like we're going to have to swim, we can always turn back."

Neither was going to be the first to admit defeat as they both looked at the swirling water lapping against the shore. "Come on then," Lenc said eventually, "let's have a go."

Slowly, he eased his horse into the water and as she went in up to her hocks, she seemed to understand where they were going and without hesitation waded deeper into the water. Not to be outdone, Alun put his knees to his horse's flanks and followed.

Lenc watched the sea water rise up his horse and his legs. The sensation when the freezing cold water crept up and over his knee-high boots was an icy shock. He wished he had thought of taking them off before attempting the crossing. Too late now.

On they waded, Lenc's horse nodding her head and snorting loudly down her nose as the sea water splashed up at her. They were coming up to halfway across when suddenly his trusty mount slipped and fell sideways, momentarily disappearing under the water, unceremoniously dumping Lenc in the sea. She quickly recovered, snorting and neighing, and made off for the far bank. Lenc felt the sea closing over his head, then surfaced, coughing and spluttering. He had the presence of mind to hang on to the saddle pommel, as his amphibious mount swam on strongly. Behind him, Alun saw his tumble into the water and started to laugh until he realised that the same thing was likely to happen to him. Two seconds' thought and he swung one leg over the saddle and gingerly lowered himself into the water. He gasped as the cold clutched his vitals, but his horse was striking out strongly, following the leader.

Both horses swam strongly for the far shore and within ten paces had found their footing again. Their riders felt the sand and stones beneath them, and holding their horse's reins walked beside them to dry land.

When they reached the shore, Lenc and Alun let their reins go as the horses shook themselves, spraying even more water over their hapless riders before strolling up the beach to placidly graze on the marsh grass. Lenc looked at a sopping Alun then burst out laughing. Alun looked up at him. "I don't see what's so funny, you Gaulish prick," he said witheringly. "I'm fucking freezing here."

"Ah, it's not that bad," said Lenc, as he pulled his boots off, and turned them upside down to release a cascade of water. "We're across on the Holy Island or White Island - whatever it's called - and we'll soon dry off. If we ride on, we may even find somewhere with a big fire and something to eat. Where's your sense of adventure?"

Alun mumbled something unintelligible which Lenc failed to catch; he could have been wrong but he thought it may have alluded to some failing of his ancestors born out of wedlock, but he thought it best to let it pass.

He gave Alun a damp clap on the shoulder then walked up the beach to find his horse.

Once mounted again, the freshening wind, although bitter cold, was at least drying their sodden clothes. Alun started to cheer up, particularly as signs of civilisation started to appear. "There should be a tavern somewhere along the path to the docks," he said. "You can stay outside and look after the horses if you like, while I go in and dry off."

"My what a fertile imagination you Ordovices have," responded Lenc.

By now they were riding steadily uphill, until they rode through some tall scrub onto a cliff path with the sea stretched out before them and the cliff edge tumbling away to a narrow beach. Lenc could see a river inlet below, then the land flattening out again and a few roundhouses set back above the flood lines.

"The port is just round this headland," said Alun, "which is where most of the islanders live. The sea port is quite big and has steady trade with Hibernia. Apparently there is a lot of trade in gold through the port, which keeps the Druids happy."

As the cliff path started to descend, they could see a small group of fishermen outside one of the small cottages, mending nets. They looked up as the two riders approached.

"Had a bit of a ducking, have we?" was the initial greeting from a red-faced man sitting on a barrel with a net stretched over his knees. Lenc registered the sitting man quietly sliding a long-bladed knife up to his barrel with his bare foot. As they spoke, the other fishermen casually moved behind their spokesman, most of them carrying fishing knives.

"You could say that," laughed Alun. "We tried to ford the sea passage and it proved deeper than we thought, but all we got was a soaking for our pains. Wouldn't mind standing with our backs to your fire for a while though."

"Where have you come from?" asked the fisherman. "We don't see too many strangers round here. Them as we do see often want to do us harm, even if we do have next to nothing. Maybe you're Hibernian pirates, anchored down the coast, looking out for anything you can get."

Alun gave a snort of derision. "Fear not," he said, "we came by land, I am Ordovician, and I promise you we mean you no harm. Some food and a warm by your fire would not come amiss, but we will pay you what we can for the privilege."

The fisherman looked at Lenc, and turned back to Alun. "If you're Ordovician, what's he?" asked the fisherman.

"He's a Gaul," answered Alun dismissively, "got lost."

So far Lenc had stayed out of the conversation, mainly because he didn't want to give away his accent, but now that little problem had been cleared up, he felt emboldened to ask: "Who are the Hibernians?"

The fisherman gave a snort. "I can tell you're a foreigner. The Hibernians are a plague - they're pirates from the big island to the west, who prey on this coast. Usually leave us alone though, because we have nothing they want. More interested in the gold that the Druids trade in. Gold ships from Hibernia put into the port regularly."

"Gold, eh?" said Alun appreciatively. "Now that could make me go a'pirating."

"You'll have not only the Druidae to deal with," growled the fisherman, "but them bastard Roman warships as well. It's not a good trade to ply."

"You make a fine point," conceded Alun. "Maybe we'll just stick to what we do - killing Romans."

"Much better idea," agreed the fisherman. "Just don't bring the bastards near here. You better get yourself dried off. Go in the house, the woman will look after you. I'll give your nags a rub down as well."

Gratefully the two swung down from their saddles, Lenc still holding his boots. Alun poked his head into the house and called hello, and was ushered in by a stout lady in a black full-length dress and a long apron who cooed when she saw her guest was soaking wet, followed by another, just as sodden.

"Ooh," she mewed in concern, "are there any more of you?" she asked.

"No Mother," replied Alun easily, "just the two of us, but standing by your fire would be a godsend."

"Come in, come in, best get those wet clothes off - you'll dry quicker without them."

The two hesitated and looked uncertainly at each other.

She caught the look and laughed, showing a mouthful of stumps of yellowing teeth. "Do you think you've got something I haven't seen before? I've reared six children, five of them boys, so there's nothing new in the world. Then when your clothes are drying over the fire, perhaps you would like some food?"

"That's perhaps the best suggestion of the day," agreed Alun as Lenc nodded eagerly. They quickly stripped off and their clothes set to steam in front of the open fire. The fisher-wife found a couple of home-spun blankets to wrap themselves in, then turned back to her cauldron hanging over the fire. She spooned two steaming bowls of broth, smelling of the sea, and added some bread from a recess near the fireplace.

Lenc gingerly tasted the thick broth, which proved very tasty. "This is good," he said. "What's in it?"

"There's turnip and some beans, but mostly what I can find along the seashore, and some fish bones to make a stock," she replied, then with a saucy wink added: "There's mussels and cockles and seaweed. Very good for you, seaweed, makes you stand up straight if you get my meaning."

"I'll bear that in mind," agreed Lenc.

The two sat quietly in their rough blankets tucking into the broth, as she bustled about her kitchen, every so often checking on the clothes drying in front of the fire.

"What brings you to these parts?" she asked Lenc.

"It was silly really - we were riding on the shore and took a notion to see the port, so we decided to ford the sea passage between the island and Mona, not knowing how deep it was, then had to swim for it. Lucky it was low tide - or maybe not so lucky, if the tide had been in, we wouldn't have attempted it."

"All I can say is that you were very lucky," replied the fisher-wife. "That passage can be treacherous if you don't know what you are doing."

"Very true," agreed Alun sagely. "I don't think we will be repeating that adventure very soon. Good job there's a bridge across near the dock."

"I suppose you could call it a bridge," conceded the woman. "It's really more a series of built-up rocks and tree trunks. The land is so flat there, the sea spreads wide at high tide, so it's easier to ford. Mind you, it would be a big mistake to wander off the path; we've lost a few people who thought they knew better than us."

After finishing their broth the two struggled into their nearly dry clothes, despite protests from their hostess who wanted them to wait while their clothes dried out completely.

"Regretfully we are mindful of the time," said Alun. "We need to be back to meet our comrades. They will be concerned if we are missing too long. But your hospitality will be remembered for a very long time."

The old lady blushed and said it was nothing, glad to see some strangers, and they must stop by again very soon.

Outside, the old man was still mending his nets, but at least he gave them a good-natured wave as the two mounted up. "Thank you for the food and the warm," said Lenc. "Both were appreciated."

"Best not try and follow the coast round to the port," warned the fisherman. "It gets very craggy and is quite dangerous. Just past here the track splits - go right, then another track joins from the east and that's where you need to go to find the crossing back to the big island. Don't know why you want to go to the port anyway; it's too shallow for most ships, just a few fishing boats that's all. Even the Hibernians have to stand off beyond Salt Island and row their cargoes in."

"Maybe we'll give the harbour a miss," agreed Lenc, "from what you say it doesn't seem to be worth seeing. Might be best if we make straight for the bridge."

The fisherman shrugged his shoulders. "Probably best if you want to be off the island before dark."

The cliff track was easy to follow, snaking through tumbled rocks, rising with a dappled mass of purple, green and red heather searching for the sun through the random stones. Thanks to the fisherman's directions they turned onto the lower trail, with the wide estuary on their right. Mud flats, isolated stands of grasses, and massive boulders formed a backdrop for a lazy sea that swirled through, looking for the easiest path. A pair of peregrine falcons caught the thermals above them, looking for prey.

After following the shore-line they could see the estuary open out to the sea. They came to another junction and steered right, away from the harbour.

The new track was easy to follow as it wound down to the water's edge and a man-made causeway of stones and soil, which marked the start of the connection to Mona. The causeway was a simple heaped pile, with smooth stones laid on top, allowing good access for carts. The two rode side by side until they came to a rudimentary bridge of tree trunks with flat planks on top, above the channel. Gingerly they crossed, their horses taking care on the slippery causeway. Along the way they could see the earthwork had been repaired in several places along its length. The wooden bridge proved to be the first of five similar structures, allowing a dry and, unobstructed tidal waterway.

"It must be almost a full-time job, keeping this causeway open," observed Lenc. "Suppose it's pretty much vital if the locals want to get off the island. Maybe the Druidae's prisoners would come in handy keeping the repairs up to date. Rather them than me."

Lenc and Alun were back at their bench outside the hostel when Madawc, Iestyn and Darren arrived back from their fact-finding mission. Alun greeted them and called for ale and when they all had a drink in front of them, Madawc described their day.

"The first thing is, if you're not a priest in this place you stick out like a man with two heads. We wandered round for a bit, looking at all the fine buildings, then we came to the head man's palace, and it's quite a building. It's a big imposing place, the biggest in town, and made of stone, with that stone tower to one side that we saw on the way in. No idea what that's for, maybe a lookout, but we saw no sign of defences at all - they obviously don't have a fear of being raided.

"The town spreads onto another smaller island with a harbour, which has a lot of trade with Hibernia, but because a lot of it is hidden in the oak groves you can hardly see a fraction of it."

"Yes, we were on the smaller island today - we know about that, just get to the point," interrupted Lenc testily.

"All right, I'm getting there. I was just setting the scene," protested Madawc. "Can I continue?"

"Sorry," said Lenc, "please go on."

"Thank you," replied a vindicated Madawc. "As I was saying, on the way to the palace there are smaller towns within the town, all set in trees. There seemed to be classes going on all over the place. Wherever there was a gap in the trees there would be these priests all being talked at by another priest. We got close enough to listen a few times but couldn't understand a word of it. They all seemed to enjoy it though. They all just sat there as this senior priest gabbled away."

"The head priest is called Delphidius, and he is as old as you can imagine. White hair, flowing beard, priest robes, bare feet. Odd that, I thought - you would think he could afford shoes as head man." Madawc took a suck at his ale.

"But what about Caratacus, did you see him or any of his party?" pressed Lenc.

"Not a sign," said Madawc, wiping his chin. "Round the back of the palace is the Druidae barracks, and guest buildings. We didn't like to get too close, as there were sentries on the buildings and more than one mobile patrol, but that's likely where they'll be."

CHAPTER VIII

When Caratacus and his party arrived at Caergybi, the town in the forest created by the Druid order, Cainos arranged for them to stay in guest houses at the rear of the Arch Druid's mansion. Cainos wasted no time in requesting an interview with the great man, but had to make do with an initial discussion with his chancellor, Alwyn.

"Come, sit," indicated a smiling Alwyn when he met Cainos in a small oak grove behind the mansion building. "You have been having adventures recently, I hear."

Cainos sat heavily. "Looking back, it has been quite an eventful time," he agreed. "As you know, I was ministering to the Silures in Gobannion and when the Romans started building forts close by, I was concerned by the threat to the tribe, and also that it brought Rome that bit closer to Mona. We all know that a single ambition of the Roman governor is the ultimate wiping out of our religion."

Alwyn nodded sadly.

"When Caratacus arrived from the south, chased by the legion, I thought that he would be able to unite the tribes, providing an irresistible deterrent to the Romans and a strong bulwark against them attacking Mona. At first everything went well and we had some successes, but then the legion, with their disciplined troops, overcame us, and when the tribes saw they were defeated, they scattered. I thought to bring Caratacus and his party, plus his bride-to-be, here for sanctuary before continuing his quest to unite the tribes of Britannia."

Alwyn sat back and ruminated. "We have a few problems with your news," he said eventually. "The first is that Caratacus has been beaten soundly in every set-piece battle he has had against Rome, losing thousands of men each time. Are we sure he is the right man for the job? What makes you think he will not be beaten again? That is, if he gets another chance? And the second is this talk of an alliance with the Silures through his marriage to Veldicca, who, now that her father is dead, achieves high office within the tribe. We can see that an alliance between the Catuvellauni and the Silures would be helpful, but is it practical? And lawful?"

Cainos hesitated; he didn't much like the way the conversation was going. Alwyn had already indicated that he had received news of the battle which Cainos would rather he did not know about.

"I confess I find myself in some confusion," continued Cainos. "It is my opinion that we should persevere with Caratacus as he is our best hope of uniting the tribes. It is true that both the Ordovices and Silures, would happily kill him after the last battle. An alliance with the Silures is just as unlikely considering the way so many warriors were lost in that futile assault of the shield wall. With his wife killed by the Romans, there is nothing to stop Caratacus taking Veldicca as his bride, which would surely have to reconcile the Silures and unite two of the biggest and warlike of the tribes of Britannia, despite what happened on the ridge."

Alwyn smiled. "I was wondering how you were going to get round to that. Our spies tell us that Vellibia, wife of Caratacus and their children are still alive. They were captured by Scapula and as we speak are on their way to Camulodunum. So how can Caratacus marry when he is still married?"

Cainos hid his start of surprise and even managed a smile. "This is certainly good news that Vellibia is alive. We just presumed that she would have been killed in the fighting. But it makes no difference. While Caratacus is free and she is in chains, she is no use to him, nor their heirs. Veldicca will make an ideal queen and the advantages to our religion will be immense. I would have thought that Delphidius would have been able to announce that because Vellibia is a prisoner of the enemy she can no longer in reality be called the wife of Caratacus. And with Veldicca taking her place as Queen of Britannia, think where that leaves us as Druids. Our place at the right hand of the first King of Britannia would give us the opportunity, once the Romans are dealt with, to make Britannia a place of peace and prosperity. We could open schools, establish government, and take our rightful place in forging a new world."

"And what of the princess, does she wish to marry Caratacus?" asked Alwyn.

Cainos spread his arms expansively. "What woman would not want to marry the future King of Britannia?"

"You paint a compelling picture, Cainos," Alwyn conceded. "I will certainly pass your words on to Delphidius. It will be for him to decide what to do. In the meantime, we must ensure that your party enjoys our hospitality." With that, he stood abruptly. "I will come and find you when I have news."

Cainos stood and bowed to the chancellor. He wondered if he had done enough not only to convince him, but to persuade the Arch Druid as well. Time will tell, he thought.

Alwyn found the Arch Druid in an open classroom with a thatched roof and slated floor, with tall oak trees surrounding the building, creating an air of quiet and stillness. The elderly priest was sitting in the centre of a group of young novice priests, avidly listening to his story of the links between Celtic Druids, the Phoenicians and Aramaeans of ancient Syria.

Delphidius was advanced in years, but carried the weight of his age well. He was tall, with no sign of a stoop, his silver hair down to his shoulders, with a plait either side of his head in front of his ears. He had a kindly, wrinkled face and startlingly bright blue eyes.

Despite himself and his need to share his news, Alwyn found himself fascinated by the old man's gentle storytelling. He stood at the side of the group until Delphidius came to a natural stop and most of his pupils stood and reluctantly moved away.

Alwyn moved into the old priest's line of vision and give him a small bow.

"What news from Cainos?" asked Delphidius.

"Lord, he has a strange and powerful story to tell, and I am not altogether sure I have heard it all, or whether there are other vested interests at play."

Alwyn sat with the Arch Druid, who listened intently as the tale unfolded.

"Yes, I see the difficulty," conceded the older man. "What does seem plain is that Cainos was prepared to lie to you, and it was a nasty shock that you already knew that Vellibia was not murdered but captured. On the other hand, we do need that bulwark against the Roman legions that the tribes can supply, if we lose it, our days could be numbered on Mona."

Delphidius leaned back and looked ruminatively up at the thatched roof. "To add to the confusion, there is another party, of five men, who arrived on the island yesterday and came straight here. The Druidae detachment at the ferry challenged them, and one in particular knew nothing of our order and was initially aggressive. They were asking after Caratacus and his party. Since they arrived here three of them have been sniffing around the town, probably getting the lie of the land."

Delphidius pondered for a second. "I think we should speak to these men and find out what their connection is." He leaned forward again and spoke softly to Alwyn. "In the meantime, choose one of our young female novices to be a handmaid to the Princess Veldicca. She must be personable and friendly and able to become a friend and confidante. Let's keep this to ourselves, no need to bother Cainos."

CHAPTER IX

That evening, Lenc and the four Ordovician warriors hunkered down in their tavern of choice before more bowls of steaming mutton stew. They were talking through their plans for the coming days but so far had failed to come up with anything, other than lie in wait for Caratacus to wander out of the Druid palace, get past his bodyguards and run him through.

"Why don't we just kidnap Veldicca and ride for the ferry?" asked a desperate Lenc.

"Because Caratacus and his men would easily catch us up and kill us before we could cross to the mainland," said Alun testily. "And forget about swimming the horses across. You have to know what you are doing on that particular piece of water. No, we have to deal with him first then assuredly Veldicca will fall into our hands."

They talked round the problem for another round of beer until eventually Lenc pushed himself back from the table.

"I for one have had enough," he announced flatly. "The key to all this is Cainos. We know Veldicca would not submit to Caratacus willingly; he and Cainos - or perhaps just Cainos - have some sort of hold over her, so we have to find out just what that is before we can take any action at all."

There were rumblings of agreement at this from round the table, but it was Madawc who raised the question they were all reluctant to ask. "Yes, but how do we do that? Isn't she a prisoner?"

Lenc pondered. "I don't think they could have taken her into the palace as a prisoner. That would look a bit odd, considering she is supposed to be Caratacus's betrothed. Again, we are back to Cainos. He has either drugged her, or more likely spun her a story that he has her best interests at heart and he is just looking for a way to save her, so she must follow his lead. At least its kept her alive.

"What this comes down to is that we must find Veldicca, find out what's happening and just whose side Cainos is on. We know he is a clever, scheming bastard who will lean towards whoever he thinks is going to suit his purposes best. Right now, that's Caratacus, but if that doesn't work out, I am sure Cainos will be quick to denounce him and change his allegiance."

Suddenly the tavern door swung open, caught by a gust of wind, and banged against the wall. A man followed and quickly shut the door and looked round. He was young, fit-looking and his hair cut short in the way of the Druid priests, but he wore ordinary clothes of a long cloak and, underneath, a woollen tunic and trousers. His shoes had leather straps criss-crossing up his calves and, importantly, he was unarmed.

Alun's eyes narrowed as he leaned towards Lenc. "Druidae," he whispered softly.

Lenc sat back as the newcomer ordered ale then looked round, and for the first time seemed to notice the table with five warriors all looking at him intently.

"Good evening," he said affably. "Can I buy you strangers a drink to welcome you to Coleg Derwyddon?"

Lenc could sense that Alun was about to turn the stranger's offer down, and put a restraining hand on his arm. "That is very welcoming of you, thank you and please sit with us."

The young stranger smiled and nodded as Iestyn and Darren reluctantly made room for him on their bench. As the beer was passed down the table, Lenc turned to him with his best smile. "What brings you here and seeking the company of strangers?"

The young man smiled back. "I can see you like to get straight to the point and have guessed I have a mission which probably concerns you. You would be correct in that; I have been sent here to invite you to meet Delphidius, our Arch Druid, who would speak with you. Apologies, I did not introduce myself - my name is Nathan."

Lenc sat back and stared hard at Nathan, who appeared relaxed and unconcerned. "Why would this important man want to speak with the likes of us?" he asked.

Nathan took a slug of beer, and setting his pot on the table, spread his arms and shrugged. "I am just a messenger," he said, still smiling. "I'm afraid the Arch Druid did not feel the need to take me into his confidence. All he asked me to do was to meet you tomorrow and escort you to a private place where he can talk to you."

Could this be a trap? wondered Lenc. He turned to Alun, who seemed to be thinking the same thing.

Nathan spoke again. "If it's any help, I can tell you that the Arch Druid really wants to speak to you and it is very much in your interests to speak to him. I can assure you that if he meant you harm, you would have been dealt with before now."

Lenc had to agree with that. He was impressed with the Druid's intelligence network, which seemingly passed the information of their arrival on the island to the head man almost before they arrived at the settlement. If he had that information, what else did he know?

"I for one would be honoured to accept. Would it extend to my friend here?" Lenc indicated Alun who was clearly still not thrilled by the invitation.

"Of course, and I will be pleased to report back that you will be there in the morning. Not too early - the Arch Druid leads our prayers from dawn. When that is over, I will come and fetch you." With that, Nathan drained his beer pot, and with a friendly nod left the gathering and walked off into the night.

For a moment no one spoke; they were all grappling with this latest development.

"It's a trap," Iestyn said firmly.

"I don't think so," replied Lenc. "As the lad said, if the Druids wished us harm, they could have captured us easily. We could be having that conversation with the head man with the help of a red-hot knife. I think the Arch Druid has heard the story that Caratacus and Cainos are peddling, but something has made him cautious about accepting it. Then we come along, obviously interested in the forthcoming wedding, and he wants to know what we know. It will be difficult for him to believe that Cainos is deceiving him, but I think that he thinks Cainos knows something he is not telling."

More for something to do than anything else, the next morning the small band filled their time rubbing down their horses and checking hooves, until Nathan arrived with a cheery greeting.

"I must say I'm looking forward to this meeting," Lenc told him. "I've never met an Arch Druid before. How do I address him?"

"Don't worry about that," Nathan reassured him breezily. "Delphidius, the Arch Druid, is very approachable. I am sure you will like him and want to work with him. Listen to what he says and be honest with him."

Nathan led his two companions up the track towards the stone tower, which appeared in glimpses through the trees. Lenc was fascinated by the way they seemed to be walking through a dense forest then suddenly an opening would appear with a large stone and timber building set back as if wishing to be part of the forest itself. The buildings were all uniform, with a waist high stone wall, and thick timbers rising to a central thatched tent shape.

Nathan saw his interest and explained: "These are our places of learning. Young scholars come here from all over Britannia, and indeed from the mainland as well, to learn the words of wisdom so that they can go back and minister to their own people. They are very dedicated and some will spend half a lifetime learning and memorising the faith of the Druids."

"And you," asked Lenc, "you are a would-be priest?"

"I am afraid not," replied Nathan ruefully. "You might have guessed that I am Druidae, which is a sort of priest, but we are soldiers too. Our vast movement needs, shall we say, a muscular arm so that our religious work and our vital assistance as judges and administrators in the community can go on undisturbed."

Lenc presumed that Nathan was taking them to the palace, but when they came to a fork in the path he led them away from the main route, round the hill. Soon the trees started closing in as the forest thickened. Light could barely penetrate the canopy, but Nathan struck on in front, followed by a bemused Lenc and Alun.

Guessing their thoughts, Nathan reassured them with a "Not long now."

Suddenly they broke out of the thick undergrowth to yet another clearing with what looked like a covered wooden stage and a horseshoe-shaped amphitheatre, opening to the west and ten great pillars of smooth standing stones. Standing by the stones was a long-haired, tall priest in a white cassock, belted at the waist and leaning on a long wooden staff. On his head was a wide-brimmed white hat, with a cap of shiny bronze. This must be Delphidius, thought Lenc, and he seems to be alone.

The priest turned as he sensed them coming and smiled. "Welcome to Mona, and apologies for the mystery, but I would rather people did not know of this meeting." He looked quizzically first at Lenc, then Alun. "You must be Lenculus," he said, "so that must make you Alun of the Ordovices. You are strange bedfellows indeed."

Lenc realised with a start that this old man knew everything about him, perhaps even that he was still a Roman legionary although officially, he thought, a deserter.

Delphidius looked at Nathan, who bowed and walked some distance away until out of earshot and sat on a fallen tree at the edge of the forest. Delphidius indicated a table and three chairs laid out within the standing stones.

"Gentlemen, I am glad you came, and believe me I owe you no ill will, but I must have the truth. Will you tell me your story? And I'll tell you what I know and from there we can decide what to do."

This was difficult. Lenc and Alun had agreed that on no account would they divulge their intention of killing Caratacus and returning Veldicca to the Silures, but on the other hand what else could they tell this perceptive priest?

Delphidius smiled as he realised Lenc's quandary. "Perhaps I should start after all?" he suggested.

Lenc nodded, smiling in relief.

The Arch Druid related how Cainos had explained that Caratacus's wife and children had been captured and killed by the legion in their surprise attack, and now he wanted to marry Veldicca, who would give him the sons he needed to help him unite the whole of Britannia.

"Unfortunately, we already knew that the wife of Caratacus and his family are still very much alive, so how could he possibly marry while already married?" explained Delphidius. "Ordinary men could have two wives if they could afford them - but not a king, that would surely create divisions, so why is he doing this and why is Cainos trying to deceive us?"

Delphidius leaned forward in his intensity. Clearly a good man, he had detected subterfuge in one of his own and it worried him desperately. He must know what Cainos was up to and, by association what was Caratacus's part in all this.

Lenc collected his thoughts and glanced at Alun who was staring fixedly at the ground. No help there.

"Lord, you have been honest with me, so I must be honest with you," said Lenc after some thought. "When the legion attacked, Veldicca's father was one of the first to die, making the Princess Veldicca a queen. She fought the Romans at the head of her tribe with Trenos, her betrothed. Caratacus and his men skulked at the rear, and when the Silures retired, incapable of defeating the Roman shield wall, Caratacus berated them until

Trenos called him a coward for not taking part in the fight."

He wasn't sure about that but it sounded right. "Then Caratacus stabbed him to death, viciously punched Veldicca and tied her to her horse and they all fled the field, guided by Cainos. From what you say and my previous experiences, I think Cainos is playing both sides. He has convinced Veldicca that he is looking after her best interests and has persuaded her to go along with the story that she is keen to wed the future king of Britannia until he, Cainos, can find a solution.

"He will try to persuade you that it is in the best interests of the Druids that this marriage goes ahead whether Veldicca is in agreement or not because it will create a bulwark against a Roman invasion of Mona. However, if you decide that you cannot support such a marriage, then he will say to Veldicca that his diplomacy prevailed and she can go back to her people.

"If that is what happens, Cainos will certainly be out of favour, unless, he can talk himself back into the would-be king's favour. By all accounts he is quite good at sounding plausible."

By now Delphidius was staring morosely into the distance. Eventually he collected himself and turned back to the other two at the table.

"As priests our sole purpose is the betterment of the people we are responsible for. If they follow the right path, they will receive their reward in another life. That is our doctrine but if their teachers are following a selfish path of their own, how can we in all honesty, preach the common good? Cainos appears to be guilty of scheming and manipulating ostensibly for the good of the movement, but he sees himself as standing at the right hand of the most powerful man in Britannia, so what would that make him? The most powerful priest in the land. That is simply not acceptable. Naked ambition is not a good thing in a priest."

Lenc and Alun sat uncomfortably in silence as the old priest brooded, before visibly collecting himself and managing a smile.

"And you two, why are you pursuing Caratacus and Veldicca? You first Alun."

Alun looked at the ground, then up at Delphidius. He swallowed. "Lord, I have never lied to a priest before and do not intend to do so now. My father and brother were killed in the fight with the Romans, and so were many more good men. I vowed at the time that I would find him and kill him, and I will carry that promise out or die myself in the attempt."

He nodded to Lenc. "This man is my enemy but he is also sworn to kill Caratacus so we will ride together until we have completed our promise, then I will kill him as well. Only then can I go back to my tribe."

Delphidius nodded and turned to Lenc. "Now you, my son, I am told you are from Gaul. Why are you here and so set on murder?"

Lenc thought a moment before replying. "Lord, you have my story. I have feelings for Veldicca as she used to have feelings for me. I believe I betrayed her by not being at her side during the battle with the Romans, so now I must rescue her and kill Caratacus. I do not believe that she will be interested in me but she will want to return to her tribe to take her rightful place at the head of the northern Silures. And that is how it should be."

"What will you do if you succeed in your mission?" asked Delphidius gently.

Lenc shrugged. "I have thought no further than killing Caratacus and setting Veldicca free, I can't think any further than that."

"Making your peace with Alun might be a good start," suggested the old priest. "You have been honest with me I know, and for that I thank you. I must decide what I am going to do. Please don't do anything dramatic and I will call for you when I have decided on a course of action."

The old priest struggled to his feet, the signal for Nathan to stand and walk towards them. Lenc and Alun also hurriedly stood.

Delphidius waited for Nathan: "Take them back to their lodgings then come and find me at the palace, I have another task for you."

Nathan bowed his head as the Arch Druid raised his hand in peace to Lenc and Alun, then walked stiffly away from them, leaning heavily on his staff.

When Nathan returned from his mission, he found Delphidius in the same spot, sitting in the glade staring reflectively into middle distance. The Arch Druid collected himself when he became aware of Nathan hovering and asked him to go and find Princess Veldicca's maidservant, a novice priest.

Delphidius watched the teenager as she walked across the glade towards him. Her hands were clasped together and she stared fixedly at the ground as she approached. She was barefoot and wore a rough tunic, tied at the waist, which hid her young body. Even as an old and seemingly venerable priest he surprised himself by thinking that although the girl was not attractive in the worldly sense, there was something about her that demanded attention. He groped for the right word. She certainly had… yes, that was it, presence. She had presence. He wasn't sure what that meant but felt it would stand her in good stead in the years to come. What certainly helped this presence was her strong red hair, her most striking feature, tied up and swept back off her face.

She stood still, staring passively at the ground, waiting to hear what the Arch Druid wanted with her. "What is your name, girl?" he asked.

"My Druid name is Branwen, Lord," she offered.

"And how are you getting on with the princess," he asked.

"As well as can be expected," she replied haltingly. "Probably in a world of men, she is grateful for another female to talk to, even a servant. She is lonely and very troubled."

Delphidius nodded understandingly. "What do you think troubles her?"

The girl hesitated. "Lord, she does not wish to marry that man, but her priest has told her to pretend she does want to marry him. She says the priest is looking for a way to rescue her, but she isn't sure whether that can happen. She has asked me where the stables are and how far away the ferry is."

He sighed and dismissed the girl with a smile of thanks and a wave of his hand, but as she turned to go, she turned and hesitantly said, "Lord I came to Mona to learn the ways of the Druids. I want to be a priest and help my people. When can I go back to my studies?"

Delphidius smiled. "Your question does you credit, my child. But at the moment you are doing a most worthy job. Being a Druid priest does not stop at ministering to your people's spiritual needs, because we are also administrators, advisors and helpers. To do this we established an intelligence-gathering network the like of which has never been seen before. You are part of that, and in time you will realise that intelligence-gathering is vitally important to us. That is how you are currently serving the cause, not just by brushing a princess's hair."

She nodded, reassured and as she left, as if waiting for a signal, Alwyn diffidently took her place, bursting to know the latest developments.

"We are not much further forward," said Delphidius ruefully. "We know the princess does not wish to marry Caratacus, irrespective of whether he is already married or not. I imagine she wishes for nothing more than to go back to the Silures and lead them as her father did, which is her rightful destiny. For me to bless this marriage would be very wrong. The marriage may help to unite the tribes of Britannia, but I rather doubt it; it would certainly not be appreciated by the Silures.

"I have spoken to the strangers who are searching for the royal party, and they are set on murder. I suspect that if Cainos gets in the way, he will also be dealt with, so now will be a good time to speak to Caratacus and Cainos together. We will get to the bottom of this puzzle yet."

CHAPTER X

Caratacus was bored. After the nerve-shredding flight from the legion, when his ambition to be the first King of Britannia looked further away than ever, then the long ride northwards to Mona, and the only good-looking female was that bitch Veldicca who looked at him like she would look at her shoe after stepping in dog muck. Now that they were relatively safe under the protection and hospitality of the Druids, Caratacus had regained his sense of entitlement and was on the lookout for excitement, at the very least a compliant serving girl.

He was idly throwing pebbles at the seagulls in the garden behind the palace when Cainos came looking for him, bursting with news.

"What do your Druids do for recreation in this godforsaken place?" Caratacus demanded. "I don't mind you lot being celibate, just means more for the likes of me who appreciate the female form. And a drink wouldn't go amiss either," he grumbled.

Cainos impatiently ignored the petulant outburst. "I think things are coming to a head. We have been summoned to the palace for an audience with the Arch Druid who I imagine must have come to a decision."

Caratacus dropped his handful of pebbles, the seagulls forgotten. "It's about time, I'm not used to having to wait on priests to make their minds up. When do we go before the exalted one?"

"Today, this afternoon," replied Cainos. "Oh, and it's just you, me and your future bride in front of the full council chamber."

"Does that mean no bodyguards?" asked Caratacus.

"Afraid so, but they won't be necessary, I'm sure," soothed Cainos. "If there was any dissension, I would have heard about it by now. Everything will be fine."

Caratacus wasn't so sure. "What about Veldicca? What if she turns on me? That little bitch could have my heart cut out if she accuses me of kidnap."

"You must remember Caratacus, that if you are accused then so am I, but I can assure you that will not be the case. Between now and then, I think I can confidently say that Veldicca will be sending her apologies for not appearing before the council, having been struck down by a mystery ailment. We just have to go along to the palace and hear what Delphidius has to say. It will be fine."

"On your head be it then, priest. But I promise you, if I end up on the fire, you will be dead first."

Down in the town, Lenc and Alun had also been summoned. Nathan found them at the hostel and quickly outlined Delphidius's plan. "Caratacus and Cainos have been summoned before the Grand Council. You must come up to the palace, which you will enter by a side door and stay out of sight during the meeting. Delphidius is concerned that his own man, Cainos is not telling the truth, which to him is more important than you wanting to kill Caratacus. He wants you to stay hidden but prepared to come forward and give your testimony if he demands it."

Lenc nodded in assent. "And what of Veldicca? Will she be present?"

"She will be there," confirmed Nathan, "but I think Delphidius is reluctant to question her until after he has heard from Cainos and Caratacus. I have also been instructed to say that you must come unarmed. You will be searched before entry to the palace, but don't worry, Caratacus and Cainos will be treated the same, and their retinue of warriors will not be present."

That afternoon, after trying to make themselves look presentable, Lenc and Alun followed Nathan to the palace. Walking without the weight of their sword belts was a strange experience for both men; they soon became accustomed to the unexpected freedom of movement, but the feeling of being naked without sword and dagger took a bit longer.

The road climbed steadily through the oak groves, past the colleges with their groups of earnest novice priests soaking up knowledge, until eventually breaking out into open ground and their first sight of the Druid palace. Up close it was certainly big, but decidedly unimpressive, thought a disappointed Lenc.

He looked left and right at the building, which curved away out of sight. From where he was standing, apart from a solid oak double door flanked by large pillars, there were no ground floor features to the wall at all. He estimated that the few windows he could see were on the third floor, and again more on the fourth, the highest floor under the roof.

Nathan saw him examining the building and explained that the ground floor was the imposing meeting room of the Grand Council. "Round the back, where we are going, there are more ground floor windows but that's because that's where the work is done to keep the whole place running properly. The building is circular, and to take advantage of the sun, the tower in the centre of the palace is hollow and open at the top to catch the sun's rays. There are brightly polished metal spheres which are angled to track the sun's path through the heavens. I have no idea how they work or how the rain is kept out but work they do. It's very clever."

Lenc nodded in impressed admiration. "I would love to see that working some time; I've never heard of anything quite like it."

"Maybe there will be time to show you round properly," replied Nathan, "but right now we need to hurry. We must be in position before the Council convenes."

As they walked round the building, Lenc tried to estimate just how big it was, but could come up with no practical point of comparison. The engineer in Lenc was slightly disappointed to see that the symmetry of the circular building was broken by what Nathan described as the "working area", which looked as if it had been tacked on afterwards as an afterthought. Standing in a doorway was a maidservant with flame-red hair, looking out impatiently. She gestured when she saw them coming.

"This is Branwen," confided Nathan, "and she has become a companion to your Queen Veldicca."

Lenc wondered whether Veldicca could be called a queen without a crowning ceremony, then decided that he didn't really care. All he wanted was to see her safe. He wondered, not for the first time if he still had a chance with her.

Branwen gestured to them to hurry and held the wooden door for them to pass through. Once inside she carefully bolted the door and led them past kitchens, down a corridor and into a side room with a brightly coloured curtain stretched along one wall. She put a finger to her lips and whispered that the council chamber was on the other side of the curtain.

"Let's go in, so you can see the chamber, then we will come back here and stay quiet until called for."

She pushed the curtain to one side and motioned them forward into the great chamber of the Druids. Lenc and Alun tiptoed inside and stood in awe. The room was vast, with a vaulted dome ceiling of white stone. It was circular, seemingly without any corners. Four massive pillars held up the ceiling, and in the centre was an altar made from a solid slab of stone, lit up by a shaft of sunlight which pierced the room through an open well in the centre of the ceiling. Lenc realised it must be the bottom of the tower. He craned his neck to try and look up into the tower in the hope of seeing the polished metal spheres, but could only see a gallery running round the well. Even so, it was an impressive architectural feat, he mused, that tower must be forty pedes (feet) wide.

An elegant painting of animals of all kinds, shrubs, trees and flowers ran round the room in a continuous, seemingly never-ending frieze. A single ornate throne made of carved oak and draped in fresh mistletoe stood near the wall facing the altar set on a small dais. On the other side were the chairs for the Druid Council, arranged in a semi-circle.

"The Arch Druid sits with his back to the rising sun," Branwen whispered, "so the council can feel the full force of the sun's rays, from where all life begins."

Lenc stared transfixed round the chamber. He had never seen anything as impressive or technically impossible.

"I thought Rome led the world in architecture and engineering, but I've never seen or heard of anything like this. It's brilliant." He looked round in wonderment, trying to grasp the enormity of the skills displayed in the chamber. Above the fresco, the curved walls were bare - no paintings, or statues, just smooth stone walls, carefully cut to be perfectly interlocking.

"Come we have been here too long," Branwen finally told them. "We must be behind the curtain before the council arrives. You must stay absolutely quiet," she added. "The Druid Council will soon enter the chamber and be seated. Only then will the Arch Druid enter and sit in the Druid's chair. He will call for Caratacus, Cainos and Veldicca to come in and stand in the centre of the chamber by the altar. You must only open the curtain if you are called forward by the Arch Druid. Do nothing untoward or threatening in any way or you will find yourself stretched out on the altar and sacrificed. This I can promise."

Lenc and Alun looked at each other. "Will we get a chance to speak?" whispered Lenc.

Branwen bit her lip, then:"That is for the Arch Druid to decide and will depend on the answers he gets from Cainos."

The two men pulled a bench close to the curtain so they could hear, while Branwen stood where she could risk a peek and keep up a whispered running commentary.

Suddenly the silence was shattered by a single long blast on some sort of horn, startling Lenc and Alun. Alun was about to say something to lighten the atmosphere but was hissed at by Branwen who put a finger to her lips.

From their concealed anteroom, they could sense the august council of Druids file into the chamber and hear the scraping of chair legs as they took their seats. Branwen hissed a quick description of their scarlet and gold embroidered robes, and the intricately worked golden necklaces and bracelets that denoted their rank in the religion. When they were settled Delphidius, resplendent in his ceremonial robes gravely entered, bowed first to the assembled priests, then to the altar before sitting on his elaborate throne. He arranged his robe, a mix of bright colours shot with gold thread, to hang simply from his shoulders. He touched a thick gold chain with a large medallion hanging heavily from his neck. The image was of a human figure which, from the waist down, morphed into intricate tree roots.

He carefully looked round the chamber then stamped three times on the floor with his staff and called for Cainos, Caratacus and Princess Veldicca to enter.

Lenc sat forward, listening intently.

Branwen twitched the curtains and whispered, "Something's wrong... The princess is not present. Caratacus and Cainos are standing in front of the Arch Druid. Caratacus is looking round... He looks bored with the proceedings, while Cainos seems a bit more anxious."

Then Delphidius spoke: "Cainos, I have summoned you here for an audience with the full council of Druids, so you can explain to them what you have explained to me about your escape from the Romans and your companion's desire to marry a Queen of the Silures when we are clear he is already married. And where is the Queen of the Silures? I was looking forward to hearing her views."

At first Cainos bowed his head then looked up and round at the council. "I apologise on Queen Veldicca's behalf. She did not feel very well and wished to be excused. She asked that I represent her at the council."

He shrugged his shoulders with an air of regret, as Branwen hissed: "She was all right when I left her this morning."

"My lords, I confess this is a strange story," continued Cainos. "We were defeated by the treachery of the Romans and fled the field. We knew that Caratacus's household had been captured, and, we presumed, killed. It was good news that in fact they live, although it does leave a problem for Caratacus and his ambitions to be king of a united Britannia.

"He feels that he must have a wife who can bear strong children to take his family line on, so whether his current wife is alive or not, she and her children cannot help him in his destiny. Rome will never let them go.

"Lord, I took this path with the best of intentions for our movement. With me at his side to advise we can raise the tribes and push the Romans back into the sea. When that happens, Caratacus will be crowned the first King of Britannia, a free country once more with the steadying hand of our movement to ensure peace and prosperity. Perhaps as our senior Druid, it would be appropriate for you to perform the crowning of the first King of Britannia?"

Delphidius looked stoney-faced at Cainos, clearly not impressed by the ingratiating coronation suggestion.

Hurriedly Cainos continued: "A union between Caratacus's tribe - the Catuvellauni - and the Silures of Queen Veldicca will create a bulwark against Rome ever attempting to invade our Isle of Mona, thus keeping the Druid movement safe while the Britannic army comes together.

"You see, lord, that crowning Caratacus would unite the whole country, with our movement the guiding hand behind the throne."

Delphidius sat back to consider this. "And what of Veldicca?" he asked. "What does she feel about this? She lost her father to the Romans at the start of the attack and her betrothed to

Caratacus at the end. Her desire to marry him seems a little strange, don't you think?"

Once again Cainos was confounded by his leader's intelligence knowledge. "Lord, you speak truly, but Veldicca is a sensible person, and she knows what is best for her tribe and for Britannia. I think I know what is best for our religion and by making Caratacus king, having a strong queen will be good for everyone – except the Romans of course."

Angily Delphidius rapped his staff on the granite floor. "Enough of this," he thundered. "It is not your place to decide this sort of policy. You wish to involve us in a war which will consume this whole country, with a man who has never beaten the Romans in many conflicts and lost thousands of good lives. Before I decide whether to have the pair of you sacrificed on the altar, we will listen to two people who wish Caratacus dead, and by default, you with him."

Delphidius stood and in a ringing voice commanded: "Come forward and speak."

Branwen quickly drew back the curtain, and Cainos gasped as Lenc and Alun stepped onto the chamber floor.

Caratacus recovered first from this bombshell and sneered: "So the Roman spy escaped as well. Surely this shows how much the Romans fear me if they are still pursuing me."

Lenc stepped forward with his fists bunched; the sight of his arch-enemy making him throw caution to the wind. "Don't flatter yourself, your over-riding ambition was more important to you than getting in harm's way at the shield wall. You murdered a good man who at last saw through your machinations and you kidnapped a good woman, needed by her tribe, again for your own ends. If I had my sword, I would kill you within the sight of these holy men."

Delphidius again rapped on the floor with his staff. "Enough," he shouted angrily. "There will be no more talk of killing, at least until I have decided on a course of action."

He turned again to Lenc and leaned forward. "I confess I am

having difficulty reconciling your part in this affair. We know you to be a Roman soldier, so I understand why you would wish Caratacus dead, but why are you pursuing the lady Veldicca?"

Lenc looked round the circular room, at the Druid Council who all seemed to be leaning forward, listening intently. By the look on his face, Cainos evidently realised Lenc was on dangerous ground, while Caratacus had a half-smile on his face as if convinced he was in the right.

Slowly Lenc nodded to Delphidius. "Yes lord, my part in this sorry tale is certainly a strange one. I was on the battlefield and witnessed the legion who somehow found a way to attack from the rear. I took a blow to the head and by the time I recovered, Caratacus had murdered Trenos, Veldicca's intended, and had her tied to a horse, then the whole band fled, leaving us to face the Romans.

"In the time that I was with the Silures, I grew to like them and particularly Veldicca, who despite being promised to Trenos, had some feelings for me. I accept she probably hates me now, but I feel I have an obligation to save her and ensure her safe return to her tribe. For her to marry this man would be a travesty, and an alliance based on deceit does not bode well for the future of this country."

Delphidius pondered Lenc's words and then came to a decision. "You are a Roman spy and for that I should have you executed or sold into slavery, but before I decide, we must hear what the lady Veldicca has to say."

He motioned to Branwen who hesitantly stepped forward. "Branwen, you must go to the lady's quarters and bring her here. Take some help if she needs carrying. We will get to the bottom of this."

He sat back and watched impassively as both Cainos and Caratacus both started to protest. Impatiently he held up his hand and roared, "Silence. You will get your chance to speak but first I will hear from Veldicca." He glared at the priest and the would-be king who were both cowed into silence. They stood, looking fixedly down at the floor.

The silence in the chamber was electric with tension, and a hush fell over the room as everyone waited breathlessly for the next chapter. Eventually the chamber door creaked open and Branwen half-carried a clearly distressed Veldicca into the chamber. There was a gasp of outrage from the Druids closest to the doorway as they took in the girl's confused look. Veldicca passed her hand over her eyes and pushed her hair away from her face. She looked round in puzzlement as if she had no idea why she was in the room with all these richly dressed priests.

Lenc stepped forward, concern etched on his face, but stopped when Alun gripped his forearm.

Delphidius stood and, smiling, hurried forward to help Veldicca. "Come and sit near me," he said in a soothing tone. "Branwen," he added sharply, "some water, and a chair, quickly."

Branwen hurried to fill a horn cup with water and, as Veldicca collapsed into the hastily found seat next to the throne, helped her to sip.

"Cainos, stand in front of me," he ordered. "Have you given this girl any treatment?"

Cainos floundered; he was obviously not prepared for the question and wasn't sure how to answer it. "Well, I may have administered a sedative, but only enough to help her to sleep," he whispered.

Delphidius snorted and looking round shouted for Nathan, who had been hovering just inside the door to the chamber. He hurried forward to stand in front of the Arch Druid but at a distance from Cainos. "When these proceedings started, I instructed Nathan to search the belongings of both Caratacus and Cainos," explained Delphidius. "Nathan, did you find anything of interest?"

Nathan reached inside his robe and pulled out a pouch with twigs sticking out from the top. "Lord, this is belinuntia which was rolled up in the bedroll belonging to Cainos. You infuse it with boiling water then drink it. A small dose will act as a narcotic and give you vivid dreams; it was a favourite of the old witches. If you increase the dose, it will cause unconsciousness, and ultimately it can be a fatal poison. Possibly Cainos wanted just to incapacitate the princess so she could not answer for herself, but I am told there is a dangerously fine line between a sleeping draught and fatal poison."

Delphidius nodded and turned back to Cainos who had visibly turned white. "Have you anything to say, Cainos?" he asked. Cainos could only open and close his mouth. He looked round for support, but found none.

"Lord, I did this for the good of the movement. If Veldicca became Caratacus's consort she could well be the first Queen of Britannia. With myself to advise them, our movement would be the most powerful religious order in the land. We would be unstoppable."

Delphidius looked at him searchingly for a long minute. Then finally he shook his head wearily.

"I had such high hopes for you Cainos. I thought you a potentially great diplomat and an ambassador for our way of life. But you have disappointed me with your greed and ambition, and I am afraid you must pay the price." He made a signal, and an older Druid came down the steps to the altar, where he placed a steaming horn chalice.

"This vessel contains an infusion of belinuntia, not a fatal dose, but enough to make you hallucinate. I want you to know what you have done to the lady you had sworn to protect."

Cainos gasped and shook his head in a panic. "No, lord, please, not that. I swear I took this action for the good of the Druids - I was not thinking of myself at all."

"Pick it up," snarled Delphidius.

Cainos took a deep breath and reluctantly moved towards the altar and stretched out his hand for the chalice. He looked once round the room, his eyes resting on Caratacus. "I hope you rot in hell," he hissed, then raised the chalice to his lips and took several large gulps.

Caratacus could not speak but just watched, horrified but fascinated despite himself.

The Druids leaned forward in their seats to see what would happen next. For a heartbeat, Cainos stood stock-still, just tentatively licking his lips. Then suddenly, his eyes swivelled up into his skull and he fell to the floor, writhing uncontrollably. The chalice rolled away, leaking the last few drops of the narcotic on the granite slabs. At this Delphidius made another signal and four Druidae marched quickly across the chamber and lifted the still writhing Cainos onto the cold stone of the altar, stripping him of his outer robe, baring his torso and quickly strapping him down in the crucifix position.

By now Cainos was mumbling, his head thrashing right and left as white liquid bubbled from his mouth.

Delphidius stood holding a bright ceremonial dagger with both hands above his head. He looked round at the expectant Druids then: "One of our number has favoured earthly gratification over our chosen path and must be punished. He will be sacrificed and our philosophers will watch the passage of his blood to see if there are omens for the future in his death."

Three elderly bearded Druids gravely stepped forward and positioned themselves round the altar. Delphidius followed them and placed the point of the wicked-looking blade just below Cainos's breastbone. The sharp point pricked the skin enough for it to bleed. Then suddenly Delphidius tensed, twisted the knife and lunged, aiming for Cainos's heart. He twisted once again and gouts of blood came pulsing out of the now inert body. The three observers stepped forward, intent on studying the way the blood gushed from the body.

Cainos lay cold and white on the altar slab, as his life blood gushed, then ebbed away; then, to the consternation of the observers, his eyes fluttered open, he tried to focus and said: "The Otherworld welcomes me."

Then he was still.

Delphidius sighed and laid the knife next to the body, where it was picked up by Nathan. The Arch Druid stood for a moment, his hand resting lightly on the altar. He sighed heavily. "Let this be a lesson to us all," he said softly.

"Administering potions can be a difficult business. The difference between the right measure and a fatal one can be infinitesimal. I choose to think that, in this case, it was a higher will that dictated that the draught administered to Cainos was a fatal one. All I asked for was that he took a small amount to see what he would confess to. That he took enough to kill himself is important justice. So be it."

Lenc and Alun stood transfixed at what they had just witnessed as the three observers reluctantly moved away to decide on their verdict on the omens displayed in the death. Hoping not to be noticed, Caratacus was quietly stepping backwards but his path was blocked by two Druidae who grabbed him by the arms and forced him to kneel.

Delphidius noticed him and half-smiled. "And what are we going to do with you, great would-be king? What do the omens hold for you?" He spoke sharply to the Druidae leader. "Secure him, and keep guard on him. You had better disarm his men and restrain them as well. We will wait and see what the omens say before I decide what to do with him.

"As for you two," he said, turning to Lenc and Alun, "I would have you and your companions stay in the Druidae barracks, while we decide on the best plan. I suddenly feel very old; I think it best if all of you leave the chamber."

Lenc looked uncertainly at Alun - what did this mean? Were they to be next to be sacrificed?

"Come," said Branwen simply, and reading their minds added: "You are not in danger, not yet anyway."

Suddenly there was an uproar as Caratacus surprised his guards, wrenched himself free and tried to run at Delphidius. The guards were quickly on him, but Caratacus would not be silenced.

"This is all that bastard Roman's fault," he shouted. "He's the one that caused all this. It's him you should be gutting."

Delphidius looked up. "Take him away," he said wearily.

Lenc and Alun allowed themselves to be taken to their new accommodation, Nathan, who had followed them promised that their companions would be informed and would bring their belongings to the barracks. When they were alone, Lenc sat on the edge of his bed in the small barrack block.

"I can't take it in," he eventually confessed. "I don't think I've ever seen anything like that in my life."

"It's not over yet," warned Alun grimly. "Those soothsayers could easily decide that the only way to ensure their safety is to kill us all. At least we would have the satisfaction of knowing Caratacus would be going with us."

"Very reassuring," added Lenc dryly.

CHAPTER XI

Lenc and Alun were lying on their cots, staring at the ceiling when the door to their stone cell dormitory flew open and the three Ordovicians unceremoniously pushed in. They were agog to know what was behind their change in fortunes and why their weapons had been taken away. They listened silently, eyes widening as the story unfolded.

Their room had little in the way of furniture - two lines of four cots and windows too high to see out of. A stout bolted oak door kept them in the room.

"Wonder how long we'll be cooped up in here before we know what's going to happen," Alun said aloud to no one in particular.

"Maybe we don't want to know," responded Darren darkly.

Privately Lenc tended to agree as he knew he was in a very awkward position. The Druids knew his background and he also knew that Rome was their ultimate enemy. Maybe they would support Caratacus after all. That being the case, he would probably follow Cainos on the sacrificial altar.

With nothing else to do, the five each took a cot and lay on it. The cots were lumpy with straw-filled palliasses supported by strung rope. "Better off on the floor," grumbled Madawc.

It was approaching dark before they heard the jangling of keys and Nathan stepped in.

"Time to go," he said brusquely. "You are summoned before Delphidius, don't keep him waiting." He stood back as they all stood, brushing straw off their clothes. Lenc was first to walk out into the corridor, but waited for Nathan to lead the way. The short walk was made in silence, each man deep in his own anxious thoughts about the outcome of the audience with the Arch Druid. They would know soon enough.

Lenc knew the way back to the council chamber but was surprised when Nathan led them past the entrance and up a flight of stone steps. They walked along a dark corridor, feebly lit by rush lamps, before stopping at another oak door. This was nothing like their prison cell; the frame of the door was richly carved with a spiralling ivy motif and the door itself arched and brightly polished. Nathan rapped on the door and at the command "Enter" pushed on it and stood aside to let the others pass. Inside, the room was lighter with a floor-to-ceiling opening looking out onto the forest. In the centre sat Delphidius at a huge white stone-topped table, and to one side, Veldicca, now seemingly recovered from her ordeal, but studiously ignoring them and staring fixedly out at the trees.

Delphidius looked searchingly at them all, then addressed his remarks to Lenc and Alun who stood together.

"Gentlemen, you have given me quite a problem," he started. "The actions of Cainos were something the Druid Council could not tolerate. He showed greed, subterfuge; he lied to a future queen and then drugged her and tried to persuade his Holy Council to accede to his request to support the marriage of Veldicca to that man, who may or may not become the King of Britannia. He had to die," he said simply.

"What to do, firstly about Caratacus and then you five, are different matters. I have had to take advice from the council and have thought hard about my duties as the leader of the Druid Council. You see, I cannot look on this as an unholy alliance between tribesmen and a Roman spy. If I did that, you would all follow Cainos." After a tense pause, he started again. "Lenculus, you are a Roman spy and I should have you executed out of hand. The rest of you, I would be inclined to tell you to go back to your homeland, taking Veldicca back to your border with the

Silures so she can be restored to her proper place with her tribe.

"But as the leader of the Druids I have a sacred responsibility to ensure that what is ordained by higher authority than mine is not interfered with. What if the Roman's fate is to pursue Caratacus and either capture or kill him? What if, aided by these men of the Ordovices, it is fate that Caratacus is prevented from raising the tribes against the Romans? What if he is not meant to be king? He has already shown he is no war leader. Perhaps we should be waiting for another to come forward and lead the tribes against the Romans?

"This, then, is my decision. I have told Caratacus that he and his men must leave at first light, go straight to the ferry and leave Mona immediately. They must seek their destiny elsewhere. You five will stay here as my guests, for two days and two nights then you must immediately ride for the ferry and also leave the island. What you do after that is your affair.

"What this means to you, Lenculus is that nothing has changed. You are free to pursue Caratacus and the Ordovicians can accompany you. Alun, you may decide to kill the Roman and pursue Caratacus yourselves and avenge your tribe. Or you may think you will have a better chance of success if the Roman goes with you. Whatever the result, I am satisfied that fate and the manipulation of higher beings will bring about the proper solution for the people of Britannia.

"As for Veldicca, I would like to think that she has a duty to her own people and will return to them. She may also think that Caratacus has a profound debt to pay to her tribe. My spies will follow your activities and report back to me, and I will watch your progress with interest. You must all follow your consciences."

With that, Delphidius sat back in his chair as if exhausted. The five looked warily at each other, and for the first time since the interview began, Lenc unclenched his fists.

He nodded at the Arch Druid and felt himself elected as spokesman. "Your decision has been difficult," he acknowledged.

"I for one am grateful for that decision and your careful words. Alun has sworn an oath that when Caratacus has been dealt with, he will kill me next, and I understand that. But before that happens, we will have rid the world of a man whose vaulting ambition could be the death of many, many warriors and for no real gain. He must be stopped."

Delphidius nodded. "Go now. Eat, rest, prepare your horses for the hard road ahead, and let the fates decide the future."

That evening, after a meal of barley broth, hard bread and beer, Lenc finally decided it was time to discuss their future.

"I confess I was relieved at the words of the Arch Druid," he said. "He could so easily have ordered my death, which would have left you free to follow Caratacus. You would still be honouring his words if you killed me on the road, so have you decided what you are going to do? You can kill me and carry on without me, or use my knowledge of both Caratacus and any Romans we may meet on the road to best advantage. There is also the small point that five blades are better than four."

"These are all good points," conceded Alun. "Yes, we have discussed it between us, and on balance we have decided that we shall all travel together until Caratacus is dealt with. Then my original promise will be honoured, but not before."

Lenc nodded. "So be it. May I suggest that because Caratacus and his band are still close, we should have a sentry on the door. Remember that door opens outwards, and he may well be tempted to send some men to kill us."

They looked around the sparse room to find anything that could be used as a weapon, but it had been cleared of everything but the rough cots. Eventually two of them were cannibalised, and the legs ripped off to make clubs. Primitive, conceded Lenc, but better than nothing especially in the confined space of the priests' cell. Madawc and Iestyn unravelled the twine matting from the smashed cots and made a trip-wire across the door opening.

"If they do come, they also will be without weapons and have to improvise, so we should have a chance," said Lenc, grinning.

"Do you think Caratacus himself will come?" queried Alun.

"It would be entirely against his nature," replied Lenc confidently. "If there is one thing that I have noticed about your future king, it is that he would far rather let other people fight his battles for him. I counted eighteen of them, without Caratacus, so if we can reduce the odds a bit, so much the better."

As darkness fell, Alun elected to take the first watch, followed by Darren, while Lenc volunteered for the middle - always the most dangerous as sleep is disturbed and nerves frayed. Alun settled down on his palliasse which he had bunched up in the doorway, and laid his make-shift truncheon down at his side.

Lenc looked up at the high window. "What moon there is should come in through that window," he asserted. "When the first ray gets to here" - he scratched a mark on the wall - "it's your turn Darren. Then when it gets to here" - another mark - "wake me."

"What if there are clouds?" asked Darren doubtfully.

"Then you have a long night of guard, and don't fall asleep," replied Lenc.

Shortly after midnight, Lenc was shrugged awake by Darren. "Your turn," he whispered. "Quiet as the grave."

Lenc blearily struggled upright. "How did you know it was my time?"

"I watched the moonbeam, just as you said."

Lenc was about to tell him that he made the story up, but thought better of it. Maybe the Druid was right - we have fate and the gods on our side. He pushed the thought aside as too dangerous to contemplate and took his place on the palliasse, his club handy at his side. He settled down and rattled some objects tied to the iron bars of the door. Hopefully they would give an advance warning of someone on the other side.

Sitting uncomfortably on the lumpy palliasse on the floor, he let his mind wander. He thought about Veldicca and whether she would ever forgive him. She knows I came after her, he thought, surely that should mean something. No, she would see her duty as going back to the Silures and being a queen.

These thoughts were trudging through his brain when he jerked into full wakefulness, alert to a faint scraping sound on the other side of the door. He used his club to prod the nearest man to him, who looked round blearily in the dark. The noise came again, and Lenc stood as the others were roused. He pulled the palliasse away from the door, and in the moonlit gloom motioned to the others to flatten themselves against the wall either side of the door.

Suddenly the door flew open, and one after another, eight men carrying clubs tried to rush in. The cell was still in darkness, but behind the invaders another warrior held a rush torch as high as possible, effectively silhouetting them. The first man caught on the trip-wire, but was pushed forward by the men behind him. As he fell to the stone floor, Lenc stepped forward and was rewarded with a satisfying thump as the two-handed swing of his club connected with a bare head. He realised the intruders had elected for stealth rather than security and had left their armour and helmets behind. They also were barefoot. Good, he thought.

As the first victim lay prostrate on the floor, the others tried to disentangle from him and the tripwire, as the clubs came down sickeningly. As men went down, they were attacked and clubbed repeatedly. There would be no mercy in this fight. The man still outside with the light realised the advantage was with the defenders and hurriedly threw his torch into a corner. He hesitantly stepped forward, but when he registered his comrades spread out on the stone floor of the cell, decided to make himself scarce and ran alone down the corridor. Lenc pulled the door shut, then turned and surveyed the carnage in the room. Alun and Madawc were striking flint to light the rush lamps and gradually the room flared into light as the rushes caught.

"Any still alive?" asked Lenc dispassionately. The bodies were quickly checked, and Alun stood and aimed a last blow at one man, groaning on the floor. He stooped and looked. "There were, but not now."

"Let's lay them out in the corridor," said Lenc. "Caratacus is sure to send more men if only to find out what happened, but I don't think they will try a repeat performance. We'll be waiting for them in the corridor, where they can only come at us two at a time. Once they see the bodies, they won't want to try us again."

The bodies were unceremoniously dragged out of the cell, leaving a trail of blood on the stone floor, and laid out so that if Caratacus decided to send his men in again, they would have to clamber over their friends' bodies to get to the cell door.

They had just finished piling the bodies across the corridor when the noise of running feet alerted them to a new danger. Alun bustled out of the cell, carrying their clubs and hurriedly passed them round. They turned to face the oncoming warriors and Lenc flexed his knees and gripped his club as he waited for the onslaught.

Then, into sight came Caratacus with his men behind him, the first two carrying torches. He stopped them just short of the pile of bodies and surveyed the damage. He was wild-eyed with anger.

"You bastards, you'll pay for this," he eventually raged. "You don't butcher eight of my men and get away with it. I'm going to...."

Lenc interrupted him with an imperious raising of his right arm.

"By the gods, you really do like the sound of your own voice," he sneered. "You have been given a chance by the Druids and a two-day start. Then we shall hunt you down and kill you before you have the chance to kill more honest men. Rest assured, we will find you and will stop you and your fantastical dreams."

Caratacus visibly collected himself. "I must say, I was surprised to see you here Roman, and in such fine company," he sneered. "Do they know you are a spy committed to Roman domination? Do they know that your mission is not only to kill me but to enslave every Celt in the land?"

"As for the first," replied Lenc, "yes, they do, and for the second they know I will do everything I can to ensure their lands and families will be left in peace. Such is our hatred of you and all you stand for, that we are working together and while we do, this strange alliance will hunt you down and stop you. This we have all promised.

"Your bluster is beginning to bore me. It will be light soon, and you need to put as much distance behind you as possible. But keep looking over your shoulder."

Caratacus contented himself with: "One day, bastard, one day," before leading his men back along the corridor.

Lenc breathed out a sigh and lowered his club. "I don't think they'll be back, but we'd better keep a guard out here. Put the lamps in those brackets further up the corridor; they should stay alight till dawn, and one of us will keep watch out here."

He turned to Alun. "Strange there were no guards out here. Do you think Caratacus dared to kill them?"

Alun thought for a second. "More likely that wily old bugger Delphidius ordered the guards to stay well clear just to see what happened. More tempting fate."

"I wonder what he will think about this then," added Lenc.

The night passed without further incident, and as the first rays of the sun peeked through the high window, Lenc was woken by a knocking on the door. He pulled the door wide open, enough to swing his club if necessary, but put it down when he saw it was Delphidius standing alone.

"You have been busy," observed the Arch Druid. "Caratacus and what's left of his followers have gone, heading in the direction of the ferry. I would be grateful if you could bury these men. If nothing else it will keep you occupied for some of the time before you leave Mona. Meanwhile you are welcome to breakfast with the Druidae."

The old man nodded and left the cell, gingerly skirting the pile of dead men in the corridor.

Lenc turned back into the cell to face the others. "Did you hear the Druid?" he asked. "For some reason I think we have his approval, and I for one am looking forward to food."

This met with everyone's approval and they hurried down the corridor, hardly glancing at the pile of bodies. Outside they found themselves in a courtyard. The block they had slept and fought in formed a section of a long building, which joined with others to make a square. Judging by the noise and the aroma, the kitchen and mess hall were immediately opposite. Lenc led the way, as they joined Druidae walking in the same direction.

"There you are," shouted a friendly voice, and Lenc turned to see Nathan, their guide from the day before, smiling at them. "May I join you for breakfast?" he said, smiling.

"Of course," replied Lenc, relieved that the good feeling from the Arch Druid appeared to have filtered down through the ranks. "In fact, lead on."

Nathan nodded and swept on into the hall. Inside there was warmth, chatter and noise as the Druidae patiently queued to receive their food and then found somewhere to sit.

Nathan led them past the main queue to what seemed to be an area for more senior Druidae. The tables were scrubbed clean and the noise was subdued. He gestured them to an empty table then sat with them.

"Your food will be brought to you," he explained, "and if you want something to drink, you get it from the table there," nodding to a side table with pitchers and beakers. I hear you had some adventures last night," ventured Nathan as they arranged themselves around the table.

"It was quite eventful," Alun agreed.

"Caratacus and his depleted band wasted no time in leaving," said Nathan with a grin. "They were off like scalded cats, didn't even say goodbye."

At this point servant girls brought out oatmeal and barley porridge, spiced with nuts and sliced apple and rounds of hard bread.

"Can I get you something to drink?" asked Nathan, looking round. "There is fresh water, also our local beer." They all nodded enthusiastically, and Alun offered to help carry the beakers.

As they ate, Lenc asked Nathan about their own duties for the day. "Delphidius has asked us to bury Caratacus's dead. Can you show us where and find us some shovels?" he asked Nathan.

Nathan nodded. "It won't be too onerous," he said. "I'll organise a horse and cart. We can load them up and I'll show you a marsh nearby where we can drop them. It's really just a case of pushing them under and the marsh will do the rest. Cainos was dealt with separately, but his Druid amulet and other trappings need to be thrown into Llyn Cerrig Bach, the Holy Lake. A priest will come with us and perform the ceremony."

Alun saw the puzzled look on Lenc's face and tried to explain. "Cainos was burnt by fire late last night, and his ashes scattered, but his Druid jewellery - particularly that big round badge he wore round his neck - cannot be given to another priest, despite their value, because their owner disgraced his calling. So when the bodies are dropped in the swamp, a priest will take the badges of office and throw them into the lake."

How odd, thought Lenc. "Would they mind if I went with them to watch this ceremony?"

"I don't think he'll mind," replied Alun with a mischievous smirk, "but as a courtesy it might be as well to ask, you being a Roman bastard and all."

"Wouldn't think of doing anything else," replied Lenc quietly.

With nothing better to do, Lenc and the Ordovicians wandered through the ornate gardens surrounding the great chamber, marvelling at the unknown plants laid out with such precision. Lenc desperately wanted to have a closer look at the intriguingly intricate system of mirrors bringing light into the council chamber, but after everything that had happened, he reluctantly decided that asking for a conducted tour might just be pushing his luck a bit too far.

Nathan hailed them when he reappeared, leading a horse and cart, filled with the bodies for burial. A bare foot sticking out over the back of the cart was pushed back behind the tailgate and carefully covered. A priest, wearing his white woollen ceremonial robes and a wide-brimmed hat with a bronze crown, sat on the driver's seat, with a muslin-wrapped package on his lap.

Nathan looked for Lenc. "I have told the priest of your request and he has no objections." Lenc nodded his thanks to the priest and mounted his horse behind the cart. Madawc was still stuffing bread into his mouth, as the Ordovices mounted their saddled horses and took their places behind the cart. Nathan climbed up next to the priest and laid the reins along the horse's back as it slowly ambled off.

"Where are we going?" Lenc asked Nathan.

"As you know, we are on fairly high ground here," he explained, "but closer to the sea, the land is very low and often gets covered by high seas. There is marsh there, which can be quite treacherous, but also has the advantage of being a handy place to consign bodies. A few stones down their chain mail and they will soon be gone."

"What about this Holy Lake, what's so special about it?" Lenc asked his question to Nathan, but it was the priest who replied.

"If you understand the Druid belief, you will know that we believe in the forces of nature," he said, still looking towards the horizon. "We revere the forests and the mountains, but also the sea; all are life-giving elements, and a lake, which is part of the land, yet also bound to the sea, must have a powerful influence. We are not offering Cainos's baubles as a sacrifice to some god or other; we are disposing of them so that no man will see them again. They came from the ground and will return to the ground, sunk in the mud at the bottom of the lake for ever."

The day was overcast and cold as the small party trundled slowly out of the Druid town and down to the marshland. They rode a well-used path, flanked by high grass and, in places, unidentified rushes. That probably meant water near the surface, Lenc guessed. He could see why Nathan was careful to keep the cart in the centre of the track.

The horse seemed to know the way as he plodded on, his head nodding almost to the squeal of the wooden wheels. Lenc stared as a band of five men moved to one side to let them pass. As they got closer, he realised with a shock that they were all chained together at the neck. The men squirmed to look at the cart and its occupants as they passed, but showed no emotion at all. Lenc twisted on his seat to look at them as they passed and noted that they were carrying digging tools, and were overseen by three Druidae who carried clubs.

"Are they slaves?" he asked in amazement. "How can the Druids own slaves?"

Nathan looked over the horse's head for a moment before replying. "I think you have been told that among the many duties of our movement, we are responsible for law and order within the tribes. So if we have to administer punishment for whatever the crime, we can order death or hard labour for as long as we deem is the right amount of time. You can see they are fit, and obviously fed. They will serve their time doing useful work, and then return to their tribes, if the tribe will have them. In the meantime we ensure that they earn their food and lodgings."

Lenc was still twisting round to see the slaves shackled together like animals. He supposed it was a solution to criminal activity, but somehow it didn't seem right for priests to be taking part in it.

They plodded on, the landscape hardly changing. Sometimes they could see over the top of the swaying plumes of rushes with glimpses of the sea to their right, and in front the unbroken vista of grasses blowing in the cold breeze. The landscape was flat for as far as they could see, with behind them only the blue-grey outline of the high ground of the Druid's Holy Island. A few solitary sea birds plunged and soared above them.

Eventually the priest touched Nathan on the knee, who pulled up on the reins and the horse patiently slowed to a stop. Lenc shivered in this cold, desolate half-land, half-sea wilderness.

"This looks like a good place," he said to the riders. They all dismounted, while Nathan pulled the blanket away from the bodies, then taking hold of an arm, head or leg, hauled them unceremoniously off the cart to land in an ungainly heap on the muddy track. Half of the bodies were picked up under the arms and the ankles, and, led by the priest, the procession moved awkwardly into the marsh. Their feet squelched in the watery mud, but the surface held under their combined weight. The priest only walked a few paces then stood aside to allow the bodies to pass.

"Here?" queried Nathan. The priest nodded and the bodies laid on the path. After they had gone back for the other dead warriors, stones were gathered and pushed roughly under the dead men's chain mail, before they were rolled off the path into the dank swamp. Almost immediately, water started to seep up and embrace the dead men, quickening their descent into the cold, grey water. The bodies bobbed on the surface for a moment before they slowly sank into the mire, and in a matter of minutes, only a few bubbles were the only evidence the victims had been consigned to the foul-smelling swamp.

The priest bowed his head for a brief moment, then led the way back to the cart. Lenc was the last man to leave and took a last look round for the bodies which had sunk into the mud. At first, he was struck by a tinge of sadness at the thought of this undignified burial, but comforted himself with the thought that less than a day ago, these bastards tried to kill him, and if things had turned out differently it could have been him sinking into the mud. He shuddered in the cold and forced the thoughts from his mind.

Once back at the track, the priest and Nathan climbed up onto the cart and once again the riders took up station at the rear. They carried on plodding for what seemed an age before the priest once again signalled a stop. He climbed down from the cart, this time with the wrapped package held to his chest for safety. They followed him on a narrow path as he walked towards rushes higher than a standing man, then entered a small clearing opening onto a dark lake. The lake was no longer than two hundred paces at its widest but seemed a sombre, almost evil place. The surface was a dark grey with hardly a ripple as the rushes that surrounded it, slowly swayed, releasing a rustling music which added to the otherworldly sensation.

Lenc shivered as the priest slowly unwrapped his package. He glanced at the others and could see they felt the same. They were all cold, but Lenc could also feel a heaviness in the air. There was something about this place that he didn't understand, it was as if time was standing still and the world was holding its breath. He shook himself and tried to dispel the tingling down his spine.

The package was opened and spread on the ground. Most prominent was the heavy Druid symbol that Lenc had first seen on Cainos's chest a lifetime ago in Gobannion. It was a spreading oak tree growing from a man's head, that had been so proudly explained as the interpretation of life reborn. There were also his gold rings, a belt buckle and a couple of brooches. Whispering an incantation, the priest held each article up to the sky before hurling them as far as he could into the lake. The heavy Druid symbol made a loud splash before disappearing from view, quickly followed by the rest of the jewellery.

Lenc wondered idly if they would ever see the light of day again. Maybe in years to come someone would come across them and make their fortune. He wondered if those people in the future would care how they got there?

CHAPTER XII

Relieved to be once again on the mainland, Caratacus and his war band lost no time in putting distance between them and the island which promised so much but proved to be a monumental disaster.

They collectively sighed in relief when they clambered from the ferry and walked their horses back onto the mainland. The Druidae were certainly present, but none came out of their small stone hut to challenge them. Until they were safely on the mainland, Caratacus for one, kept looking round, fully expecting vengeful priest-soldiers to ambush them with freedom in sight across the waterway. Once across, he noted a rider, trying to look inconspicuous as he sat motionless in a small copse of trees. "I see we're being observed," he said loudly to his men. "No matter, once he has reported that we have finally left their thrice damned island, his interest in us will be gone."

Nevertheless, he was still there for some distance as they followed the coast path, before finally turning away. That night they took shelter in a farm, despite the farmer's protestations that he had little enough food for his family, let alone a hungry war band. The farmer was careful to keep his daughters out of sight, something that Caratacus noticed with amusement. He was very tempted to have some sport with them, but reluctantly agreed with his lieutenant Aeron, that to alienate more people on their journey was probably not a good move. The farmer did not offer any drink, but he did grudgingly spoon out a watery barley broth. At least it was hot, conceded Caratacus.

They bedded down where they could in front of the fire, then saddled up early the next morning, as the farmer was tending to his animals. Having a band of hungry warriors and their horses descend on a small farm was a huge imposition, thought Aeron, who tried to be friendly to him. "I am afraid we have no coin to give you, as we fell in with a bad lot on Mona and lost everything but our horses and weapons. And we were lucky to escape with them," he said.

"Sorry to hear that," replied the farmer. "I wasn't aware there were bandits on Mona. The Druidae are usually pretty good at keeping undesirables away."

"Afraid it wasn't bandits, it was the Druids themselves," replied Aeron. "They seemed to take exception to us, and we were lucky to escape with our lives in the end. I thought at one stage they were going to execute us on their altar."

The farmer shot him a puzzled look, then grunted and decided that he would keep his questions to himself.

As the small band finally clattered out of the farm yard, the farmer spat on the cobbles, "Good riddance, bastards," he said venomously.

For once Caratacus was in high spirits, as they cantered along the coastal path. To their left, the sea looked cold and inhospitable as it smashed up onto the rocky beach just below. To their right the mountain range crowded in. On the lower slopes, a jumble of rocks had come loose from the mountain and tumbled down towards the track before coming to rest in the gorse. But the road was easily passable and they made good progress.

"Keep this up and we will be with the Brigantes sooner than we thought," said Caratacus.

The landscape changed little until the path bent to skirt the start of the estuary they had been told about. The many rivers tumbling down to the sea from the mountain range cut channels through the well-trodden path, but it was easily followed. As they left the coast, the open landscape closed in with thick forest from the high tide mark and spread upwards through the jumble of rocks. Aeron edged his horse closer to Caratacus, "We should beware here, lord," he warned. "This looks like perfect bandit country. A few determined men could give us some real problems."

At first Caratacus laughed away Aeron's fears but on reflection decided to humour him. "It is a good place for an ambush," he agreed, "so pass the word to be vigilant. If attacked, we will ride through, then regroup at the other side, then decide how to exact retribution."

Aeron nodded and jerked the hilt of his sword, freeing it from the scabbard.

They travelled carefully through the gloomy forest, and just as the band was starting to breathe easier, they came across a small clearing.

"If it's going to be anywhere, this looks like a likely place," whispered Aeron drawing his sword.

Caratacus agreed. "Perhaps two men should go ahead and scout the path," he suggested tentatively. Aeron nodded, and motioned to one of the riders. "We'll go ahead," he said, "If anything happens, don't stop to pass the time of day, get your heels into your horse and ride through."

The tribesman nodded and drew his own sword. "Let's go," he said through gritted teeth.

The two horsemen cantered up to the front of the small column, both on high alert. Everything seemed peaceful, but the woodland could easily hide an army. Aeron swallowed and knee'd his horse forward. They clattered into the clearing, he kicked his horse forward, and the two suddenly charged across the open ground yelling loud war cries. They were nearly at the other side when an arrow thudded into the second rider. He swayed, managed to stay in the saddle, but had been hit hard. Aeron grabbed his reins and the two carried on, crouched low in the saddle. Caratacus quickly signalled his men to ride left and right.

"Let's flush these bastards out," he yelled.

The band were all seasoned warriors, who plunged into the undergrowth, searching for their attackers. There was a crashing and shouting as the ambushers, thwarted by their victims' aggression and surprised at being assaulted, vanished into the woods. Caratacus waited under cover until his men rode slowly back into the clearing, chests heaving. One small group was prodding a prisoner forward.

Caratacus spurred his horse forward and confronted the man who stood with his head down, blood pulsing from a cut on his shoulder. He was barefoot and in rags. He made a sorry bandit.

Caratacus leaned down to him across his horse's neck. "Tell me why I shouldn't stretch your neck, you sad piece of shit."

"Lord, we only steal because we are starving. We are forced to live in the forest, and we cannot feed and clothe our children. If you kill me, then you are sentencing to death my wife and our two small children as well." The would-be bandit looked up imploringly, at the horsemen surrounding him, but shrank back when he saw the implacable look of contempt on Caratacus's face.

Aeron also saw the look and nudged his horse forward so he was between Caratacus and the kneeling bandit.

"Lord, we should think this through," he warned softly. "Why don't we move away from him and discuss matters sensibly."

Caratacus was inclined to dismiss what seemed suspiciously like a plea for clemency from his second in command, then thought he owed him the chance to at least explain himself. Then I'll kill the thieving little bastard, he thought venomously.

The two horsemen moved away from the main party where they could be alone as Aeron leaned over to talk quietly to Caratacus. "Lord, I understand this goat's turd and his band set out to kill and rob us, but why don't we make use of them? We will soon be followed by an armed war band, which may well outnumber us and certainly wants us dead. Why don't we spare this gang and let them do their worst with that Roman renegade and his Ordovician mates?"

Caratacus looked at him steadily then slowly nodded. "You are quite right, as usual. If they kill a few of our pursuers then it's a few less for us to deal with. Tell our prisoner he can go before he dies of fright. Explain to him he has been spared so that he can rob and kill the band that should be coming through here within two days. They'll have to have their wits about them though."

Aeron nodded and swung his horse round to the now terrified and piteously whimpering prisoner who was convinced he was about to die. When Aeron contemptuously shouted at him to be quiet and listen, he gulped and took a deep breath, his chest heaving. Aeron motioned to the two warriors gripping the frightened thief to let him go, which they did and laughed when he fell to the ground, grovelling at their feet.

Aeron crouched and put his hand on the terrified man's shoulder.

"I am not going to repeat myself or explain any further than I need to," he said in a voice dripping with menace. The prisoner nodded frantically, his eyes wide with fear.

"We are going to let you and your band go free, but there is something we want you to do in return. It may even be to your advantage. A small band of men, maybe as few as five, are tracking us. They are two days behind us, but a group that small will be moving fast and may be making up time, so you will have to be ready. They will all be on good, valuable horses, and one of their number has a large purse of Roman silver, so it will be very much worth your while to ambush and kill them. Don't give them a chance to fight, just lay your ambush and kill them before they have a chance to fight back. Believe me, if you let them fight, you will be the worst for it."

The pathetic prisoner looked up, beginning to realise that his life was going to be spared after all. He nodded eagerly, keen to show that he would do whatever was wanted and at the same time scrabbled to get up. He started to gabble his thanks before Aeron contemptuously put his booted foot on the man's chest and pushed him back hard to the ground.

"Now fuck off and find the rest of your sorry gang and tell them what they have to do. And don't forget to tell them that there is a bag of silver to be won if you do it right. Do it wrong, and either they will kill you or I will find out and come back here and stretch all your necks."

CHAPTER XIII

When the small group returned from its gruesome task in the swamp, Nathan was met by a messenger who took them to the Arch Druid's rooms. "He wants a word with you," was all that the Druidae would offer. When they were shown into Delphidius's room, the priest was sitting at a rough wooden table covered in parchment. Standing to one side, looking imperious was the Lady Veldicca.

Lenc hurried forward, smiling. He wasn't sure what his reception was going to be but did not expect a warm-hearted embrace. He could tell from the look on her face that he was less than popular.

She looked at him in rage and loathing, then gathered herself, and launched forward.

'Crack'.

Lenc blinked back the tears as he took the stinging blow high on his cheekbone. Veldicca stood in front of him, a furious expression on her face and her small fist still bunched.

Ruefully Lenc touched his swelling and reddening cheek as he stared at the woman who had occupied his thoughts for so long. "I take it you're not pleased to see me?" he eventually managed.

This seemed to enrage the princess even more as she took another step forward obviously about to land another blow.

"Whoa, whoa," said Lenc quickly. "I give in, no more. Please, let me explain."

"Explain… what have you got to explain?" shouted Veldicca.

"Other than you're the Roman bastard who was instrumental in getting my father, my betrothed and half my tribe killed by your treacherous and conniving ways. And to think I cared for you."

Lenc stood quietly against this onslaught, his chin on his chest. Alun and his men watched, fascinated. Delphidius, stood, gazing fixedly at the floor.

"There's nothing I can say that's going to help," Lenc said eventually. "Yes, I was a Roman spy, but when I met you and the tribe, my loyalties were shaken. I did not want to do what had been hammered into me... my duty. Yes, I provided the plan which caused your defeat, but I tried to save you. I should have known that you would never desert the tribe and escape with me. I know you will never want to speak to me again and I accept that although half of my mission - your rescue - is now complete, I cannot in all conscience complete the second part, which is to kill Caratacus until I have ensured your safe return to Gobbanion."

Veldicca stared at him, still seething but rapidly calming down. "What makes you think I am going home?" she asked. "I'm coming with you to find Caratacus, and if I get to him first it will be me that runs him through. Only then will I go home."

Lenc looked searchingly at her, then Delphidius, then the Ordovicians. "Do you mind if I sit down?" he asked of the room. "I think events are moving faster than I can cope with."

At this Alun snorted with laughter, which he quickly strangled as Veldicca whirled to glare at him.

"And as for you, you snivelling Ordovician bastard, what are you doing riding with the enemy, when there are real enemies to kill?"

Alun nodded, still trying to hide his smile. "Lady, you speak truly. Lenc is my sworn enemy, and when our mission is over, I shall kill him. Until then he will be useful should we meet the legion and he will be able to get us into places we cannot access by ourselves. We have all sworn an oath that we will kill Caratacus for what he did on that hill."

Veldicca looked round for a seat, hurriedly carried over by Delphidius. She thanked him and sat.

"This is a strange war band. Enemies coming together to fight an even bigger enemy. Very well, I shall join you, and together we will find Caratacus and kill him," she turned to Lenc. "And then either the Ordovicians or I will kill you. Only then will I go home and take my rightful place in the tribe."

Lenc shrugged but Alun was disconcerted. "Lady, you cannot come with us. The road will be hard and dangerous and we will have enough to do keeping ourselves alive without having to defend you as well."

With that Veldicca jumped up, eyes blazing, "While the Ordovices were watching, I was in the front line that ran at the Roman shield wall. I saw my father and my betrothed murdered, and in my grief and anger, I killed Romans. Then when we had to accept defeat, Caratacus turned and ran, taking me as a prisoner. Don't you worry about me, I don't need defending. I have revenge to take."

"Well I'm glad that's all settled," Delphidius sighed as he sank onto his chair. "You will all pursue Caratacus and by the time your quest is over, you may have resolved your differences and not have to resort to slaughtering each other."

Lenc contented himself with another shrug of his shoulders. As they were trooping out of the chamber, Delphidius called out to Alun. "Ask the others to wait for you outside," he said. "I have something I wish to say to you."

Puzzled, Alun told the others he would meet them in the garden.

"Take a seat," Delphidius asked with a distracted air, then pulled his own chair round from his desk and sat facing Alun.

After summoning his thoughts, Delphidius leaned forward and spoke urgently. "Alun, you know me as a man of peace, but you also know that I can take life if I think it necessary. I have seen you with the Roman, and despite your oath, I cannot believe that it is the right thing to kill him when your mission is accomplished. An oath is an oath, but it doesn't need to be binding. When Caratacus is dead, can you not just shake hands with Lenculus and both ride away? I know he is Roman and the enemy, and you would want him dead without your special quest, but I detect a bond between you, and if you were to kill him, you will regret it till your dying day."

Alun looked down at the floor, twisting his hands in his lap. "Lord, I can see now why you are the leader of your people. You see things that others do not. Yes, I will regret killing the Roman, but I have made a solemn oath, which I still think is right and just, despite your persuasive words. When Caratacus dies, so will Lenc, and if I die before that, then my tribesmen will honour the oath in my place. Lenc is a viper in our bosom, and no good will come from letting him live after his usefulness is over. Yes, I may be saddened by it, but he must die."

Delphidius sighed. "And so it must be. I am truly sorry but also understand the importance of the oath you have made. In all other matters, please take my blessing and the knowledge that your quest is an honourable one."

Alun bowed his head for a second, then stood and forced a smile. "With your blessing, lord, we will achieve our mission."

Delphidius nodded and clasped his hands in prayer as Alun strode from the room.

Dawn on the second day of their imposed stay with the Druids saw the small band finally saddle up as a weak sun tried to burst through a leaden sky.

Delphidius had wished them success the evening before at a celebration dinner. "I won't be joining you in the morning," he confided. "I start my devotions early. I find, as I get older, it's easier that way. But I do wish you every success, although given your mission I probably shouldn't."

Waiting for them in the stable were their new-found friends, Nathan and Branwen who wanted to see them off and wish them well. The pair watched as saddles were cinched and bedrolls strapped behind.

"The Druidae at the ferry have been told to mark which way Caratacus and his men rode," confided Nathan. "I think it's fairly obvious they will head east along the coast, but when they get to the estuary at the edge of Deceanglian land they will probably head north for the Brigantian capital on the other side of the Penninus."

In answer to a questioning raising of eyebrows from Lenc, Nathan explained that the Penninus was a range of mountains forming the spine up the centre of Britannia.

"Brigantia is an absolute nest of vipers, and one of the biggest tribes in the whole of Britannia. Their ruler is the Queen Cartimandua who is kept on her throne by the Romans. She knows what's good for her and she keeps the peace with Roman gold and a strong militia. She kicked her consort Venutius out of her bed and banished him to a hill fort high in the Penninus, just so she could install a young warrior in her bed. Venutius hates the Romans and would love to overthrow the Queen but he would have to defeat her warriors, as well as make terms with the Romans. The Queen has taken hostages from Venutius's family who will be the first to die, if Venutius moves against her.

"His hatred and jealousy, not to mention his manly pride, could make him a good ally for you. He could, of course, also appeal to Caratacus, who will probably get to him before you do. Whatever happens, you are going to have to be very careful because every man's hand will be against you."

Lenc shrugged, and grasped Nathan by the arms. "Thank you for all your help, and please pass on to Delphidius that we leave this holy place enriched by meeting him and his Druids."

As Nathan stepped back, Branwen stepped forward and shyly offered a package of food to Veldicca. "It's not much," she whispered, "but I hope you enjoy it."

Veldicca smiled and impulsively embraced the girl. "Thank you, Branwen, and I hope we shall meet again some day."

"I hope so too, but I think it unlikely," replied Branwen.

"When I finish my studies, I shall go back to Camulodunum which is about as far across the country as you can get from Silurian territory."

Veldicca had to agree but added: "That is true, but you were very friendly to me on Mona and I shan't forget that. If I ever hear of a priestess called Branwen I will know you are doing good work."

Branwen smiled. "No lady, it is the custom of the Druids to give novices another name. I have not used my true given name since I arrived here, but when I leave, I shall revert to that and that is how I shall be known."

"What is your true name?" asked Veldicca curiously.

Branwen hung her head, then looked up, straight at the princess. "Lady, my birth name is Boudicca."

CHAPTER XIV

There was little activity on the trail that hugged the northern coast at that time in the morning and the small band made good progress. They clattered through groves of oaks before passing out onto the open drover's trackway, and as they turned onto the bigger trail, they could see far in the distance, once again, the looming shape of Yr Wyddfa with the peak shrouded in mist. Lenc shuddered at the thought of their near brush with death on the snow-capped mountain.

They rode mostly in silence, with the four Ordovicians close together and a pointed distance between Lenc and Veldicca. He thought he really ought to try and mend fences with her but feared that rather than mend the fence she would probably hit him with it. He decided to stay patient and let her make the first move. Besides, he had already felt her stinging right hook.

Then at last Veldicca glanced across the Ordovicians at him. He caught the look but she quickly turned away. Still Lenc waited to see what would happen next, and to his surprise, he didn't have to wait long. They were riding through open country with just the odd farm roundhouse to break the monotony, when Alun suggested a stop to rest the horses. Gratefully they stiffly slid down from their saddles and led the horses to a copse of trees where they were tethered on long ropes so they could graze. The men were thankful for the respite and stretched their arms and legs, while Veldicca slipped from her horse and sat demurely on the grass. When she thought Lenc wasn't looking, she sneaked a glance at him through long eyelashes.

Alun paused after taking a long swig of water from a leather flask and looked carefully at both Lenc and Veldicca. He put the flask back on his saddle and turned to the small band.

"I think we need to decide how we are going to reconcile our differences, because if we are all hating each other and wondering whether we are going to wake up with a knife in the guts, it's not going to help us succeed and may well cause us to fail in our mission," he said finally, before turning to Veldicca. "Lady, you have every right to hate this man," he said, gesturing at Lenc. "I have told him we would ride together until this bastard Caratacus is killed. Then I or one of the other Ordovicians will kill him. It's as simple as that. I don't have to like him, but I can see that in the days and weeks to come, he could be useful, especially if we run into the legion. So, until we kill Caratacus, we will be civil to him so we can work together."

His gaze swept the group, then he looked pointedly at Veldicca: "It would be a big help to the harmony of the group if you could do the same thing. I know he has wronged you badly, but I think it would make our task so much easier if we could all get along. When we complete our mission, I would be happy to stand back and let you kill him, but until then, as we Ordovicians can get along with a Silurian and a Roman, could you get along with all of us as well?"

Veldicca stayed thoughtfully silent for a while. "I can see the sense in what you are saying," she said finally. "I don't like it, but I will co-operate. We are certainly strange companions, but we do have a common cause. Yes, I agree, until we kill Caratacus we should work together."

She turned a cold face towards Lenc, and with eyes blazing said: "But as for you, don't think you will worm your way into my affections. If you put one hand on me or say anything that offends me, I promise I will kill you, even if it makes the finding and killing of Caratacus more difficult."

Lenc nodded and leaned back on the grass. "We have some hard riding to do, and life will be much easier if we can rely on each other. When Caratacus is dead and our alliance is over, then we will see about you turning on me, but have a care and do it properly or you may be in for a surprise."

The baleful grey of Yr Wyddfa, its summit hidden in the mist, was their landmark. The mountain range rose from the sea on the mainland, and for many hours of riding never seemed to get any bigger. The mist never parted, but Lenc, for one, was quite happy not to gaze at the blue line of hills. The memory of the cold and freezing danger of their journey through the mountain pass would take a long time to fade. Eventually, as Lenc eased forward on his saddle to try and change position, Alun pointed forward. Lenc could see a line of trees and, through them, the glint of the sea. All of a sudden Yr Wyddfa loomed higher, the mist shredding as wind whipped across the estuary to batter the mountain range. A thin drizzle added to the gloom of the day.

"The Druidae at the ferry may have some information for us," shouted Alun. "It's just ahead."

The small party clattered on, spirits rising at the thought of stretching their bones after a full day's riding. There were few buildings to mark the ferry port, just the end of the road, which petered out on the hard-standing that the ferry tied up to. A few low thatched buildings stood damply tucked into a screen of oaks, but there was little sign of life.

Better things to do than stand outside in the wet, thought Lenc sourly. As they approached, the beaten earth track changed to rudimentary stone, then at last a face poked out of a doorway at the sound of the horses but quickly withdrew. The small band cantered towards the building and gratefully dismounted, which signalled the appearance of the man in the building who finally ventured out into the strengthening rain and beckoned them inside. By his long woollen robe and sword strapped to his waist, he was Druidae. Lenc and his companions tethered their horses under a lean-to shelter and followed him, hoping for a warm fire to banish the keening wind.

Lenc pushed open the door and walked through into a dark room with benches round the walls, and three men sitting there, who nodded a greeting to the visitors. They all wore the simple uniform of Druidae. They were the same ones on duty when they had first arrived on the island, seemingly so long ago.

"Greetings," Alun said affably. The Druidae responded with a mumble.

"We have some warmed cider we can offer you," said one after a pause. "It will help with the cold."

Lenc noted that their welcome was a lot more positive and certainly less suspicious than the previous meeting and nodded appreciatively. As one of the shaven-headed priests poured the steaming cider from a large pot held on chains over the open fire, Alun asked if they had any news of Caratacus and his party.

"Yes, they came through as expected. They had ridden their horses hard," said the cider pourer. "The Arch Druid had sent word that we were to mark which direction they rode off in, which is why I had Brother Ethan here posted on the mainland."

Ethan nodded. "By being on the mainland, I could keep my horse hidden, then follow them until I was sure which direction they were taking, although that seemed in little doubt," he explained. "They took the drover's track skirting the sea eastwards into Deceanglian country. Where they were heading is anyone's guess."

Lenc thought hard. "They could be heading for Catuvellauni country, their tribal home, but I doubt it," he mused. "We know that Caratacus's family were afraid of the Roman reaction to his raiding, so they came up with a plan to pretend to disown and kick him out. He promised he was going to unite the tribes, and then sweep down on the Roman army and drive it out of Britannia for good. He would, of course, be at the head of that army as the king and the Catuvellauni would be well placed to ride with him and take the spoils. That was foiled when he got his arse kicked once again, so for him to go home now would be to admit failure. No, I think he will continue his ambition to form another army and where better than Brigantia, one of the biggest tribes in the country."

The Ordovician tribesmen looked puzzled at this; their understanding of tribes only stretched as far as their neighbours and they neither knew nor cared about anyone further away.

Lenc saw their confusion and explained: "Brigantia is a vassal state of Rome, a buffer against that bunch of savages further north. It stretches all the way across the country, from the west coast to the east, and from the border with Caledonia down into the middle of Britannia where they meet the Catuvellauni. It's a very big tribe by anyone's reckoning, and if Caratacus can form an alliance, when he rides south and gets the Catuvellauni to join as well – which they will - he will have a formidable army."

Alun shrugged. "I would say that sounds like the best bet, but didn't you say it's a vassal state which bends the knee to the Romans?"

Lenc conceded that point. "Yes that's true, but if the Brigantian leaders see a good chance to stop paying taxes to Rome and maybe take over Britannia, wouldn't that be a temptation?"

They had to agree it was a possibility. "I think we should head that way and take a look," Madawc said eventually. "We know that's the direction they are headed, so as long as we keep asking if people on the road have seen the war band, we may just as well head for the Brigante stronghold, wherever that is."

As they sat huddled close to the fire, one of the Druidae poked his head round the door to announce that the ferry was on its way. "I can lead your horses on board if you like," he offered.

Alun thanked him graciously, then stretching his legs out added: "I must say, sitting in the warm, drinking cider is far more agreeable than going out there to suffer the wind and rain and the gods know what else, but I suppose we have to follow our destiny."

"We are a strange crew indeed - Ordovicians, a Silurian and even a Gaul - and we are chasing the would-be King of Britannia who we would kill," added Veldicca. "Every man's hand, and by that, I mean Brigante, Catuvellauni, even bastard Romans, will be against us. We are going to have to be clever and very careful."

They were all silent for a while reflecting on the journey ahead, when a shout from the dock made them shake off their dark thoughts and start bustling about gathering up their kit and thanking the Druidae for parcels of food.

Lenc stood and thrust his arm out, which was grasped by the senior Druida. "I didn't know what to make of you when we first arrived here," he said gruffly, "but I know better now. Many thanks for your understanding and assistance."

"We are often misunderstood," the Druida said simply, "but we have a task, and that is to protect our religion. The Arch Druid has told us that you are doing his work and that's good enough for us. May your gods watch over you and your mission successful."

Lenc nodded as the others echoed his thanks before they shouldered their way out into the wind and now slashing rain. Their horses were already on the ferry, peacefully tethered, and there was the same woman sitting at the helm, leaning on the tiller. She raised a laconic arm in recognition.

The tide was running hard and she wasted no time in ordering her scraggy crew of urchins to cast off, allowing the heavy ferry to drift away from the jetty into the full force of the tide. Lenc looked back at Mona, breathing in the salty air, his face lashed by the rain. He had conflicting thoughts on this strangely mystical sect of Druids. They worshipped no gods, believing nature to be their divine inspiration. They preached that being a human was just part of a cycle so you never died, just went on to be something else. It was sort of comforting, he supposed, and a good reason for the Celts not to fear death, but all the same, surely it was just as much wishful thinking as believing in all the gods or even one man like that one in Judea whose religion seemed to be spreading everywhere. It was too big a question for him, he thought. I'll just be polite and not disagree with any of them.

The journey across the strait was uneventful and the small party stood aimlessly on the mainland jetty as the urchins led their horses off.

"Which way is the eastern coast road?" shouted Lenc to the ferry mistress.

She raised an arm and pointed. "Just follow the sea and you'll come on it. You will have a day's ride through Deceangli country with the sea on one side and the mountains on the other. The Deceangli are peaceable people but beware, there are bands of outlaws - people displaced either by the tribes or the Romans - who would kill you for your horse."

Lenc nodded his thanks. "Don't worry, we'll take care."

The woman shrugged and went back to stowing ropes.

Lenc looked round to try and identify where the sun should have been behind the dense dark cloud. "The horses are well rested and we can still make a bit of time before we find shelter for the night. Alun would you like to lead?"

Alun nodded and steered his horse to the front, closely followed by his tribal friends, Madawc, Iestyn and Darren. Veldicca hesitated then snapped her reins and fell in behind, with Lenc taking up the rear behind her.

He wondered whether he should move up and talk to her, try for a reconciliation. Maybe not, he thought. The wounds are still too fresh, best to wait awhile.

As they left the jetty, they kicked up onto higher ground, overlooking a drop down to beaches framed by black rocks jutting out to sea. Across the strait, Mona looked low and peaceful, with just the odd plume of smoke from a kitchen fire to mark any habitation at all. The landscape on the mainland side was bleak - the sea to their left and the lower slopes of the mountain range to their right, covered in trees bent sideways by the almost constant wind. Not a soul showed themselves.

They rode on, hunched into their cloaks to try and keep out the persistent rain, while Lenc started to worry that, with dark approaching the lack of shelter may mean a wet night on the ground. Then with almost all hope gone, Alun let out a shout and pointed ahead to a farmstead with a welcoming light in the one window. They dismounted in the farmyard and Alun splashed forward to bang on the wooden door. He put on his best grin as the door opened and a querulous voice asked: "who's there?"

CHAPTER XV

With his grin still firmly fixed, Alun raised a sodden arm, palm showing, to mean he meant no harm. "We are tired, wet travellers, looking for nothing more than shelter and warmth for us and our horses. We have some food and are willing to share it with you in return."

"Yes, but who are you?" demanded the farmer, a stout man with hands like shovels, grasping the door as if he would slam it in their faces at the wrong answer.

"We are Ordovicians," shouted Alun, "and we are friends with the Deceangli. You are Deceangli I hope?"

The farmer nodded, "Aye, that I am, but the last lot of strangers we welcomed pissed off, not only without paying but they stole any food they could lay their hands on, not only that, I had to hide my two daughters or they would have stolen them too - their virtues anyway."

"Would this band be led by a big man, blond hair, well dressed?" asked Alun. "Only we are chasing him and would like to offer him some cold Ordovician iron, if you get my meaning," he added darkly.

The farmer beamed and let go of the door. "In that case, come in and welcome. You can bed the horses down in the stable and I'll bank the fire up. You have some food, you say?"

The small band gratefully shed their cloaks after drying the horses off and filling a trough with feed for them. The one-room farmhouse was warm and dry, and when the farmer realised that his visitors had a woman with them, he allowed his two young daughters and wife to join them. The farmer's wife busied herself at the fire, while the two teenage girls stared at Veldicca with big round eyes in dirty faces.

She smiled at them and asked their names. At first they were too tongue-tied to answer before the older one plucked up her courage. "She is Gwyneth and I am Helen," she shyly managed.

"I am very pleased to meet you," replied Veldicca. "I have been in the company of men so long it's a pleasure to talk to two young ladies."

The girls weren't sure how to take this and giggled uncertainly. The farmer smiled at their confusion. "Come along girls, these are our guests. Find them a warming drink."

As the girls scurried around the kitchen, glad of something to do, Alun quietly asked the farmer about his other visitors.

"Arrogant bastards. Especially their leader. Nothing was good enough for him. Our food wasn't to his taste, my cider was rat's piss, and he wasn't impressed about sleeping on the floor in front of the fire. I told him he could sleep out in the stable if he wanted, because that's all there was. That shut him up," he said with satisfaction.

"Did they say where they were going?" asked Alun quietly.

"They did ask about the road to Mamucium and whether it passed near any Roman forts," replied the farmer. "I told them there was only Deva, but that's easily avoided. There's a lead and copper mine near the end of the Deva estuary; from there you follow the sun across a small landmass to another estuary, then pick up the trail for Mamucium. Anyone will put you right; it's a well-trodden path," he added vaguely. "Although why they wanted to go there, the gods only know - that's deep into Brigantian country and they're a warlike lot, all of them. I hear they're deeply divided between Rome-lovers and Rome-haters, but you wouldn't want to get on the wrong side of either lot," he added, shaking his head.

Lenc sat back, nursing his warmed cider. He wondered whether they would catch up with their enemy on the trail or pursue them all the way to the Brigantian stronghold.

The conflict over allegiance to Rome was interesting though; it possibly meant that Caratacus would be met with less than open arms. We shall have to tread carefully, he thought.

The next morning, Lenc and his companions gratefully accepted some warm porridge which even included some honey, served by the farmer's daughters.

"Thank you for your hospitality," said Lenc to the farmer as they were saddling up.

"Don't mention it," replied the farmer. "My daughters will be talking about your visit for a long time, especially about the young lady; they were quite taken by her.

"If you carry on along the trail you came in on you will soon come to forestry. Be very careful going through the trees, there are bandits who would kill you for your boots."

Lenc thanked him for the warning, then pressed some food on the farmer's wife, who had left her hearth to see them off. Hiding behind her skirts were the two daughters, who wanted to say goodbye to Veldicca. Shyly, they left the security of their mother and stepped forward. Veldicca saw them and, before mounting her horse, made a point of smiling at them and giving them both a big hug. "If I come this way again, I will be sure and call to see you," she said warmly.

The tongue-tied girls could only beam at her as they watched her mount her horse.

Once in the saddle, the small party waved goodbye to the family before heading for the coastal trail once again.

"From what the farmer was saying, we should be turning into the estuary before long," shouted Lenc against the wind. "The hills come down close to the shore, then when we come to forest, that's where we will be attacked if we are going to be. I think we should probably scout ahead on foot rather than just blunder into an ambush."

Alun nodded. "That will also hide how few we are. If there

are bandits we should come on them by surprise, we may even find a way round without having to fight them. Maybe they did our job for us by killing Caratacus."

"It's a nice thought," conceded Lenc, "but I think Caratacus is too slippery to be caught like that."

"I think we should expect the worst, and that's an ambush. When we are in sight of the trees, I will go ahead on foot and at the very least try and find out how many of them there are and how they aim to receive us."

Lenc took the lead on the rapidly narrowing trail as the rocky cliff pressed down further as if trying to slide into the sea. Lenc wondered idly what the legionaries shivering in their Deva stronghold thought of this wild country.

Up ahead, the rocky hills were finally receding, giving way to the start of what seemed like a dense forest, climbing up from the shore to disappear out of sight in a jumble of valleys and peaks.

Lenc led them into a windbreak caused by fallen rocks, and dismounted. "If they have any sense, they'll have a lookout on the path where it enters the forest," he said. "I think I'll climb up higher and enter the forest where hopefully no one can see me. I'll go further in, see if I can find anyone, then come back along the path and deal with the lookout."

He grinned reassuringly as the rest of the band dismounted and led their horses out of the wind howling from the sea. He looked round for Veldicca and was gratified by the concern on her face before she saw him looking and quickly turned away.

Maybe there's hope for me yet, he thought.

A rockfall masked his approach to the forest as he climbed higher. He was sure there would be a lookout watching the trail, but felt he could stay out of sight until he could hide himself under the canopy of trees. For once he was grateful for the rain, which, although not heavy, was an insidious drizzle that seemed to hang in the air, rather than actually falling. Any lookout would care more about shelter than concentrating on the job, he hoped.

Carefully he peered round the rock face. Away in the distance was the estuary with the flatter far shore, the jumble of rocks which tumbled down to the seashore and into the trees, with the trail snaking the easiest route before disappearing into the forest. If there was an ambush, the lookout would be somewhere on the edge of the tree-line. He would watch out for travellers, then step back into the foliage before raising the alarm with the rest of the war band. It still remained to be seen how many of them there were and how resolute they would be in a fight.

Lenc slipped round the side of the rock, watching where he put his feet, and using it as a shield, crept forward before reaching the cover of the damp trees.

He paused as he crept in under the canopy, and looked round carefully. He could see no sign of life but knew that near the track would be a person. He slowly drew his gladius then sat patiently for some minutes before quietly moving forward keeping a wary eye all round.

Aside from the steady drip from every leaf, there was no sound or sign of animal life in the silent forest, which told Lenc that there were humans around somewhere - not that it helped, but it underlined his instinctive caution.

When at last he crept cautiously onto the path, he crouched down once again. He felt sure that he would be behind the lookout by now but resisted the temptation to try and find him. Once again he retraced his steps away from the path into the undergrowth. He moved back until he could still just see the brown of the dirt-path, then cautiously walked alongside it, constantly scouring the surrounding terrain, on the alert for signs of life.

Just as he was beginning to wonder whether Caratacus had decided to give up on ambushing his pursuers and put more distance between them, he froze as a sharp sound came from ahead. He crouched down, slowly moving his head around, looking for whatever made the noise. He flinched as the noise came again. He licked his lips as he tried to identify the sound. Slowly and carefully, he inched forward, studying the ground before moving, wary of giving himself away.

Ahead, he could make out a clearing, perfect for an ambush, he thought. As he crept nearer, he realised with a start where the noise was coming from. There at the edge of the clearing, a small group of ragged men struggled with a dead body. Two of them strained to hold up the body, which had a rope round its neck, with the other end looped over a strong tree branch. The rest of the tattered gang were hauling on the rope, trying to pull the body up into the tree.

With a start, Lenc recognised the once proud warrior, still with an arrow embedded in his back, as a member of Caratacus's bodyguard. At first Lenc was puzzled as to why they would try and string up an obviously dead man, then as more of the bandits appeared in the clearing, he realised the dead man would be a frightening warning to any passers-by. He ducked quickly as another group of ragged men came into view. They were laughing and jeering at their friend's ineffectual efforts to string the body up onto the branch.

Looks like Caratacus and his party bumped into the bandits and not only bested them but persuaded them that a much more lucrative group would be following in two days' time, just ripe for the plucking, he thought.

Slowly and carefully Lenc backed away from the clearing. He had seen enough and although the band outnumbered his group, he was under no illusions about their fighting ability. Now I know what the plan is, we can soon sort this lot out, he thought. When he judged himself far enough out of sight, he dropped down to the path and, skirting the edge, walked back to where he expected to find the look-out.

His thinking was that the man - or men - would not be expecting danger from behind, so he would be fairly safe until he came to the edge of the forest. Then just as expected, as he caught sight of the clear path and the jumble of rocks, there, sprawled with his back to a tree, was the solitary lookout. Lenc smiled to himself as he crept up on the unsuspecting watcher. He quietly unwound a length of rope hanging from his sword belt, then stepped carefully up to the tree. It was an easy matter to loop the rope round under the man's chin and catch it on the other side and pull it tight. The man yelped with fright and pulled frantically at the rope as Lenc tied it off behind him. When he was satisfied that the rope was tight enough, but not so tight it would throttle his prisoner, he walked round to the front. The man's eyes widened in fear as he took in the drawn gladius, and the obvious military air of his captor.

"You are very close to leaving this world," said Lenc with a smile. "I can't have you crying out, so you have one chance to tell me or I will have to silence you permanently. Do you understand?"

Terrified the man nodded as much as he could with the rope round his neck.

"Good, I see we understand each other. How many of you are there, for a start?"

"Ten of us, Lord, but we wouldn't want to harm you, we would be looking for easier prey."

Lenc laughed; it wasn't a pleasant sound.

"You're only looking for easy pickings, are you? You wouldn't have been told to expect a small band from Mona by any chance, would you?"

By now the prisoner was terrified and in a deadly dilemma. He was sure he would be killed if he gave the wrong answers but would probably still be killed if he gave the right ones. His eyes rolled as he tried to come to a decision about what to say.

"Yes, lord, you are right," he eventually blurted when Lenc prodded him none too gently with the point of his gladius. "Two days ago, we stopped a war band led by a big blond man. We killed one of them, but fled when they turned on us. The blond man said he would spare us if we lay in wait for a group of riders coming on the coast path a day or so after them."

Lenc nodded. "What were you supposed to do when you saw this party of riders approaching?"

"I have to run back into the forest and alert the rest. There is a clearing back there, and by now there should be a body hanging from a tree. We thought that would make you pause and help with the ambush."

"It's possible, I suppose," conceded Lenc. "And would you have archers in the trees as well?"

"We have two archers, lord, but I am sure they would be no problem against a military man like you."

"Do you have a camp nearby?"

"Yes, lord, further up the hill, in the rocks."

Lenc grunted. The lookout was a sorry bandit, much like the rest of the group he had seen. But even so, the man had given him a problem. By rights he should run him through - one down, ten to go. But the man was terrified and was really no threat, probably hungry, he thought.

He reached for the rope round the prisoner's neck and hacked a length off the end.

"Hold up your hands." Meekly the man did so. Lenc tied his hands together then hauled the rope up and tied it off on a low branch. Then he hacked a length off the man's tunic and used it as a gag.

"Now I want you to sit still while I go and get my comrades, then we are going to come through here and take on your mates. If I hear one sound from you, I will do what I should have done already and run you through. Do you understand?"

Vehemently the man nodded.

Lenc took one last look round then moved out onto the path towards the sea. It was a short walk back to where the others were waiting and Alun stepped out as he approached.

"Any difficulties?" he enquired.

"No, it's not Caratacus and his men lying in wait for us but some apologies for bandits, about ten of them, but they are no warriors. Caratacus must have been as wary of ambush as we are; they lost one man to an archer but apparently scared off the rest of the bandits. There are two archers, and they think they will distract us with the body of the dead man strung up from a tree. Let's join the rest and I'll go through what I propose."

Alun stood back as Lenc walked round the fallen rock to where the others were waiting. Veldicca was sitting on her cloak on the wet grass, and looked up at him then looked away.

He quickly explained what he had seen and done, then outlined his plan. "As we expected there's a lookout on the edge of the forest, and when he saw us, he was supposed to run back and warn the rest so they could set up an ambush, only it was him that got caught in the ambush," said Lenc with a grin. "From what I can gather they're a pretty poor lot, but there are at least ten of them. If we split into two groups, either side of the path, we should be able to come up on them through the undergrowth. We can reduce the numbers before they realise we're among them, and if we attack hard, I'm certain they won't hang around long."

Lenc looked at the four Ordovicians who seemed to accept the plan.

"So that's two on one side and three the other," said Alun. "Darren and Madawc, why don't you come with me and Iestyn can go with the Roman."

He turned to Veldicca: "And you, Princess had better look after the horses."

Veldicca had been listening with rising fury as the threadbare plan was discussed and she realised she was to have no part in it.

She jumped to her feet, red spots on her cheeks and small fists clenched. "How dare you discount me? I attacked the shield wall while the Ordovices lay about watching. If anything, it should be me leading the way against these bandits - at least I have proved myself in battle. Besides, the horses don't need minding. This is a good spot, out of the way, and they can be hobbled so they won't wander off."

Lenc had rather anticipated this outburst from the princess but thought it more tactful to keep a dignified silence. Let the tribes sort this out, he thought.

Alun shrugged and spread his arms expansively. "Lady, once again you have caught me," he said disarmingly. "I had forgotten you had every right to be part of the fighting. You have proved that already. Please forgive a mere man for thinking otherwise."

This took the wind completely from Veldicca's sails. "That's all right then," she said imperiously. "Let us have no more of this poor, frail little woman nonsense. I can look after myself."

Lenc looked away and half-smiled. He wondered whether Alun was looking to get into Veldicca's favours, although putting her in danger seemed a strange way of doing it. He would not only have to keep her out of danger but keep Alun at arm's length as well.

"Lady, I think it best if you come with Iestyn and me," he said. "That way we have equal numbers."

Veldicca clearly had an opinion on whose gang she would be in, but before she could speak, Alun offered: "Why doesn't Madawc or Darren go with Lenc, then the princess can come with me? Under the circumstances it might be more beneficial," he smiled disarmingly.

The princess opened her mouth to say something but was forestalled by Lenc who could see he had been outmanoeuvred. "Why not," he agreed. "If that's settled, can I now outline what I suggest we do against these thieves in the forest?"

No one objected, so he carried on. "Right, thank you," he said with only a hint of sarcasm. "The lookout has been taken care of, unless someone has been along to relieve him, in which case they know we're here and will be waiting for us. Either way we have to proceed with caution. They have a camp, which the lookout told me is on the hillside above the ambush clearing, so I propose we make for that, and if we catch a few of them there, so much the better. The only way we will succeed is to split them up and deal with them in small groups, agreed?"

Grudging nods met his question.

"Right, the longer we wait the more chance there is of the look-out being found, or freeing himself, so we'd better get started."

The group stood, checking sword belts and hobbling the horses. Lenc led the small party further up the hill to the edge of the forest. He paused and beckoned to Alun.

"Chances are we are at the same height as the camp," he whispered. "If we stay at this level, we should eventually come across them. The clearing isn't too far into the forest, but I don't think it will be far from the camp either, so if we can deal with whoever we find quickly, that will reduce their numbers and make the rest more manageable. Speed and silence," he emphasised.

Alun nodded. "Seems simple enough. Let's hope they haven't been reinforced."

Lenc smiled, "There's a saying in the legion that the plan never lasts longer than first contact with the enemy. We shall just have to put as many down as possible and hope for the best. Try and watch out for Veldicca, when we get into the fight, she can be prone to be over enthusiastic which could get her killed."

Alun gave a wolfish grin. "Don't worry I will take good care of her."

That's exactly what Lenc was afraid of, but he let it go, just nodded and led them under the canopy on the old drover trail. They drew their swords and picked their way carefully through the trees, stopping whenever they heard a suspicious noise. A track forked off to the right and seemed to climb higher. Lenc pointed at it with his gladius, then silently stepped onto the new trail, with the others following at a crouch. Abruptly, he stopped, held up a clenched fist and sank to one knee. He leaned back to Alun and made a gesture as if sniffing the air. Alun did the same. He nodded in confirmation. "Woodsmoke."

Lenc nodded. "Just ahead, not far I think."

Carefully they crept forward until they came to a jumble of

rocks with crude shelters fashioned from scraps of material and rough thatch. At first glance the camp seemed empty, then Lenc saw the odd outline of a figure sheltering from the elements. His eyes widened as he gripped Alun's shoulder. He leaned in and whispered, "That's a complication I didn't expect - there's women, possibly children as well in there. Pass the word back about the women. We don't know how many of them there are, but leave them alone unless they offer resistance; if they do, then kill them. Got that? It's them or us. Take your party up the hill and work further round the camp. When you're ready, come in shouting and yelling and cut down anyone who offers resistance. As soon as we hear you, we'll do the same from this side."

Alun nodded and gestured to Veldicca and Darren, pointing up the hill. Quietly they moved off while Lenc repeated the instructions to Madawc and Iestyn. The three of them watched as Alun's small group disappeared into the trees above the camp.

They spread out among the rocks and trees and waited patiently for the other group to get into position. They didn't have long to wait before there was an ear-splitting yell as Alun, Veldicca and Darren jumped into the small camp with swords raised, ready for battle.

"Come on then," yelled Lenc as he jumped up, gladius at the point. Without looking for support, he crashed through the trees and into the camp. A wild-eyed man was in front of him, vainly trying to tug a rusty longsword from its scabbard hanging up in a shelter. He shrieked as Lenc took him in the neck, killing him instantly. Lenc jumped over the body and plunged into the camp, aware that the two Ordovicians were either side of him. They all skidded to a halt as they met Alun's band in the centre of the camp.

"How many?" demanded Lenc.

Alun shrugged. "Just the one, he was no bother." Veldicca and Darren were busy going through the crude shelters looking for fighters.

"That's two down. We'd better get ready to welcome the rest of the bastards. We need to think of something that will make them come after us up the track in a hurry."

Suddenly a wild-eyed young woman barefoot and dressed in filthy torn rags burst out of a shelter but tripped almost straight away. Darren who was the nearest to her, laughed at her predicament until he saw that her ankles were manacled together so she could walk, just, but with great difficulty. Awkwardly he reached down and tried to help her up, but stepped back when she screamed hysterically.

Instinctively Veldicca went to the distraught woman and tried to calm her. The presence of another woman seemed to help and she visibly quietened, although she looked round with fear-stricken eyes. Veldicca spoke to her, holding her with both arms round her tattered tunic.

She nodded as the woman poured out her story. When she paused, Veldicca looked up with tears in her eyes. "There are more women, in the shelters. They were all caught in raids and their men killed. These bandits used them and passed them round then when they got new ones, the old ones were killed. Bastards."

The woman shrank away when Lenc reached out a hand to her. He turned to Veldicca. "Take her to the others and see if you can free them. Tell them we will keep them safe. If any are able, they can help us fight these bastards."

Veldicca nodded and helped the still sobbing woman to stand.

Lenc called to Darren who was busily searching through one of the shelters. "Darren, we need a lookout on the path. Can you find a place where you've got a decent view? The more notice we get, the better prepared we'll be."

Darren nodded and disappeared down the path. Lenc turned to Alun. "We need to set up an ambush somewhere on the path. Ask Madawc to drag that bastard I killed along the path then cut him about and leave him in plain sight. Hopefully it will make them so angry they'll rush us and that could give us the edge."

Alun nodded and before long returned with Madawc. Both Ordovicians were dragging the second dead bandit along the path. Alun looked up and smiled at Lenc's questioning look. "If they get angry at one dead comrade, how angry will they get at two?" he asked.

Lenc had to admit the logic was sound. As the two Ordovicians dragged their victims down the track, Lenc went looking for the slave-women, and found them in one of the shelters with Veldicca. To his surprise, she was two-handedly waving a longsword, and the women were watching avidly. She broke off when she registered Lenc approaching and rested the point of the sword on the ground.

"We managed to knock the pins off their shackles and now they all want to fight," she said. "We haven't enough swords to go round, but we have knives, and there are plenty of rocks to throw."

Lenc looked silently at the women. He counted ten of them and nodded. They were all in rags, with hair hanging like lank rat's tails, but were certainly not cowed, and after recovering from their ordeal seemed excited at the thought of vengeance.

"Is this all of you?" he asked.

The women seemed to be aged between thirteen and mid-twenties, he could only guess at the nightmare they had been living after being torn from their homes and families. One girl, who seemed one of the oldest, hesitatingly stood. Like the rest, her hair was wild and uncombed. Her long shift was torn and grease-stained, her hands filthy and covered in open cuts and insect bites.

"I was kidnapped about a month ago when these bastards attacked my village, just inside Brigantia, while our men were all away, helping to swell Venutius's army of true Brigantes. They killed my children and my elderly parents in the vilest way possible, although I wished they had dealt with me the same way. Since then, I have had to make their food and been passed round like an animal to satisfy their lust. I don't care, in fact I would welcome the chance to die if I could kill these cruel and heartless bastards."

"I do understand," said Lenc soothingly. "And don't worry, you'll soon have your chance to get your revenge." He looked at her appraisingly. "We need to get the rest of the band so angry they will come racing up this path from their ambush – now, can you think of a way to do that?"

She looked at him, then looked down the path. "If I crept down to where they are, I could cut one down, then let out a scream. That should get them running, I reckon."

"Perfect," said Lenc with a smile. "By the way, what is your name?"

"My name is Brianna, and I am Brigantian. I welcome the chance to drop one of the bastards by myself, and will resist the temptation to stay and fight the rest of them." For the first time since he had met the woman, Lenc was surprised and pleased to see her wolfish smile in anticipation.

"No, you cannot, it's far too dangerous," protested Veldicca, who had been listening to the exchange. "You will be killed."

Brianna smiled again. "No, lady, he is right. If one of the men attacks, they will be cautious. They are all cowards and will scent a trap. But if I appear on my own, they will think I have escaped, and it will be good sport to catch me and take my life as slowly as possible, so I welcome the chance to take the fight to them."

Lenc nodded in agreement and could see that even Veldicca saw the sense in using the freed slave-woman as a decoy. She saw the sense but didn't like it, and bit her lip in anguish.

"Right, everyone, to your positions," said Lenc busily. Brianna hefted the rusty longsword and walked purposefully down the track, disappearing into the trees. Lenc watched her go, then turned to the others. "When they come, they will be running up the track looking to kill Brianna and avenge their dead comrades, so hurry, we must get into position to give them a big surprise."

Lenc led the women down the track and checked when he heard a low whistle. He squinted into the dense undergrowth and made out Alun, who waved and gestured to them to join him. Lenc led the way and the women followed, ushered along by Veldicca. The two dead bandits lay in a heap on the track, their wounds on gruesome display.

"Darren is down the track," whispered Alun. "He should give us plenty of notice."

Lenc turned to the women. "Separate into two groups, one either side of the track, then find a place where you can hide and not be seen. You must be about an arm's length apart and ready to jump out when you hear the command, but don't get up until I say," he hissed. "It's important we hit them hard all at the same time, so wait till I give the word."

The nearest women to him nodded and gripping what weapons they had, silently moved into their positions.

Lenc heard Madawc before he saw him, running up the track. He put his arm out and Madawc swerved into the undergrowth and knelt down.

"They're just behind me," he whispered, "and coming up fast - we don't have much time."

Lenc looked at his small group. He knew the Ordovicians and Veldicca would fight like demons, but the women were an unknown quantity. Would they just mill about in fear and get in the way? That would get them all killed, he thought ruefully. Oh well, we'll soon see.

He drew his gladius when he heard a new commotion from down the track.

"Remember," he said grimly, "on my command."

The silence was split by Brianna holding her tattered skirts up and running hard on the track. Behind her they could hear the clear sound of running men as the bandits burst round a bend in the track into sight. Their swords were out as they ran and their wild expressions showed they were looking for blood.

Brianna cleared the dead bodies without breaking stride and ran on for another ten paces before turning and hefting her sword, legs braced and shouting wild threats at her pursuers.

The men stopped when they saw the mutilated, dead bandits lying on the path, then shouted obscenities and threats about what they would do to the women when they caught them.

Lenc was impressed with Brianna's courage and fighting spirit, but had a moment's concern at the danger she was willingly accepting. Too late for that now, he thought.

Lenc had just opened his mouth to scream out his command when, almost as one, the women jumped up and lunged through the undergrowth, throwing themselves at their hated kidnappers. He could only stare, still open-mouthed as the women tore into their oppressors, battering them with swords, knives and rocks. Seeing this, Brianna ran past him back down the track, waving her big sword above her head. She arrived at the fight in a rush and without pausing brought her sword down with a sickening thud on the nearest bandit who was trying desperately to fend off three screaming women. As the blade sank into his shoulder, he went down as if pole-axed. She screamed in triumph and looked round for her next victim as the women kept up their frenzied assault.

To his horror, Lenc saw Veldicca in the middle of the women and with the first swing of her longsword almost decapitate one of the bandits. His shriek was choked off as blood bubbled from a gaping neck wound. She hardly glanced down at him before swinging again.

"Come on," yelled Lenc finally, "we can't let these women do all the work."

By the time Lenc and the Ordovices jumped onto the track, it was littered with dead bandits. Some had their hands up and two were being pursued down the track by Brianna and two vengeful women, carrying a big stone apiece. As they watched, the two women raised their stones as they caught up with their prey then, together, hurled them at point-blank range. They couldn't miss, both scoring direct hits. As the bandits stumbled, they were tripped, sending them sprawling and skidding on the ground.

As they turned and, wild-eyed, held their hands up in abject fear, Brianna panting heavily, stood over the nearest bandit and changed her grip on her weapon holding it two-handed, pointing down. She paused and looked directly into the terrified man's eyes before plunging the blade into his chest. The force of the blow skewered him into the ground, wrenching the sword out of the woman's hands. The second man gaped in disbelief as she put her bare foot on the dead man's chest, the better to pull the sword out. She wrestled it free then pointed the blood-stained blade menacingly at him.

"No, no," he pleaded, cowering, trying to inch backwards while at the same time holding up his open hands in supplication.

"You bastard, you didn't take any notice of me pleading when you were pulling my legs apart, did you?" She took a step forward, her voice spitting with fury as the now sobbing man tried to slide away from her.

"Go on, Brianna," encouraged one of the other women, "cut his balls off." The others nodded eagerly.

Lenc was about to step in when Alun held his arm and stood in front to block him getting past. "I would say these women have earned the right to do what they want with this piece of shit, don't you?"

Brianna looked up impatiently and Lenc was forced to agree. He gave a reluctant nod. She looked intently at him and turned back to her victim, hefting her blood-stained sword. He could not take his eyes off the wavering point, and swallowed fearfully.

"What should I cut off first?" she cooed softly to him. "My friends think your balls. Would you like to lose your balls?"

He shook his head vehemently as he put his hands down to protect his bits. The point of the sword followed his hands as they cupped between his legs. She smiled at him as she enjoyed his fear. Then the smile turned to a grimace of rage as she pushed down with the blade into his yielding flesh. He screamed in agony as the blade went through the back of one hand and sank into his body. She twisted the sword with a vicious grunt, oblivious to her victim's screams for mercy.

"A woman's revenge is a powerful weapon," muttered Lenc to himself.

Brianna and the other women watched fascinated as life ebbed from the man. Eventually he gave a last sigh and lay still. Only then did Brianna grasp the hilt of the longsword and pull it out of the dead body. She wiped the blood from the blade on the dead man's jerkin then almost tenderly put the tip of the heavy sword into the ground next to the man and rested her head on the hilt.

Two of the other women hesitantly moved to her and put their hands on her shoulders. She looked up and smiled tiredly. Then shaking herself, she slung the sword onto her shoulder and looked round at the scene of carnage.

"Have you got them all?" asked Lenc quietly.

Brianna looked round, then considered. "You killed two, there were seven killed here, so one is missing. In the end I never got to kill any of them at the ambush; they saw me coming and I just started running. I can run quite fast with my skirts up." She grinned impishly.

"The missing one will be the lookout," replied Lenc. "With a bit of luck, he'll still be tied to a tree."

With the immediate danger over, Lenc breathed a sigh of relief. He motioned to Veldicca, the Ordovicians and Brianna, who seemed to be the dominant figure with the newly released women. As they gathered round, he tried to assemble his thoughts. They seemed pretty safe, but they still had a long way to go. He knew there could well be more hostile groups on the road, and that included Roman patrols. Still, the Brigantian women could be useful.

He turned first to Brianna. "You have had a terrible ordeal," he said, "and I am pleased that we were able to help you. We are travelling to Brigantian country and would like you to come with us. We are strangers here and you can help us find the way. You vouching for us when we get there might be crucial, and if we meet more bandits, we have seen what you can do."

He looked round his small band for confirmation, and was pleased to see them all nodding. It made sense.

"We would very much like to accompany you to our homeland," agreed Brianna, "and of course when we get there, we'll explain how you helped us escape from these bastards. I must say I am a little curious - you are a long way from home, what do you seek from my tribe?"

Lenc considered. "We will explain fully, of course, but what you said about Brigantia interests me. Tell me more about the tribe."

Brianna hesitated at first. "This is quite a long story, but I shall try and keep it as brief as possible.

"When the Romans came, they wanted a buffer between their conquered lands and the Caledonians who they are yet to try and conquer. Three tribes were joined together, stretching from Caledonia down to Catuvellaunian land and from the east coast to the west coast, taking in the Penninus mountain range in the middle. Then this huge territory was given to the Roman vassal, Cartimandua, and her man Venutius, who in return for being appointed as queen and consort, had to keep the Caledonians out, keep the peace and pay taxes. This worked surprisingly well to start with. We were at peace, the Caledonians did not raid us - probably because they were afraid of antagonising the Romans - and as long as taxes were paid, the Romans left us alone. They called us a client kingdom, which meant that as long as we behaved, they wouldn't need to keep a garrison there, just keep taking the taxes. Bastards," she added bitterly.

"Unfortunately, the Queen gave herself airs and graces she had no right to. She kicked out Venutius and installed his squire, the much younger Vellocatus in her bed. Even that would have been all right, but she then announced that she was going to marry Vellocatus and make him king even if he wasn't of noble blood. When we were kidnapped by these bastard bandits, Venutius was raising an army to kick Cartimandua off her throne, so what's happening now, I have no idea."

Lenc thought hard as Brianna spread her arms in confusion. "I really don't know any more than that," she added.

"Can you take us to Venutius?" he asked her finally.

She nodded her head emphatically. "He is building a stronghold at a place called Rigodonum, you have to cross the Penninus which, I'm told, runs all the way up the centre of Britannia like a sort of spine.

The Ordovicians and Veldicca listened closely to Brianna's words and when she finally stopped speaking, Alun snorted. "What a mess, trust that shit Caratacus to think he can profit from this lot." He looked at the others, "I think our road is set out for us - looks like we're going mountain climbing again. Let's hope this Venutius is prepared to listen to our story."

Darren was despatched to bring the horses, while the rest searched the camp and packed what little food they could find into saddlebags. Brianna confidently led the group, mounted on a dead bandit's horse. They skirted the Dyfrdwy Estuary, balancing the need to stay as far away as possible from the new Roman fort at Deva with the ever-present threat of marshes the closer they rode to the sea. They made a strange sight, with Lenc and Brianna in the lead, followed by Veldicca and the Ordovicians, then the gaggle of freed women slaves, most riding on single horses but four sharing two horses.

"From here we go straight across to another estuary, bigger this time, then north-east to Mamucium, then climb the pass through the Penninus and down again to the plain on the other side. Should take about two days' riding," said Brianna breezily.

That's if a legion patrol doesn't happen on us, thought Lenc uneasily.

The journey across the marshy estuary was windswept and cold, and out to sea wading birds chattered and swooped under the big sky. Lenc thought it a profound area of sea grass, dunes and flatness, utterly desolate and devoid of land life, the only sound that of the wind keening through rustling grass.

"Once in sight of the next estuary we should be safe from Roman patrols," continued Brianna. "We will be in Brigantian country, which the Romans think settled. They may have another think coming." Brianna looked closely at Lenc. "I've been meaning to ask, what's your part in all this? where are you from? What is your tribe?"

Lenc shifted uneasily on his saddle, not sure how to answer. He was put out of his quandary by Veldicca who had been riding behind and nudged her horse up between the two front riders.

"Brianna, you should know our self-appointed leader is a Roman soldier, or rather a Roman deserter. He actively plotted against the tribes and helped in their downfall at a big battle further south. My father was killed by the Romans, and my future husband was killed by Caratacus and I was kidnapped, prompting Lenc the Gaul here, to come to my rescue. On the way he picked up the Ordovicians who also want Caratacus dead. As soon as he is dead, they have sworn to kill the Roman as well before heading home."

Lenc wisely decided to keep silent as Brianna digested this unexpected series of revelations. He felt that Veldicca had described the situation fairly accurately.

Eventually Brianna cleared her throat. "Firstly, it matters not to me that the Gaul is a Roman deserter. What is more important to me is that he rescued me and the other women from a living nightmare. I was quite sure that the only way out was death. I was even trying to think how I could do it. I am happy to ride with him, and fight for him. As for this Caratacus I can see that you all have an interest in his death, but what makes you think he is in Brigantia?"

"His tribe is the Catuvellauni," explained Lenc, "which is below Brigantia. He could have gone there when his plans turned to ruins, but he had officially been cast out of the tribe and he can only go back with a massive victory under his belt. I am sure that he is in Brigantia and will try and persuade Cartimandua to rise against Rome."

Brianna looked dubious. "If it was Venutius he was petitioning, I would say that he was in with a chance, but not Cartimandua. She was made queen of one of the biggest territories in Britannia by the Romans - she owes everything to them. Besides, if she decided to throw in her lot with Caratacus and take an army south to join the Catuvellauni she would have to share her crown with him, and possibly lose it to him. She knows where her fortunes lie."

Lenc nodded as he conceded the flaw. "I would agree, but for one thing. Caratacus has an over-riding conceit; he would be quite sure that after an hour or so in his company, Cartimandua would be swooning at his feet, ready to agree to anything such a highborn handsome man suggested. He could then ride south at the head of the Brigantes to link up with the Catuvellauni, giving him the Army of the North."

With plenty to think about, the rag-tag band rode on, making good progress on a drovers track which took them north, detouring round the new Roman encampment of Deva dominating the river estuary and surrounding countryside. They stopped for the night at a small settlement, where they were allowed to camp in a disused barn, after Brianna told the village elders their story. A fire was lit, and after the horses had been settled down, their food, including some bread and vegetables donated by the village, prepared for the pot.

"By tomorrow afternoon we should be at Mamucium," said Brianna happily as she stirred a bubbling pot of barley and vegetables. "At least we will be back in Brigantia."

After the meal, with the group realising how tired they were, the women gravitated to the back of the barn and laid out whatever bedding they had, and the men stayed round the fire. Eventually Lenc announced that he was going to stretch his legs before bedding down. Outside, dark was falling, although there was still enough light to see clearly. Somewhere a lonely owl hooted as it started its evening hunt.

What a day, thought Lenc. What more can possibly happen before I get back to normality, whatever that is.

Suddenly his thoughts were interrupted by a rustle behind him. He turned quickly, hand on his sword, then relaxed as he realised it was Veldicca who had followed him from the barn.

"Did I startle you?" she asked as she caught him up.

"Not really," replied Lenc steadily, "but if you had got closer to me before I realised you were there, I might have taken you for enemy and stuck my sword in you."

Veldicca's eyes flashed. "Obviously I did startle you. I will give you more warning of my approach in future; I would hate to frighten a warrior of Rome."

Suddenly Lenc felt tiredness wash over him. He sighed heavily.

"Yes," he said eventually. "As usual you have bested me. Now why don't you go back to the other women and get some sleep? I need some time to think, and I can't do that while you're picking fights with me."

Veldicca stopped in her tracks, eyes wide. "I never meant that," she protested. "This has all come out wrong. I followed you out to talk to you, to try and tell you how I feel about you, our quest, and what can happen in the future. But if you don't want to hear it, yes, I will go back."

As she turned, Lenc reached out for her arm, and although she stopped, she did not turn round.

"Once again I am apologising," Lenc said to her stiff back. "That seems to be all I do with you."

Slowly she turned and quietly said, "I followed you out because I thought we needed to have a proper talk, so that I could try and let you know how I feel, although I must say I am still very confused."

Lenc said nothing but steered her towards a fallen log and motioned for her to sit. When she did so, he sat next to her.

She was silent for a while, collecting her thoughts. At the same time, Lenc was a maelstrom of emotions. Was she forgiving him? Did she want him back? Or had she decided to give up the quest for Caratacus and to go back to Siluria? He shifted uneasily on the log.

Veldicca looked fixedly at the ground, her hands clasped together on her thighs.

Hesitantly she spoke. "I don't think I have ever been so confused in my life. Everyone I know is either dead or has betrayed me. I find myself on a mission far away from my home with a man who betrayed me in the worst possible way, three sworn tribal enemies and a group of women rescued from bestial rape and slavery, in order to kill a man who is attempting to unite this island." She turned and looked at Lenc despairingly, with tears in her eyes. "Is it any wonder I am confused?"

Lenc hesitated then took her hands in his. She didn't resist. He swallowed.

"I don't think I can say anything that is going to help," he said eventually. "Everything you say is true. In my defence all I can say is that what started out as my duty to spy on the tribe became the worst actions of my life. In the beginning my biggest fear, if found out, was death. But something worse than that happened. I met the tribe, and you, Veldicca, and suddenly I did not want you to be beaten by Rome, but I was realistic enough to know that there will be no alternative. You will accept rule from Rome or die, simple as that. All those days and nights living a lie, enjoying the time near you, liking being with the tribe - I even got to like Trenos." He looked up hoping for a smile, but Veldicca's face was like white stone.

"It is possible that after all the things that have happened to you in the last few days, you are finally seeing reality, and you have to decide on your future actions," said Lenc softly. "Will you ride with us to help rid of us of Caratacus, then will you return home to try and claim your birthright after the death of your father? Either way, I don't know how, but I will support you."

Veldicca nodded, but still not looking at Lenc, she snuffled and drew the back of her hand across her nose.

"I thought I hated you - I did hate you," she said in a small voice. "When my servant knocked you unconscious in my father's tent, I was determined that when we had beaten the Romans, I would come back and kill you for your betrayal. I had never felt like that about a man. As you know, I was betrothed to Trenos, which was the way of the tribe and I accepted that. But you came into my life and I had never felt anything like that before. I wanted to spend my life with you, but knew that could never be. I was bred to bear fine sons and one day lead the tribe with my husband. Now he is dead, and you are still a traitor."

Lenc hung his head. "Everything you say is true," he said quietly. "But you must believe me that I had no choice. My sense of duty is as strong as yours, although I am just as much an outcast as you, except that you still have the chance to return to your tribe. I cannot return to the legion - I would be crucified as a deserter. I accept I don't deserve your love and want only two things, to kill Caratacus and then return you to your people. What happens to me after that, I don't care. Let the gods decide."

After several silent minutes, Veldicca stirred. "I don't condone or forgive, but I do understand. I will come with you till we find Caratacus and kill him, then I will return to Siluria. You may escort me if you wish, and I would like that, unless Alun and his Ordovicians carry out their promise to kill you as soon as Caratacus is dealt with." She looked up at him with the makings of an impish smile. "We'll see. Till then we can be friends but what we had before can never return."

"I can live with that," Lenc replied softly.

Veldicca rubbed her eyes with her knuckles and stood. "Come then, we have a long day tomorrow."

CHAPTER XVI

The march of the Twentieth from the hills was covered in good time. The legion was on top form, with a crushing victory against the numerically superior Celtic tribes, and looking forward to wintering in a stone barracks. On the march, rations had been plentiful, even beef and mutton in good supply and there was, unusually, a supply of decent wine to help wash it down.

Agrippa, the pathfinder and his ragged band caught up with the Twentieth at Mediolanum, more than half way to the legion's new home at Deva. The legion was quartered outside the fort in a marching camp, thrown up in an evening then dismantled the next day before marching on. Agrippa was still dressed as a local, in a rough woollen cloak, covering a checked shirt down to his knees and heavy trousers held up with a sword belt. On his feet, rough working shoes, shod with iron hobnails.

He was not looking forward to his interview with Quintus Equitius, Legate of the Twentieth because he respected his commander, and his fear was that by telling him of their activities, even as orders of the Governor of Britannia - it could be his death warrant. If the Emperor and the Senate had so much as an inkling that Quintus Equitius knew about, let alone condoned the murder of a legion legate, it could signal his return to Rome in disgrace, where no doubt he would meet an untimely death. Traditionally the Senate, a hotbed of rumour and intrigue saw insurrection in every corner. The murder of a high-ranking officer and friend of the Emperor, even in this far-flung corner of the empire could well be a signal for rebellion and would be stamped on hard. If the legate could honestly say he didn't know anything about the murder of Sabinianus, legate of the Fourteenth, he, Agrippa, certainly wasn't going to mention it.

His firm intention was to say as little as possible about the incident while stressing that he was following orders from the late governor.

Agrippa left his men out of sight of the marching camp and went on alone. He tethered his horse and went forward on foot with his hands raised to show he was not gripping a weapon. The perimeter guard stood waiting for him, with his spear jutting out aggressively. "Halt," the guard commanded. "Identify yourself."

"I am Centurion Agrippa, commander of the Twentieth's Pathfinders," came the reply.

The sentry still stood braced, ready to stab the suspicious stranger if he made a wrong move. "I will need proof of that."

Agrippa nodded. "Pathfinders carry no identity," he said. "You must be new to the Twentieth or you would know me. Call your guard commander."

The sentry bit his lip then nodded. "Take two steps backward," he ordered. Then shouted: "Boss, entry sentry."

The stentorian shout triggered a commotion from a tent just behind the newly dug trench - the camp's defence, and three legionaries came boiling out, pulling on their helmets and drawing swords.

Agrippa relaxed as he recognised the leading man. He smiled as he shouted: "Josephus Cerialis, still getting the plum jobs, I see."

The leader squinted at the dishevelled civilian standing in front of him, then frowned, looked again and finally smiled. "Centurion Agrippa, you're a sight for sore eyes." Then he turned to the sentry. "Stand down, lad, he's one of us."

The guard nodded and put up his javelin.

As Agrippa walked past the sentry now standing to attention, he paused and said to the young soldier: "Well done lad, you did the right thing. Never let your guard slip."

The guard smiled briefly at the praise then reset his face to stern, although now he stood a bit straighter than before.

"So, what have you been up to, while we've been marching all over this mountainous dump, or shouldn't I ask?" queried Josephus as he poured two beakers of wine.

Agrippa took the proffered drink and smiled. "No, you shouldn't, but I do need to see the legate, and quick."

Josephus took a draught of his wine and nodded speculatively. "Yes, of course. Young Cassus who you have already met, will take you to the legate's tent. He's just about to come off sentry duty to go onto digging duty, so escorting you can be his reward for receiving you properly."

Agrippa was escorted through the rapidly forming tented camp by a proud Cassus, grateful to be excused digging but also in awe of the man at his side.

The command tent in the centre of the marching camp was bigger than those surrounding it, with two sentries standing outside the entrance. Agrippa nodded to them, "I need an audience with the legate, take me to him," he said curtly.

The nearest guard looked at the scruffy vagabond in front of him and sneered, "Fuck off, you Brit bastard."

Agrippa smiled and raised his hand to Cassus who had indignantly stepped forward to proclaim the "bastard's" position as a centurion of the Twentieth. Cassus stood to attention but his face betrayed his outraged emotion.

The smile stayed on Agrippa's face as he leaned in to the still sneering sentry. Softly, he whispered, "How would you like to end your time in the legion slopping out the shithouses on the Caledonian border? Because if I tell your principalis that you told me to fuck off without checking my credentials and finding out who I am, that is what you will be doing."

The man blanched and snapped to attention, as Agrippa nodded at Cassus who swallowed, and stammered: "This is

Centurion Agrippa of the Pathfinders. He needs to speak to the legate urgently."

The white-faced guard nodded. "Apologies sir, please follow me."

The guard lifted the tent flap and beckoned Agrippa inside, where an orderly was sitting at a desk, shuffling wooden tablets. The guard waited for him to look up, then announced Agrippa.

He was immediately shown into the legate's private quarters, where an agitated Quintus Equitius was waiting. And he was a worried man. A despatch had arrived from Deva, announcing the murder of Sabinianus, but not the circumstances. This followed the news of the death of the Governor, Scapula, not unexpected, but certainly unfortunate. He wondered if the two deaths were something more than a coincidence.

Confirmation of his promotion to Governor, however temporary, had still not arrived from the Senate, but as the senior legate, he had to assume the role until those self-congratulatory bastards in Rome decided who was going to rule Britannia.

"Good to see you back Agrippa, what news have you for me?"

Agrippa sighed. "Very little, sir, and nothing very good. Caratacus is still on the loose, although I think that Auxiliary Lenculus is hot on his trail. We followed his path over the northern mountain range and confirmed he and a small band of Ordovices which he seems to have teamed up with, have taken the ferry to Mona. I am prepared to follow him onto the island, but in the meantime, I have two men watching the ferry. Realistically, it's the only way off the island. Although the tribes were given a hiding, they're a sullen and resentful lot and still close to rebellion. One thing is for sure, we cannot drop our guard."

Legate Equitius looked thoughtful. His eyebrows nearly met his hairline. "I feared as much, but um, have you heard anything of the deaths of Governor Scapula and Legate Sabinianus at all?"

Agrippa thought hard; the governor's death was straightforward enough, he had not been a well man and the current campaign had been hard - but Sabinianus? That was a different matter.

"I did hear of the deaths, sir, the governor was a tragic loss and will be missed, he was a good soldier and a good leader, Legate Sabinianus not so much."

The legate pondered this and hesitated. "Are you able to tell me anything that the governor said to you before he died?"

This was the question Agrippa had been dreading, but he was ready for it.

"All I can tell you, sir, is that Governor Scapula was most insistent that I follow Auxiliary Lenculus in his pursuit of Caratacus. We trailed him across the mountains in the north to the Isle of Mona, where we believe him still to be. If he or Caratacus returns to the mainland, we will know and they will be followed. As for the legate, I am afraid I know nothing more than he is dead. I and my men were on the coast when it happened."

The legate looked keenly at Agrippa. "Are you sure about that?" he demanded.

Agrippa's eyes opened wide. "Of course, sir, I cannot lie to you."

"Hmm," was all the legate would allow himself.

"In that case you had better resume your search for Caratacus. He needs to be dead or in front of me in chains."

"Sir, I need to get onto Mona, but without being seen. Could you authorise a galley to take me there, wait for me and bring me back to the mainland? I will take only one man with me as a messenger, but I think it would be too dangerous to use the ferry, as we'd be marked as strangers and arouse curiosity. We could try and steal a boat, but it would attract unwelcome attention if we were caught."

"Yes, I take your point. Actually, you're in luck, there is a galley, a trireme, *Minerva* which has just escorted a grain ship into the Deva estuary. I will send a messenger straight away with the captain's new orders. She will be waiting for you."

With the interview over, a thankful Agrippa left the tent, pausing to nod to the sentry, who snapped to attention, staring fixedly into the distance.

Once alone, Quintus Equitius let out a sigh of relief. He did not believe for a minute that Agrippa and his bunch of desperadoes were not involved in the death of Sabinianus, but he had asked the question and been given an answer. It could not possibly be traced back to him, he was blameless.

"Serves the bastard right," he muttered.

After a convivial meal with his old friend Josephus, Agrippa rode back to the pathfinder camp with a renewed sense of excitement in the chase to find Caratacus. Getting onto Mona undetected was going to be tricky but had to be done. He was relieved at being able to avoid the ferry, having the trireme available made getting onto the island much simpler. They would find a secluded cove, where the ship could tie up for a day or so, giving him time to find out what Caratacus was doing on the island.

The pathfinders, Agrippa and his chosen man, Caius Bellus, found *Minerva* at anchor where the Deva estuary met the river and were quickly packed on board.

The skipper of the *Minerva* was a tousle-haired, weather-beaten Sicilian, Trierarch, or Captain, Marcellus Cassis. He commanded thirty seamen, two hundred marines and one hundred and seventy slaves who rowed in three banks on either side of his ship. Whenever possible two sails could also be used. The *Minerva* was one of the older ships in the fleet, but her strength and the prowess of both the ship and the men who crewed her had been more than tested in several sharp encounters. Her hull was freshly painted in a dark blue with the topsides in red, belying her formidable military power. At her prow was the wooden figurehead of the proud goddess, Minerva, dressed in armour and carrying a spear. Minerva fought for just causes and was seen as a civilising influence, in contrast to the god Mars, who just wanted to kill everyone.

Behind the figurehead was a catapult, a large weapon that could throw a fair-sized stone with devastating accuracy against a stone wall or another ship. At the stern, in front of the helmsman, stood two smaller ballistae, rigged to fire multiple bolts by using levers pulled back by ratcheted torsion springs, fearsome close-quarter weapons which could sweep the deck of an enemy ship clear of anyone unfortunate enough to be still standing.

"I hope your change of orders isn't too inconveniencing," Agrippa said to the skipper, "but if you can drop us on Mona without being seen, you will make our job there much easier."

"Of course, of course, glad to help," responded Trierarch Cassis. "Our task was to escort that old tub of a grain ship back to Dubris, wait for it to be filled up again and come straight back. Not exactly taxing, so your little job is a welcome diversion. I can put you ashore at a quiet secluded bay we have used before, and if it's Druids you are looking for, their main centre is Caergybi, on the far coast almost due west. I've never been there but I don't think you can miss it.

"My people have cleared a bit of space for you, but it's a short journey, so you are welcome to some food and you can bed down for a while. We should be there by nightfall."

The pathfinders welcomed the chance to rest and, helped by the motion of the ship against the wind and tide, would have liked to extend it to some shuteye. But all too soon, as their eyes were drooping, they were roused by a sailor with a lantern who escorted them to the upper deck.

Agrippa grasped arms with the skipper. "With a bit of luck, we will be back here this time tomorrow," he said, then smiled. "If we miss tomorrow night, then hopefully will be here the next night. If we miss that, then you might as well sail away, because we won't be joining you."

They coaxed their horses into the cold water from a platform lowered from the deck to the sea, and swam beside them, holding onto their saddle pommels, for the short distance from the trireme to a secluded beach on the mysterious low-lying island. They swam towards a small golden beach, hemmed in by a sheer rock face teeming with noisy bird life. Dusk was settling as they swam in the cold but placid sea. Once ashore they lost no time in splashing off the beach through rocky shale onto rough clumps of grass.

Agrippa looked round then nodded up to where the two sides of the cliffs lowered and converged. They could dimly see a stream taking the easiest route down the hillside. "Where the stream comes down will be the easiest way up," he said, as he led his horse to a barely discernible path running alongside the stream.

Roughly halfway to the top of the cliff, Agrippa turned and, in the gloom of falling night, could still see the trireme anchored in the bay. He was under no illusion that the skipper's warning that if they were surprised, they would have no choice but to cut and run. Whether there was a ship anywhere off the coast of Britannia that would take on a trireme of the *Classis Britannica* was another matter.

After the numbing cold water of the Oceanus Hibernicus, the pathfinders soon dried out on their stumbling walk up the narrow path. Finally, at what appeared to be the top of the cliff, their path became more substantial, allowing them to risk mounting up as they rode away from the sea. A safe distance away from the coast, Agrippa called a halt in a small sheltered wooded valley as the moon made an appearance.

"We'll camp here," he said. "I think we can risk a fire; we seem to be the only people on this island, but we'd best keep the noise down."

The night passed without incident, and shortly after dawn they were saddled up and on the trail again, riding hard through the green and fertile countryside with just the sun to guide them westwards. When they stopped at midday, Agrippa motioned to Caius as they sat on the grass, munching cold meat and hardtack biscuit.

"We are looking for information," he explained quietly. "We need to know where Lenc and his new Ordovician pals are and what they are doing. We know they are following Caratacus who, through that damned priest, may be here looking for sanctuary, although somehow I doubt it. Our goal is the capture or killing of Caratacus, but we are going to have to tread very carefully as the Druids have a very clever intelligence network. As we get closer to their stronghold the more we'll stick out like tits on a bull.

"I think the best plan is to go quietly from here until we get in sight of the Druid's town; you find a place to hide and observe, and I'll walk on and see what I can find out. It's highly risky, but if I'm not back after one night, you will have to make your way back to the *Minerva*, and report to the pathfinders at our hideout on the mainland coast."

Caius nodded assent as they packed up their frugal lunch and rode on, passing a couple of lakes and then pausing at a strange grassy mound, clearly man-made, surrounded by trees.

"Mark this place well," said Agrippa. "If we are close enough to the Druids, this should make a decent hideout."

They rode on until Caius reined in. "I can smell the sea," he said.

"We must be getting close," agreed Agrippa. They carried on, along a rapidly improving track and after climbing a short rise, there were the oak trees masking the town that Agrippa had been told to look out for.

Agrippa made up his mind, this was far enough for his companion. He dismounted and handed over the reins of his horse. "Back you go to the location we agreed and find a suitable hiding place, but keep an eye out for me." He watched as Caius turned his own mount and leading the riderless horse, cantered back down the trail, then he turned and headed towards the Druid town, wondering whether he would return in one piece.

Agrippa had been in Britannia for two years before Emperor

Claudius invaded in AD 43. He spent the time learning the basic Celtic language and picking up the various idioms of the many different tribes. His paramount task was to gauge the ability of the warrior tribes to fight, which appeared to increase the further away from the south-east coast he wandered. By the time Claudius unleashed his legions on the invasion, Agrippa, travelling the country as a horse trader, felt confident he could fit in as a local without too much difficulty.

He was particularly struck by the influx of traders from the mainland, eager to bring trade-goods to the south. The tribes here seemed much less likely to fight than their counterparts away from the "more civilised" parts of Britannia. In fact, he was able to report back confidently, that in his opinion, a combination of factors, the deep-seated mistrust of the tribes for each other, and the increasing enjoyment of Roman luxuries in the south, pointed to an easily managed invasion. The problems would start when the tribes finally banded together, that is, if they could ever stop arguing among themselves.

Following the successful invasion, he resumed command of the XX Valeria Victrix Pathfinders and trained his men to carry on their clandestine method of warfare.

He felt no qualms in putting his head in the lion's den once again, talking like a Briton, dressing like one, for all intents and purposes being one. Unless he made some monumental slip, he felt confident he could find the information he needed without raising suspicion. That was the plan anyway.

As he approached the outskirts of the town, he noticed a building made of rough-cut wooden planks under a thatched roof with a swinging sign above the door. Painted on the sign was a jolly priest about to drink from a foaming mug. As good a place to start as any, he thought. He tied his horse to a railing close to the door and went inside. Once he'd accustomed himself to the gloom and the acrid smoke from a guttering fire, he found an empty table and thankfully eased himself onto a bench.

"Ale, please," he said to a young girl in a homespun dress protected by some sacking material. She half-smiled and disappeared through a door by the fire, reappearing with a full beaker. He gratefully took the brimming mug and raised it to his lips. It was good, he decided and most welcome. He licked his lips and looked round the gloomy room. There were eight long benches, but only five or six men staring into their beakers. He decided not to waste his time on them; by the look of them, they wouldn't notice if Caratacus himself had come into the place waving a great sword about. He smiled at the thought.

At that moment the door swung open and two young men wearing long brown woollen habits in the way of priests came in. Agrippa looked at them with curiosity, noted the swords on shoulder straps and their obvious fitness. They're dressed as priests, but they have a look of something else - certainly not religious, he thought, they must be Druidae. He had heard of these priest soldiers but never encountered them.

The two looked round and one smiled at Agrippa. "Do you mind if we sit with you?" he asked pleasantly. "We don't see too many strangers around here."

Agrippa moved along the bench; "Please sit where you will."

The two nodded their thanks and sat at the long table and ordered beer from the young girl, who this time clumsily curtsied to the two young men. This just gets more curious, thought Agrippa.

"Forgive my question, but I couldn't help noticing the servant girl's deference to you, and I notice you are dressed as priests but carrying swords."

The nearest one smiled and explained: "We are on holy work, but our work can be, shall I say, more robust than perhaps priests are usually expected to do. We are Druidae, the eyes and ears of our Arch Druid, and when strangers come to our town, we like to know what their business is."

"That's impressive," returned Agrippa. "I am a horse trader, and wanted to see this Druid town of yours, but I have only been here long enough to drink half this beer, yet you knew I was here."

"Actually, you were seen on the road into town by one of my colleagues. He watched you head into the tavern, which we thought was a good enough excuse for us to break off from our onerous duties for a drink and justify it with checking on the stranger. No harm done. My name is Nathan and my companion is Owen," said Nathan with an expansive smile.

"Even so, pretty impressive, Nathan," returned Agrippa, "and I'm flattered that you should take such an interest in a humble horse trader."

At this the servant girl returned with the priests' beer and curtsied once again.

Nathan thanked her, then turned back to Agrippa. "To be honest we have had a bit of excitement in the town just lately and we are sensitive about strangers, especially if they mean to stir up trouble."

Agrippa opened his hands in supplication. "Don't worry about me. I decided to take in the sights after I heard about Caergybi and its wonderful architecture. Once I have had a look round, I shall head back for the ferry and the mainland. I came here looking for horses but haven't had much luck. I have a couple of recommendations to look at on the way back to the ferry, so you never know. You say you have had some excitement just lately?" he enquired, as innocently as he could.

Nathan looked at him steadily for a few heartbeats. "I suppose there's no harm in telling you - you will find out anyway." Nathan related the tale of the failed betrothal between the would-be King of Britannia, Caratacus and Veldicca, a Silurian princess and their flight from the disastrous battle with the romans. He casually finished with: "Oh, and their priest was poisoned for his trouble."

"That's quite a story," said an impressed Agrippa. "Are they still here?"

"That's the interesting part," added Nathan. "Hot on their

heels came another gang, a mixed bag of a Gaul and four Ordovicians, who were chasing the so-called King with a view to running him through. The Gaul was apparently a Roman soldier, so what he was doing tied up with four Ordovicians is anyone's guess. All we know is that all five were determined to kill Caratacus, so the Arch Druid decided that he and his men could have a head start of two days, then the Gaul and the Ordovicians could chase him, by which time he would be off the island, and the will of the gods would be heard, but nothing to do with the Druids."

Agrippa sat back on his bench astonished. At least Lenc was still alive and in pursuit of Caratacus he thought with relief. "And the Silurian princess, what happened to her?"

"She cleared off with the Gaul and the Ordovicians," added Nathan airily, "I understand she has as much interest in killing Caratacus as the rest of them."

"When did all this happen?"

Nathan counted on his fingers. "Caratacus and his band left four days ago, and the other lot followed two days later."

Agrippa called for more beer for himself and the two priests, all the while thinking furiously. He was two days behind Lenc. They would have to get back to the mainland as quickly as possible, without a moment to lose. He thanked the gods he had left lookouts on the coast road.

"That's quite a story," he conceded. "Where do you think this Caratacus is now?"

"As far as we know, he is heading for Brigantian country where he thinks he can raise an army to join forces with the Catuvellauni then sweep south, killing as many Romans on the way as possible."

Nathan paused and took a long swig of his beer. "One thing puzzles me a bit; according to the Druidae on duty at the ferry port, no one of your description has used the ferry in quite some time. You did say you came by ferry?"

"It's interesting that you took the trouble to find out, but you're wrong, I'm afraid. I arrived about four days ago, and I did come on the ferry. I remember talking to the lady who runs it and negotiated a price if I bought some horses," replied Agrippa, thinking furiously and banking on Nathan bluffing. He couldn't possibly have got information of that sort so quickly, could he?

"Never mind, it's not important," smiled Nathan. "If there is anything particular you want to see, you can leave a message for me at the Druidae barracks near the Arch Druid's palace. I'd be happy to show you round. Now I'm afraid we have to take our leave. I hope you enjoy your stay on our island."

The two drained their drinks and stood; both smiled at Agrippa who also stood as they waved to the servant girl and left.

Agrippa sat back thinking hard. He was pretty sure that Nathan did not believe his story. Maybe someone was even now checking with the ferry port. Either way it didn't really matter. His work here was done; all he had to do now was get back to the mainland and try and catch up with Lenc who was trying to catch up with Caratacus. Mind you, he thought, priests or no, these people had a hell of an intelligence network.

He waited a few minutes to allow the two Druidae time to get clear, then headed for the door. Outside, he looked round carefully, but in his hurry to get back to the rendezvous, failed to see Nathan duck back out of sight further up the street.

I wonder what that stranger is really doing here, thought Nathan. He seemed very interested in our bit of excitement. Maybe he is looking for Caratacus as well. I think we should keep an eye on him.

He gestured behind him to his companion, Owen, who by now was mounted on a roan horse, his priest's habit tucked in his belt.

"Follow him but try not to be seen. We need to know where he goes and what he does."

CHAPTER XVII

Agrippa quickly walked from the town back to where Caius was keeping watch on top of the curious grass covered mound. When he saw Agrippa and his shadow approaching, he quickly scrambled down and lay in wait in the trees. "You're being followed, boss," he said in a low voice.

Agrippa tensed, kneeled, and looked back along the trail. "How far back, how many?" he asked tersely, annoyed with himself for not using the standard operational practices of constantly checking he was not being followed. Getting back to the ship was the priority, but even so, this lapse was criminal. Quickly he dived into the cool woodland, and registered Caius stretched out on the leaves matting the copse floor.

"Just one man," Caius reported. "He has a horse, but is on foot. He couldn't get too close to you in case you saw him, so he is hanging quite far back."

Agrippa thought furiously. "Right," he said. "It's not the end of the world. If we mount up quickly and keep this mound between us and him, we should be able to get some distance before he realises we are on to him. Then we should be able to lose him before we get back to the *Minerva*."

Caius stood and shook the leaves off his cloak. "Follow me," he said brusquely, then led the way through the trees at a fast pace, skirting the grass mound. "I didn't expect you back straight away, so I had a quick look round for other ways to get back to the ship," he said over his shoulder. "If we get a move on there's a track that runs at an angle away from the coast, but once we're sure we've lost him, we can swing back onto our road."

"Good man," conceded Agrippa, still annoyed at his lack of concentration.

Despite the diversion to lose the Druida, the two pathfinders arrived back at the small bay before dark. The *Minerva* warped in as close to the shore as the skipper dared, even with a sailor in the bow, depth sounding with a lead line. When the trireme could get no closer, the two pathfinders dragged their horses into the sea and swam the short distance out to the *Minerva*. They stayed in the water as slings were dropped down to them to fasten round their horses' midriffs. The sling ropes went up to an A-frame stepped into the deck, so it could swing out over the sea. On the signal, a team of sailors pulled in unison on the soaking rope, lifting the squealing horses one at a time out of the sea.

Only when the horses were safely aboard did Agrippa and Caius clamber up a ladder onto the deck where they were met by the skipper, Marcellus Cassis.

"Any chance you can drop us in the strait between Mona and the mainland?" asked Agrippa as he towelled the freezing cold seawater from his shivering body. "Only I need to pick up a couple of my men who have been watching the coast road."

"We can do it," said the trireme skipper thoughtfully, "but it's a swine of a coastline. Lot of rock, and nasty tides. If we run aground, the locals will have a field day. We might have to stay nearer the estuary before we can put you down.

"There's also the small matter of a storm out at sea. It's settling down now, so we should be able to drop you off safely."

Agrippa nodded in agreement. "We were followed some of the way by the Druid secret police, but we managed to shake them off. If you can put in anywhere you consider safe, that would be a big help."

As the trireme, backed and filled and headed out to sea, the rider in a monk's habit stepped down from his horse to watch the graceful ship put on sail as one hundred and seventy oars were lowered into the water to pull out of the bay.

Owen had realised almost straight away that he had been fooled by the two pathfinders who had taken their chance to sheer off the path. No matter, he'd thought, they were clearly heading for the coast where they must have a boat hidden. He'd head for the sea and with a bit of luck would pick them up again. He'd arrived on the headland just in time to see his quarry disappearing below deck on the magnificent Roman trireme.

Well, well, now the Romans are involved, thought Owen. This is proving a very meaty stew. I'd better get back to report, Delphidius will be most interested in this new revelation.

"Thank the gods you're back, boss, I was getting close to sending men after you."

Agrippa arrived at the pathfinders' camp, an abandoned lead mine, completely shrouded in trees near the Deva estuary. His second in command, a German auxiliary with wild black curly hair and a shaggy beard, who only answered to the name Wilhelm, looked up anxiously at Agrippa as he stiffly dismounted his horse.

"Caius, take the horses, would you, and give them a rub down and some food, we may be going out again fairly soon."

The lead mine was a few scattered thatched round huts, and a buttressed entry into the mine, set into a hill. There was a general air of abandonment which suited the pathfinders as it meant that visitors were unlikely.

Caius nodded and took the horses' reins leading them to a makeshift corral.

Agrippa turned back to Wilhelm. "Tell me," he demanded tersely.

"We had two watchers on the coast as ordered, then three days ago, one reported in with the news that Caratacus and eleven of his men were spotted on the drover's path skirting the coast, heading this way. He reported to me, then returned to his post. I detailed two men to try and pick up the trail of the band. Two days later the scout again returned to say they had sighted Lenc with five natives, one of whom was a woman, going in the same direction, so again I detailed him to follow Lenc and sent another rider back to bring in the scout who was still watching the road. I felt that we had accounted for everyone we were interested in and it was simply a job of keeping eyes on both parties until you returned."

Agrippa allowed himself a smile of triumph as he digested this news. "Good man, you did exactly right. I think we need a hunters' meeting, because I also have news."

After eating and a short rest, Agrippa called a meeting of the entire pathfinder group to brief them on what had happened and what he planned for the future. This was unusual practice in the army of Rome, but fairly standard in its special forces. These men were trained to think and act independently, so it was vital they knew the big picture and their part in it. Just over thirty men sat patiently waiting for Agrippa to speak. They all seemed to be between twenty and thirty and the most unlikely looking Roman soldiers. They were all in rough civilian clothing, wool tunics over trousers, caught at the waist with a leather belt.

Without exception they all wore adapted issue shoes, which unlike the standard soldier's sandal, were fully enclosed, giving more protection but did include the hobnails on the thick soles, which not only extended the life of the shoes but were a handy weapon if fighting got personal.

Each man carried a cavalry longsword, a dagger and a war-bow. A sheaf of arrows with heavy metal barbed points was tied to their saddle pommels. The men all looked disreputably dirty and unshaven, fit to give the vapours to a Praefectus Castrorum, the legion's dispenser of discipline.

When all the men were gathered into a circle, with even the outlying sentries called in so they could hear but still keep a look-out, Agrippa stood and quickly described his adventures on Mona. "It looks as though our scouts saw Caratacus after he was kicked off the island by the Druids. A couple of days later he was chased by Lenc with some natives we don't know. Interestingly, Lenc has a woman riding with him, and from her description I would bet a flagon of wine she is the Princess Veldicca." He looked round at the attentive faces and smiled. "I would very much like to know how she left Caratacus and then decided to join Lenc, especially as she must know that the beating the Celtic army took was pretty much Lenc's doing.

"According to the Druidae, Caratacus is heading for Brigantia to try and persuade them to turn against Rome and throw in their lot with the Catuvellauni. Brigantia is a vassal state of Rome, a buffer between Caledonia and the rest of Britannia. If the Brigantes do decide to ally with the Catuvellauni, they would create an army which could quite likely throw us back into the sea, so as well as catching or killing Caratacus, we have to stop any possibility of this alliance happening, however unlikely it may be.

"At present we have two scouts ahead of us, one following Caratacus and the other following Lenc. When we catch up with the second scout, we will have to work out a plan to contact Lenc without the rest of his party knowing, and see what his plan is. At present he is badly outnumbered and is following his prey into dangerous territory. Our first priority is to catch up with him and find out exactly what he is up to. All agreed?"

There was a general air of acceptance and no questions. Each man knew that their job took them beyond the range of conventional Roman warfare. As a unit, they were on their own and could only rely on their comrades. There were always problems along the way; the trick was to knock those problems over, one after another, until there were no more problems. Then no doubt their bosses would find them more problems to deal with.

Agrippa was speaking again: "We will have two scouts ahead

of the main party, as far ahead as possible but always within eyesight. If the scouts see something, it will be their decision what to do. Take individual action, call for help, or, if there is time, come back to the main party and report. Let's make our preparations and get the horses ready; we leave shortly."

When the men had been given sufficient time to prepare, Agrippa mounted up, which was the signal for everyone else to do the same. There was a flurry as horses were mounted and Agrippa indicated the two pathfinders who would be point scouts.

The nominated scouts walked their horses forward, leading the way, followed by the main band, Agrippa in the lead, his men following in two columns. The day was sultry and overcast, but at least the rain stayed away. Agrippa took his eyes off the scouts ahead and looked round at the surrounding countryside. To his right, just off the drover's road, the land rose to a range of hills, not that high, with plentiful trees and bracken. He turned to the left and there was the sea, the Deva estuary and beyond, another land mass which he knew to be a low-lying peninsula with another big estuary the other side. Not for the first time he wondered at the Senate's desire to conquer new land and extend the might of the empire.

His thoughts were suddenly interrupted by a hissed warning from Wilhelm, behind him. "The scouts, boss."

Agrippa started and raised his hand in acknowledgement, furious at himself for daydreaming when he, of all people, should be alert. He looked up the track and registered the start of woodland, from the edge of the sea, climbing up the hill range. One scout had his arm in the air, and the other was on the ground, on one knee. Agrippa squinted but could not quite see what had made the scout dismount.

"Wilhelm, take over, I am going forward," he said and nudged his horse into a canter. As he approached, the mounted scout wheeled his horse and waited, sword in hand. The scout on the ground was tending to a man, leaning against a tree and eagerly drinking water.

"We found him tied to the tree, boss," said the mounted scout. "Don't know how long he'd been there, but it must have been a fair while, judging by the amount of water he's taking on board. Doesn't smell too savoury either."

Agrippa dismounted and knelt with his scout in front of the man who reluctantly put down the water flask. Judging by the foul stench coming off his torn and filthy clothing, he had probably been tied up for at least a day and night, thought Agrippa. There was a wary look about him as if his gratitude at being rescued was being replaced with a dread of what was likely to be coming next.

"Has he said anything, can you understand him?" Agrippa asked the scout.

"I can understand him, but he just keeps gabbling that he was surprised by several men armed with swords who for no reason tied him up and left him here to die."

What a load of bollocks, thought Agrippa. Silently he drew his knife. The man shrank back in fear, eyes locked on the fearsome blade. Agrippa leaned forward. "Now why don't you tell me the truth. What were you doing here?"

The man opened his mouth, then shut it again. He swallowed, and finally, the words came out in a rush.

"We didn't mean to harm anyone, but we were hungry. I was supposed to keep watch, then run back to the others if I saw anyone coming that may have been carrying money or goods, then we would rob them - only to feed our children of course. We have been starving for ages, forced to live here in this forest, sleeping on the ground." The man tailed off to a piteous whisper.

"It was one man, wasn't it?" guessed Agrippa.

The man nodded shamefacedly.

Agrippa stood and moved away. With a jerk of his head he indicated to the scout to follow him.

The freed man stayed sitting on the ground looking fearfully from Agrippa to the scout. He sensed his future was being discussed.

"This looks to me like Lenc's work," Agrippa whispered. "This sorry piece of shit has been abandoned by his mates, who were either frightened off or killed, so tie his hands again and tell him to take us to their camp. Promise he won't be hurt if he tells the truth. Give him some food - that may make him believe you."

The scout nodded as Agrippa walked back down the track to Wilhelm and the pathfinders.

"The scouts have come across a wretched bandit tied to a tree. Apparently, they were waiting to spring an ambush against Lenc's party but got ambushed themselves. He is going to take us to their camp, I don't think there is any danger, because I imagine the rest of the band will be dead or have fled, otherwise they would have come to find him. I should think Lenc and his party will have resumed their pursuit of Caratacus.

"Mount up and tell the men to keep well apart through the forest, just to be safe."

With the unhappy bandit in the lead, hands tied together, followed by the scout with his sword at the ready and his other hand holding his nose and complaining about the smell, the pathfinders walked their horses into the forest, warily checking the undergrowth as they went.

After a short walk the man stopped in a clearing, where a body was still swinging slowly from the tree branch. "This was where the ambush was to be," he said quietly then motioned with his head, towards a narrower track leading uphill, "and our camp is up there, but I imagine everyone has gone."

"We'll take a look anyway," retorted Agrippa, slightly puzzled by the resurgence of the fear on the man's face. Wonder why he doesn't want us to go there, he thought. We'll soon find out.

Before leaving the clearing he detailed two men to cut down the corpse hanging in the tree, then motioned to the prisoner to lead them up the path. As they left the main track, the overhanging trees created a dark, tunnelled glade, heightening the sense of danger. Quietly Agrippa unsheathed his sword. Behind him, he could hear the scrape of iron on iron as his men pulled theirs as well. They tiptoed up the path, alert for an ambush in this threatening place.

At the front the bandit paused and looked round to Agrippa. Near his feet, sprawled in the undergrowth were two bodies, badly mauled, one still with an almost severed hand between his legs. Agrippa moved up to examine them, turning one over onto his back with his foot. He let out his breath in relief as he saw they were strangers. Must be bandits, he thought.

"This one's been deliberately stabbed in the bollocks," Wilhelm said dispassionately. "Wonder what he did to deserve that?" This excited some ribald comment from the pathfinders, until Agrippa hissed at them to be quiet. He gestured to the now terrified bandit guide. "Are these your men?"

The man nodded, eager to please.

"Carry on then, I can't wait to see what else is up this track."

Nervously the man licked his lips. He looked as though he really didn't care what else was lurking up the track, he would rather be anywhere than here. Only when Agrippa pricked him with the point of his sword did he turn and start walking up the hill again, shoulders hunched and dragging his feet.

"Go on, get a move on," rasped Agrippa, losing patience.

As they walked, they passed three more bandits lying dead with severe head injuries. "These have been killed with rocks," noted Wilhelm.

Agrippa could see a clearing up ahead when suddenly their guide let out a hysterical wail, and turning, tried to run past his guard back down the hill. Agrippa still had his sword in his hand and instinctively raised it to the attack position as the bandit, in his terror, ran onto the point and skewered himself on the blade. Agrippa was braced for the shock, as the bandit, eyes wide with fear could not stop his momentum and ran himself further onto the blade. Agrippa grabbed a handful of shirt with his free hand then hauled the man round, dropping him next to the path. Agrippa put a foot on the man's chest and hauled his sword from the now dead body.

Without a second glance he gestured to his men. With the noise that had been made by the terrified bandit, any pretence at stealth was pointless.

"Come on then, let's get this camp searched quick time. Wilhelm, what put the fear of god into that fool?"

"Here boss - he saw his mates," replied Wilhelm and matter-of-factly pointed with his sword at the collection of dead bodies lying on or near the path.

Agrippa went down on one knee to quickly examine the bodies. They were all dressed in tatters, certainly none of Caratacus's or Lenc's men.

"Looks like Lenc took them by surprise," he surmised. "Good odds though."

At the camp Wilhelm held up a pair of ankle restraints. "They seem to have had prisoners," he said. "If Lenc freed them, that would have swelled their band. It certainly explains why so many were killed by rocks - probably the best weapons they could find."

Agrippa nodded. "Cast around and see how many horses left here and what direction they were travelling. We can't be far behind them by now."

CHAPTER XVIII

Wearily Agrippa swung himself down from his foam-flecked horse after a long journey through potentially hostile country. But the journey was necessary because it was vital to keep contact with the nearest Roman forces, even if they were heavily outnumbered.

The pathfinders had ridden hard to catch up with and overtake Lenc and his group. He left two men on the Mamucium to Rigodunum road to watch for them with instructions not to make contact, but for one to discreetly follow and the other to report back to the pathfinders' temporary camp. He left the pathfinders at a settlement a short distance away on the east-west drover's trail, while he rode to Eboracum to introduce himself and his men, but also to warn the garrison that they were operating in the area.

"Centurion Agrippa, commanding the Pathfinders of the Twentieth Valeria Victrix reporting."

Facing him was his opposite number, and commander of the fledgling outpost, Centurion Gaius Hospes. His 'kingdom' was little more than a marching camp, in the first stages of building. The legionaries had dug a square ditch as a defensive boundary, with turf ramparts on green wood foundations. Inside the square, wooden buildings were being constructed in the same style as everywhere else in the empire.

The fort was a frontier post on a well-developed drover's road on a wide plain, with the Penninus on one side and the Oceanus Germanicus on the other, many Roman miles to the east. It also had significance because of the importance of the vassal state, Brigantia, providing a buffer between Caledonia and the rapidly colonising south of Britannia. Even although Brigantia seemed to accept Rome's domination, the fort and its troops were there to ensure that the natives 'never got too restless'. As Rome's conquering path spread steadily north it would one day be one of the Empire's most significant garrisons, but when Agrippa visited, the first foundations had only just been dug by sweating legionaries.

Centurion Hospes was initially wary of Agrippa's visit. The pathfinders had a reputation for stirring the locals up, and the last thing the commander needed was an insurrection when his men were so badly exposed. Agrippa was aware of this and sought to allay his fears.

"My mission was given to me by Governor Ostorius Scapula," he explained. "Unfortunately, since then the governor has been taken by a long-standing illness. But it doesn't affect my mission, which is to find and deal with Caratacus who we believe to be with Cartimandua in Brigantum. I have a man who is travelling with tribespeople, and he will be trying to infiltrate the town as we speak. I intend to move up there to support him."

Centurion Hospes nodded thoughtfully. On the face of it, there seemed no obvious way this could affect his building work. Trouble was always pretty close, just over the horizon, but every day the fort became stronger, and it sounded as if the pathfinders were moving north.

"I wish you well with your task," he said eventually. "Tribal politics are often muddy, but the Brigantes are renowned for being devious bastards. We are out on a limb here, and I am only too well aware how precarious our position is. If the Brigantes decide to take up arms against us, with our present manpower and state of our defences, we would make a stand - but knowing we were going to die for the Emperor." Centurion Hospes looked up with a twisted smile. "I think it would pay you to make friends with the Queen. I wouldn't be the least bit surprised if she didn't betray Caratacus, maybe already has."

"Wouldn't it be nice if something was straightforward," smiled Agrippa. "Anyway, I thought I would just report in, tell you what we were doing, and of course I will report back before we leave, hopefully with Caratacus in chains or his head on a spear."

After his meeting with the garrison commander, Agrippa rode back along the drover's road to find his men. He wondered whether there had been any report from the scouts on the Mamucium road yet. Lenc couldn't be that far behind.

He found the camp without difficulty, a clearing just off the road in a thick forest. It was a good vantage point, on a slight rise, so users of the road could be seen some way off. The first sentry was grinning as he stepped out of the shrubbery.

"Good to see you back, boss," he said. "One scout is in and the other is trailing Lenc and his gang."

"That's good news. Where is the scout?"

"He's at the main camp, just up ahead." The sentry indicated a narrow path which led further up the hill. Agrippa nodded his thanks and led his horse up the track. When he reached the top of the rise, the trees opened out to a clearing which had been taken over by the pathfinders. Wet clothing was laid out on top of the low shelters the men had constructed and there was a tantalising smell of something roasting on the fire. Agrippa tethered his horse to a tree and went for a closer look. Sitting on the ground near the fire was the scout, slicing a large lump of meat with his dirk. On a spit over the fire was the rest of a deer, basting slowly and dripping fat into the fire.

"All the comforts of home, eh, Valerius?" joked Agrippa.

Valerius the scout raised his dirk. "Beats cold flatbread and water, boss."

Agrippa squatted by the scout. "What have you got for me?"

Valerius rested his bowl on the ground and collected himself for his report. "We set up just past Rigodunum on the most obvious route to Isurion. It was still hilly, so we had plenty of cover. Caratacus was at the front of the group, with 11 warriors. Quite honestly they didn't look like an effective fighting force, so what the Brigantes make of them is anyone's guess.

"On my way back, I checked in with the pair of scouts trailing Lenc. He was with four tribesmen and a gaggle of women, some riding two on one horse. About fifteen in total.

"They must have picked up the women in that raid, the other side of Deva."

Agrippa nodded thoughtfully. "So he is still on track for Isurion," he said slowly. "I wonder if these women are Brigantians. If they are, it won't hurt his cover.

"Either way we need to make a contact with him before he gets much further."

At that moment, Lenc and his motley band were on higher ground, looking across a river towards Mamucium, a settlement on an important crossroads between Deva and Eboracum and the west coast across the Penninus to Aquae Arnemetiae, famous for its natural warm springs. They had skirted the fledgling fort at Deva, then made good progress towards the grey, shrouded mass of the Penninus, the so-called spine of Britannia.

Brianna edged her horse up next to Lenc as he eased himself forward in the saddle and gazed at the village, a rudimentary earth wall encircling roundhouses and farm buildings. Outside the wall was a series of wooden walled corrals, to house the drover's stock. A fog of woodsmoke, drifting from the houses, hung over the thatched roofs. "We could do worse than ride down there for the night," she said. "There are no Romans, but there are Brigantians. I know people there, and we would be assured of a decent night's rest. We would certainly pick up some useful current information about what's happening between Cartimandua and Venutius."

Lenc nodded; up-to-date information would be very handy. "Good idea, Brianna. You better lead the way."

As they rode, Brianna explained that she had relatives who

lived on the east side of the settlement. "We can skirt round and come in on the Penninus road. It's only a small place and really only exists because of the crossroads. The Romans leave it alone until it's time for their bastard tax collectors - that shakes things up a bit."

They rode on in silence with the village gradually coming more into view. From what they could see, it seemed to be a jumble of low wattle-walled roundhouses with tall, thatched roofs. Swirling woodsmoke escaped through the thatch, creating a haze at roof top height. Brianna steered them between houses, solemnly watched by grubby, barefoot urchins, before she finally announced a halt outside another nondescript roundhouse. Except this one had a chequered blanket hanging as a door, and two goats tethered outside.

"This family is related to mine," she explained as she dismounted. "They will find us food and shelter. As for information, you will find that in the alehouses, nearer the crossroads."

Wearily they all followed her lead and climbed down from their horses, stretching and yawning. As they did so, the chequered blanket was pushed aside to reveal a white-bearded older man in a long wool shirt and leggings, and bare feet. He took in the number of riders, both male and female, then demanded to know their business at his home.

Brianna stepped forward with open arms. "Don't you recognise me, Alwyn? It's Brianna from Melandra? I married your brother's son, Brodie."

Alwyn stepped forward, a puzzled frown on his face as he concentrated on Brianna. A sudden smile of recognition lit up his face. "We heard you were dead, that raiders killed you all and set fire to your homestead."

Brianna hung her head. "That's true, we were raided. They took us by surprise, the few men-folk were killed, the children too. They carried off every animal, every bit of food and anything of value. That seemed to include me and some of these women here." She gestured to the women behind her. "We have endured a living hell ever since, until we were rescued by these four men and this lady. Now we are helping them in their mission, before returning to what was our homesteads."

The old man stepped forward and embraced Brianna, tears running unashamedly down his face.

"Brodie was a good man," he sobbed. "And your fine sons? Not them as well?"

Brianna could only nod as she blinked back tears.

Alwyn visibly tried to get control of himself and ushered them all into the gloom of the roundhouse. Inside, a woman about the same age as Alwyn ground wheat between two circular stones. She looked up in surprise when all these strangers filed into her home.

Alwyn quickly blurted out as much of the story that he had so far gleaned, which was that his niece, thought dead, was very much alive, but his nephew Brodie and their boys were dead. The old lady tried to take in this devastating information and the conflicting emotions that confirmed family had been killed, but one at least had returned from the dead.

As she listened, the woman put her hands up to her mouth then brushed away her tears. Wordlessly she walked past her husband and drew Brianna to her, pulling her into her breast. The two stood together, both quietly sobbing, before Brianna looked up and smiled through her tears.

"Don't worry," she said softly, "It's over and at last I am at peace. We have been through a terrible torment, but what I am clinging onto is that at least we took our revenge. Those evil men will never defile a woman again."

Alwyn bustled about, finding things for their guests to sit on, then asked if they had eaten. Lenc thought it time to introduce himself. "We don't want to be a burden on you, Alwyn. We have some food - perhaps we can share with you. We would be grateful for shelter tonight, and we're looking for some information about your Queen Cartimandua and Venutius before we continue."

"Of course, of course, you are all very welcome here." He paused and stroked his beard. "You can't all stay here, but I can arrange for the women to stay with a friend. As for finding things out, there is a place near the crossroads, it's where drovers and other travellers stop on their journey."

They decided that Lenc and Alun would go with Alwyn to the cross-roads tavern. A small number would not arouse interest, good or bad. Veldicca bristled at this, she thought it a good idea if she went as well. Alwyn hesitated and looked at Lenc and Alun for support, but being only too well aware of her wilful determination, they stayed quiet, studiously looking at the sparse furniture in the round house.

Reluctantly Alwyn spoke again. "Lady, let me explain that only a certain type of woman would go to a place like this, and you would certainly draw attention. Far better that you let the men do this and they can report back afterwards. We wouldn't want to spoil things by those men taking an unhealthy interest in you."

Veldicca was still bristling, but had to accept the sense of Alwyn's words. "Very well then, if you think you can do better without me," then flounced over to Alwyn's wife and asked if she could take over from the older lady at the grinding wheel.

Clearly relieved, Alwyn suggested they leave straight away, as Lenc and Alun hastily stood. Alun asked the other Ordovicians if they would take care of their horses, then hurriedly left before Veldicca could change her mind.

Out in the street Alwyn said, almost to himself, "That young lady certainly knows her own mind."

"That she does," said Lenc ruefully.

Alwyn led them confidently into a roundhouse with rough wooden tables and benches outside, where a few patrons sat and sipped at horn mugs. Inside, through the fug and gloom, Lenc could see a makeshift counter with barrels behind, and a fat man wearing a leather apron standing to one side. A serving girl poured ale and cider from the barrels. The fat man saw Alwyn and half-raised a hand in greeting.

Alwyn caught the serving girl's attention and ordered ale, then pointed at an empty table, which Lenc and Alun claimed. Alwyn waited for the beer to be poured then carried it over. Alun and Lenc took a first tentative sip, then finding it to their liking, took a good glug. Lenc wiped his mouth with the back of his hand and looked round carefully.

"I think we are in your hands, Alwyn. We are looking for someone that has recently come over the Penninus and knows what's going on. But how do we find them without prompting more questions?"

With a slight gesture of his head, Alwyn indicated the fat man at the bar. "That's the landlord," he said quietly. "He makes it his business to know what is happening, and he is a distant relative of mine; we'll start with him."

Alwyn took a slug of beer, then stood and threaded his way through the drinkers to the landlord at the bar.

"Hello, something's happening," said Alun quietly as he nodded his head at Alwyn and the fat landlord leaving the bar and walking across to a knot of men all wearing oiled wool cloaks. "Probably drovers," he whispered.

The landlord moved back to the bar as Alwyn, with a drover in tow, walked back to their table.

The drover was thin and wiry with strangely large hands, his skin a weathered brown from too much time out in all the elements. He nodded comfortably at Lenc and Alun as he sat at the table.

"Let me get you another beer while you talk to Lenc and Alun, friends of our family," suggested Alwyn.

Lenc took the lead. "We're following a small band of warriors, Catuvellauni actually, led by an imposing man - blond, with a beard - who we think is trying to form an alliance with the Brigantes." Lenc pressed forward. "Have you seen this band?"

As Lenc paused, Alwyn reappeared and put the beer down in

front of the drover, who picked it up and took an appreciative swig. He sat back and looked at Lenc and Alun.

"I don't normally get involved in other people's matters, but you are apparently friends of the Brigantes, so I must think there is a reason why you want to find this man and that somehow he is no friend of our tribe."

Lenc nodded. "It's a long story, but I can assure you that this man is no friend of the Brigantes. He will use the tribe for his own ends and will discard you when your use is over."

"They have been seen on the road," conceded the drover. "The blond man and his band stayed overnight at Isurion as the guest of Venutius, then left for Rigodonum where I understand he had a proposition for that bitch Cartimandua. What happened then I don't know, but I do know that he and his men definitely went to the Queen's fort."

Lenc nodded again as the drover continued: "He is playing a dangerous game, Cartimandua is beholden to the Romans. She is on the throne because they want her to be, and the moment she is no further use to them, she will be replaced. Venutius, who once shared her bed, is violently opposed to being ruled by Rome and would dearly love the tribe to fall on Cartimandua, who humiliated him, first by throwing him out, then moving his spear carrier, who is much younger, and low-born, into her bed.

"When Venutius finally deals with Cartimandua, only then can he turn on the Romans. It probably won't happen because Cartimandua is holding some of his family hostage and they will be the first to die if she feels threatened. She will never turn on Rome because it is not in her interest to do so, and your man has a vastly inflated sense of his own self-importance if he thinks he can persuade her to take up arms against the Romans."

Lenc agreed. "Unfortunately this is a man who is so swaggeringly self-confident that he cannot conceive of any woman being immune to his charms."

"He has never met a woman like Cartimandua," replied the drover. "She is an attractive and very strong woman. She knows what she wants and what she has to do to keep it. She would be quite capable of playing with this visitor, maybe even using him in her bed, but he will never persuade her to turn on Rome."

Lenc sighed. "That's quite a story, and I agree with you. The problem is that the man we are looking for only cares about one thing and that's himself. He is sure to try, and if he succeeds with Cartimandua, he will drag the Brigantes into a war they cannot win. If he loses, then his death will be a good thing for the tribes.

"We will follow him and watch what happens. Our intention is to kill him but if this mighty woman will do our job for us, I for one will not complain."

CHAPTER XIX

"That's close enough, state your business". The challenge, though expected, startled the riders. As the words rang out, they jerked their horses to a stop, making the front riders wheel. Staring over the rampart, on top of an earthwork, was a sentry, arrow nocked to his bow and trained at the front rider.

Despite a weak sun, a chill wind blowing from the north seemed to cut through to the bones of tired men riding the high Penninus. They had ridden hard from the north Cambrian coast, skirting the new Roman fort at Deva and picked up the drovers trail from Mamucium across the forbidding Penninus.

At last the warband approached the outer wall of Rigodunum, a fortified stone village in a windswept valley. Caratacus pushed forward so that he could be seen by the sentry.

"We come in peace and would have an audience with your master, Venutius. My name is Caratacus formerly of the Catuvellauni, but lately the tribes of the west, where we fought the Romans."

"Wait there," demanded a stentorian voice from behind the wall.

The riders hunched into their cloaks against the biting wind that swirled down the valley, until finally the sentry beckoned them forward and through a series of stone obstacles with a gap just wide enough for one horse to walk through at a time.

"Take it easy everyone, and hands away from swords," warned Caratacus as he pulled his horse round and led the band through and into a courtyard with high stone walls. On top of the wall were more guards with spears and bows at the ready. The courtyard was quite compact, especially for twelve horses, and at the far end was a large wooden gate, tightly shut.

"Stay where you are," shouted the voice, "Venutius has been informed and is on his way."

Caratacus looked round for the source of the voice and thought it came from a slightly better dressed warrior, who seemed to be the only one not pointing an arrow or spear. His hair was as long and wild as the others, but his beard was trimmed and beneath his cloak, Caratacus observed that he was wearing boots, which marked him as a Brigantian leader.

"Can we dismount?" asked Caratacus.

"Of course," came the reply. "There is water in the trough for your animals."

Gratefully the band led their horses to the trough and watched them drink. One of the men put a hand in the water and wiped his face with it.

"It's understandable that they are cautious," said Caratacus to one of his men. "We are strangers, and I don't suppose they see too many of them in these parts."

As if on cue one of the end gates was pushed open by two warriors to reveal a warrior standing with hands on hips, every inch a leader.

"Your leader plus one more may come through to the hall of Venutius," he said. "The rest of you will be taken to a place of shelter where you can rest."

There was some muttering among the men, who sensed an ambush, quickly quelled by Caratacus. "Don't worry, if they wanted to kill us, they could have done it by now. I will speak with their leader and assure him we are on his side."

He motioned to Aeron, and the two unbuckled their swords, hitching them to the pommels of their saddles, and followed the Brigantian into the hillfort. They walked between low stone roundhouses with thatch on the roof and cobbles covered in mud outside. They soon gave up trying to steer clear of the mud lapping up their boots. It was everywhere; only the depth varied.

Caratacus felt there were people in the houses peering timidly at them, even although he could not see them. He tried to dispel the uncomfortable image of being an object of curiosity and tried to look forward to their destination. Of course they're interested, he told himself. It's the first time they will have seen a future King of Britannia, probably the last as well. He straightened his shoulders and, with head held high, strode imperiously along the muddy street until it led them to an open square, where at least the air was fresher.

In front of them was a more imposing building, slightly higher, again thatched but bigger. This must be the great hall, reasoned Caratacus. Their escort pushed aside a leather cover which hung over the door and motioned to them to enter. Inside Caratacus nearly retched at the foetid stench of woodsmoke, bodies, and who knew what else in the semi-darkness. There were no gaps in the walls to allow light in, what light there was, came from rush torches which guttered in holders on the walls.

At the other side of the room, Caratacus could make out an imposing bench covered in furs, with a man sitting, watching them intently. There seemed to be more light nearer the man, and as Caratacus approached he felt a slight breeze, a welcome relief from the stench near the door. They stopped in front of him and bowed.

The man stirred on his bench and indicated to Caratacus and Aeron to sit. His long black curly hair was caught in a leather bow and, unusually he was clean shaven. He had an imposing look, as if used to authority, and his long shirt was brocaded in many colours. Underneath he wore rough-spun trousers, tucked into leather boots. "Welcome to my home," he said finally. "I am Venutius, the warrior leader of the Brigantes. Caratacus… I know this name. You fought at Medway and Tamesis?"

Caratacus inclined his head, "Aye, lord, that we did, then lately we took the Romans on again in the west, beyond the river Sabrina, and gave them something to think about."

The man leaned forward without taking his eyes off Caratacus. "But not enough to stop them I think?"

"Yes," conceded Caratacus. "Luck was against us, and although we outnumbered them, we were too busy fighting each other to make an impression against a disciplined foe. That is why I am here. The Brigantes are the biggest tribe in Britannia, with the Catuvellauni the second biggest. If I can persuade the Brigantes to join the Catuvellauni, we will surely have an army that will sweep the legions all the way back to Rome. We have had enough of their taxes and their riding rough-shod over us, stealing what they need - land, food, cattle, women."

Venutius leaned back on his bench. "Come, sit, have some ale. I have some things to explain to you, which will make our present position clearer. But before that, let's take the time to get to know each other. We don't get many visitors up here, especially famous ones like you. Let's eat and drink and get down to business a bit later, maybe tomorrow, when you are rested. I take it you do have business here?"

Caratacus smiled at the flattery. He realised he was in the presence of a wily horse trader - he would have to keep his wits about him - and waved an arm in resignation. "You are, of course, quite right. You must pardon my manners but I was – am - keen to get to grips with this thorny problem. But I am happy to let it fester for an hour or so. Perhaps a stroll round your hillfort to work up an appetite?"

After a bracing walk round the top of the outer wall, Caratacus could see that the hillfort was well defended. He confessed to Venutius that he had doubts when told the fort was in a valley, straddling the important trail, with high hills either side, but saw immediately with his professional eye that the fort would be easily defended, and any assault costly. The swell of the hills either side of the trail started well beyond arrow range, and they were well above the treeline with only gorse and bracken clinging onto the sides of the hills.

The wind whistled and moaned down the pass, with only the stone hillfort to cramp its progress.

Venutius pointed out the embrasures either side of the only gate they had come through that morning. "You see where we heat up oil," he said, pointing out the brick kilns above and either side of the thick oak gates, studded with iron. "A frontal assault would be met with molten oil and pitch and that's after they have got past the slingers along the wall."

"Looks very secure," conceded Caratacus, "but tell me, what does a fellow do for fun around here?"

Venutius smiled, "We are simple people here, and we have to make our own fun, perhaps I can introduce you to a couple of young ladies who have very healthy appetites?"

"Now you are talking," exclaimed a beaming Caratacus, "Let me send my lieutenant back to the men, then lead me to these young fillies."

Later, after a highly satisfying game of hide and seek with two servant girls, both of whom found their hiding places in adjoining bedrooms, Venutius and a grinning Caratacus met back in the great hall. They were joined by a disgruntled Aeron, who could only guess at how his leader had spent the afternoon. Venutius poured ale from a pot pitcher into horn beakers while collecting his thoughts and visibly putting the afternoon's frolics behind him.

"The story you are about to hear does not reflect well on me," he said. "I suppose I should have seen it coming and done something about it, but by the time it was on me, it was too late.

"I was married to the Queen Cartimandua way before the Romans arrived. They knew I was their enemy, certainly not their friend, so I was isolated. This was before they gave her more territory to improve the buffer between the south and the Caledonians. They saw the Brigantes as their protection in the north.

"Cartimandua didn't mind because her prestige and power grew as a vassal of Rome. She only had to crook her finger and the bastards would come running. I minded because I hate the Romans and want them gone, but I was powerless while she had their support.

"Over the years she became more and more imperious and demanding, and even tried to get me to bend the knee to her. I wasn't having that I can tell you. She was getting tired of me - I knew that, and I was sick of all the tantrums, so when she suggested I move out of the royal bed, I agreed. I didn't know then she was bedding my squire, Vellocatus, a lad I thought was my liege man. What the Queen wants, the Queen gets," he said bitterly.

"She must have found out, probably from Vellocatus that I was plotting to have her killed, because one evening she called for me to join her in the bedchamber. I was wary, but had to go. She seduced me, and for a short time it was like the old days before she prostituted herself to Rome. So there I was, lying naked on her bed having just had great sex, when all of a sudden four men with knives burst in and jumped me. They tied me up like an animal, and all the time Cartimandua sat there watching with a smile on her face. Didn't even bother to cover herself.

"I spent the night freezing in a cell, then next morning she coolly informed me that I was to be banished here to Rigodunum and four of my brothers and their children had been kidnapped and would be held to ransom in return for my good behaviour… the bitch."

Caratacus listened, fascinated by the tale, and stole a glance at Aeron, who was also listening avidly with his mouth wide open. Caratacus tore himself back to the bitter Venutius who was rounding off his tirade against his ex-wife.

"You see, I don't have much choice," he said piteously. "I have to do what she says or my family will be decimated, and all the while she is humping that young ingrate Vellocatus. I know what I would do with him if I caught him."

Caratacus leaned back thoughtfully. "I have heard some tales in my time, but that just about tops the lot. Is she an attractive woman this Cartimandua?"

Venutius grimaced. "Yes, she is, the gods rot her. She is a strong woman, hair down past her bum and very fit. I've heard that when the Roman lords come from Lindum, Vellocatus is banished to the barracks, so she can further cement her relationship with the Romans."

Caratacus leaned back with a thoughtful expression. "If I should go and visit the lady, maybe I can gather some intelligence about the hostages. Just say we could free them, how much support would there be from the tribe if you were to march on Isurion?"

Venutius sipped his beer, giving him time to think before responding. "I believe that the Brigantes have a traditional view of their leaders," he said finally. "Cartimandua is doing herself no favours with her flagrant sex habits. Her desire to marry Vellocatus, who is low-born, actually outrages a lot of ordinary people, so, yes, I think that if the hostages could be freed, and Cartimandua overthrown, the tribe would follow me to war."

Caratacus smiled with satisfaction. "That sounds like something I could help with. If I was to get an audience with her, on the face of it trying to persuade her to take up arms against the Romans, perhaps I can find out where the hostages are being held. Then we could come up with a plan to release them. After that we can deal with this baggage of Cartimandua."

Venutius looked dubious. "That would be a very tall order. She holds the throne entirely because of her protection by the Romans. They tolerate her while she holds their northern border secure, but she would soon be replaced if she threatened the stability of the northern frontier."

Caratacus leaned forward with a wolfish grin. "What if I offered her the queenship of the whole of Britannia? If the Brigantes joined forces with the Catuvellauni, we would be unstoppable. We have learned a lot since we were defeated by

Rome and we can pick our time and place to take them on. We can hit them so hard, they wouldn't stop till they reach Rome."

Here we go again, thought Aeron ruefully.

Venutius still looked dubious. "You don't know her. She is as devious and dangerous as a bag full of snakes, and most importantly she knows that her future prosperity is entirely dependent on keeping the Romans happy. She would be risking everything if she cast her lot in with you."

"I think it's worth a try," said Caratacus flatly. "A woman like her will be happy with her lot until she sees far greater wealth and glory can be had with a bold stroke. Why stick with the Kingdom of Brigantia when she could be queen of a united Britannia?"

CHAPTER XX

Venutius was right, she was a looker, thought Caratacus admiringly. He and his small band had ridden hard to the stronghold of Brigantum with the dire warnings of Venutius ringing in their ears. They arrived in the middle of the day, and despite himself, Caratacus was impressed with his first sight of the fort.

It stood atop an earthwork, surrounded by a ditch; its dry-stone wall at least the height of one man standing on another man's shoulders. The entrance to the fort lay in the western corner, where partially cut rock had been hammered down, making a smooth road across the ditch. The wall at the entrance was shaped into a perilous zig-zag, easily dominated by slingers.

Caratacus craned his neck to examine the top of the wall, where a sentry armed with a spear watched him impassively. Aeron shouted up to the sentry that they were travellers looking for an audience with Queen Cartimandua. The sentry curtly told them to wait while he roused the guard commander.

Eventually the commander and his retinue arrived and leaned over the wall. The commander studied the dusty band of warriors below suspiciously. "Identify yourself," he demanded.

Aeron wheeled his horse round and yelled back that they were warriors of the Catuvellauni seeking an audience with the Queen.

"What about?" the commander fired back.

By now Caratacus was getting the feeling that things were not progressing quite as smoothly as they should do, and now would be the time for more forceful intervention. "None of your fucking business," he yelled. "Go and find your Queen. Caratacus of the Catuvellauni wishes an audience."

Caratacus sat proudly, every inch the warrior king, while above him the guard commander opted for discretion rather than valour and sent a runner off to ask the Queen to attend the front gate.

Whether from curiosity or boredom, there was suddenly another commotion on the top of the wall as more warriors gathered to look down at them, and then a female thrust her face over the parapet, demanding to know who dared to summon the Queen of the Brigantes.

Caratacus could only see her face and long hair disappearing down behind her back, but even that glimpse was enough for him to welcome the thought of bedding her. He licked his lips in anticipation. Not bad at all.

By this time he was getting impatient with the yelling to and fro and shouted: "Lady, I have come a long way to see you and I have something I know you will want to hear. If you would let me in, I will explain all."

At that, she disappeared and at the same time the solid double gates below creaked open. A soldier, by his bearing a man of authority, wearing chain mail and carrying a sword, stood in the gateway and beckoned Caratacus to come forward. He nudged his horse with his knees and motioned to his small band to follow. The soldier stepped to one side as they ducked under the low entrance roof.

Inside the gates, the town opened up in front of them, to a narrow street with low wooden roundhouses either side. The roofs were thatched, and the roadway, a swamp of churned-up sludge. A huddle of interested spectators stood gawking at them; strangers must be a rarity, thought Caratacus. Reluctantly he dismounted and grimaced as his booted feet sank into the cloying mud.

As he did so, the guard in the chain mail strode confidently across the muddy trackway and raised his hand in greeting.

"Our Queen asked me to escort you to her in her council chamber. She says she has heard of you and wants to hear what it is you have to say. But have a care, if you upset her, or me, you will not leave here with your head still on your shoulders." His eyes glittered as he made his threat.

This is going to be easy, thought Caratacus. Out loud he said smoothly: "I have no intention of upsetting your queen; as for you, I couldn't care less if I upset you. Now why don't you be a good manservant and take me to your Cartimandua?

"Would I be right in thinking you are Vellocatus, and you serve Cartimandua in a special, shall we say, intimate way?"

Through gritted teeth, the chain mailed warrior confirmed that he was Vellocatus, that he did serve Cartimandua, but how he served her was no one's business but his own – and hers. He was a well-built, fit-looking young man in his early twenties, and quite handsome, thought Caratacus, reluctantly, but no competition at all really.

"Of course, of course," said Caratacus soothingly, then spoilt it by adding: "She is certainly a big one. Do you have trouble holding her down?"

Vellocatus visibly seethed and half-wrenched his sword from its scabbard. He fought to gain control of himself, took a step towards Caratacus and thrust his face forward to just inches from his ear. "Keep talking, you sneering piece of shit, and I will take great pleasure in separating your head from your body, and don't think your men will be any help to you. There are twenty slingers aiming at you right now and just a simple signal from me will see you all dead."

Caratacus looked round carefully, and sure enough, there were the slingers with their leather pouches ready to loose, ranged along the parapet.

Vellocatus smiled grimly when he saw Caratacus blanch and swallow. He nodded contemptuously then stepped out into the bog with a curt "Follow me."

Caratacus recovered and smiled to himself. He had made an enemy, but the young whippersnapper should know all about the new competition. Should add a bit of spice if nothing else. Besides, the jumped-up little shit would never dare to have me killed, he thought. His queen would at least want to talk to me first and would be a bit pissed off if her boy-lover spoiled the possibility of a good tumble with the future first King of Britannia. With this comforting thought, Caratacus hitched his cloak and smiled at Vellocatus's back.

Cartimandua's palace was bigger than the surrounding wattle and daub buildings, but not much more, and certainly no grander. Inwardly Caratacus sneered at the makeshift building, especially compared to his own father's lodge. Not called a palace, but at least it was fit for a tribal personage. "What a fine building," he said out loud. "Fit for a queen, and a king of course, eh, Vellocatus?" Who scowled and tried to ignore the taunts.

Vellocatus stood by the open door and tried to collect himself, swallowed and then spoke. "The Queen awaits Caratacus alone, I am to see about accommodation for your men and horses and will join you later."

Caratacus nodded and for once kept his opinions to himself as he walked past Vellocatus into the dimly lit so-called palace. He paused, eyes adjusting to the gloom as they immediately started to prickle from the woodsmoke swirling round, looking for an exit through the densely thatched roof. Caratacus could see a beaten-earth room, capable of holding a decent-sized gathering with a built-up stone fire pit in the centre. Behind the fire against the wall, he could make out drapes of some sort pinned to the wall.

In front was a low couch, covered in furs, and by the great god's balls, Caratacus thought excitedly, it's her, stripped for action. He stepped hurriedly round the fire and was disappointed to see that Cartimandua was fully clothed, but at least she was reclining on the couch, in what he took to be a provocative manner. She wore a homespun gown down to her ankles, and rather more gold bracelets, necklaces and rings than Caratacus thought seemly. She doesn't know how a queen should behave, he decided, because no one has taught her. It will be my mission to teach her - that and a few other things. Caratacus positively salivated at the thought.

He bowed to the recumbent queen. "I have been looking forward to this meeting ever since I heard of your astonishing beauty, especially as you are a queen of one of the most important tribes in Britannia."

Cartimandua smiled as she accepted the flowery compliments and languidly lowered her feet to the floor. Caratacus could see she was tall and looked strong, her shoulders and arm muscles suggesting a powerful woman. Auburn hair tumbled down her shoulders, framing startling blue eyes and a square chin. Up close she was more arresting than beautiful, he thought, but no less desirable for that. Momentarily he forgot domination of the Romans in exchange for domination of her. What a prize!

"Come sit, I am intrigued to know what you want of me." Cartimandua's voice was low and smoky, giving Caratacus another tingle of excitement. He quickly sat on a covered chair, near to the Queen's couch, and leaned forward.

"Madam, you are being direct, which I admire, so I too will be direct. I wish to suggest to you an alliance of the Brigantes with my own tribe, the Catuvellauni which will make us the biggest army ever seen on these shores, and more than a match for the Romans. Instead of being queen of a province, you will be the rightful Queen of Britannia, and you will go down in history as the leader who rid this country of the Roman tyrants."

Caratacus sat back after delivering his short but impassioned speech, then continued: "The Romans are building forts and roads all over the country, and each one makes their position stronger. But they are spread very thinly on the ground. With two legions campaigning in the north and the west, it would be an easy matter to fall on them in Camulodunum then

Londinium. When they realise what we have done, they will be forced to march their legions from Deva and Eboracum to meet us. They will be tired from the march, while we will be rested and waiting for them in prepared positions, and we will destroy them," he said with satisfaction.

Cartimandua looked steadily at Caratacus as he outlined his vision. Inwardly she seethed. What a pompous prick, she thought contemptuously. Did this Catuvellauni turd think I would give up being Queen of the Brigantes to go on a fool's errand, which would probably end with my head stuck on a pole for all to laugh at?

'Even if his ridiculous plan did work, how long would it be before I became a nuisance to his ambitions, then despatched with a cup of hemlock?

'But he is handsome though. Maybe I can put him to some use another way. She mentally shook herself to banish these increasingly lustful thoughts to concentrate on the matter in hand.'

"Your plan has the merit of being simple," she conceded out loud, "but there are some worrying parts which I would know more of. Firstly, the Romans have bested you, not once, but three times. First at Durobrivae, then Tamesis, and then in the western hills. The Catuvellauni were badly mauled which is why you were exiled to the west after you were kicked out by the tribe, so how can you come here to me and claim to be speaking on behalf of your tribe?"

Caratacus opened his mouth to speak, but the imperious queen peremptorily raised a hand to silence him.

"I will let you speak soon," she said, "but first I want you to know that I rule here with the approval of the Romans. They have been fair to me and we get on tolerably well. Why would I want to upset that when there is a very good chance that I would lose my head and that of a good many of my people should I agree to this dangerous plan. I don't doubt it's possible, but it's also possible that you would get your arse kicked yet again."

Caratacus blanched, he was clearly not prepared for this, to be dictated to, especially by a woman, even if she was a queen. He stitched a smile onto his face.

"I can see you have a good network of spies, to know all this," he said smoothly. "But you should know that my banishment from the tribe was a mere contrivance to persuade Rome not to attack and destroy us. I suggested it myself in fact, and my father agreed to it. By all accounts my ruse worked. As for the battles on the Tamesis and Medway, we outnumbered the invaders but still couldn't beat them. Their discipline and tactics were just too much for us. But we learned from that and an army that we raised could benefit from my knowledge. The mountain tribes were poor fighters and simply ran at the first hint of a fight. I won't make that mistake again."

I bet you won't, thought Cartimandua, who held the fighting prowess of the western tribes in high regard. Especially the Silures. She came to a decision.

"You have given me much to think about, Caratacus," she said finally. "You and your men are welcome to eat and drink with me and my council this evening after you have washed the dust of the road off you. At the very least we can show you some true Brigantian hospitality."

Caratacus realised the initial interview was over, and he had an uneasy feeling he had been bested by this imperious woman. When I get her naked and give her a damn good seeing to, she'll see the error of her ways, he thought vindictively.

Cartimandua acknowledged him as he nodded curtly. "Thank you, lady, I and my men will look forward to this evening with great anticipation. Will Vellocatus be present at all?" he asked innocently.

"No, he won't," said the Queen coyly looking at Caratacus through lidded eyes, "I am afraid I have an errand for him to run, which will keep him occupied for this evening."

"Good, good," approved Caratacus. "Till then."

He wandered thoughtfully out into the sunshine where his men were waiting, taking turns leading their horses to a stone trough. Aeron sprawled on a bench, but stood up when Caratacus walked towards him.

"What news?" he asked.

"Good and not so good," replied Caratacus. "I have her interest, but she doesn't like the idea of taking on the Romans. I told her that if the Brigantes were to join forces with the Catuvellauni we would make an army bigger than anything ever seen on this isle. I don't think she thought that an altogether good idea. She is happy being queen of the tribe, and Queen of Britannia is too big an idea for her, but I can work on that. She is laying on a banquet for us tonight and has sent Vellocatus away on an errand, which means I can work my charms on her and see if I can get her to see the sense of my plan. Should be easy enough," he added airily.

After Caratacus left Cartimandua's lodge, she paused for a few moments, then said loudly: "You can come out now."

There was a rustle and Vellocatus stepped into the room from behind some drapes. He had been given express orders not to show himself during the interview with Caratacus, but that didn't mean he had to like it. In fact he was fuming with a face like thunder. Cartimandua pretended not to notice and indicated he should sit near to her.

"You heard me say that you would be running an errand for me?" she asked in her best come to bed voice.

Vellocatus could only nod, he knew better than to argue.

"You realise I said those things to put that posturing fool off his guard," she asked. "I need him to think he is going to take your place and that is why I am getting rid of you for the evening. The reality is that I want you to ride to the Roman fort at Eboracum and tell them of this development. Caratacus is a wanted man and the Romans will pay heavily for him. That is why I deceived him, you do see that don't you?"

By this time she was stroking Vellocatus's thigh and looking deeply into his eyes. She slowly licked her lips, making them shine, as she slowly moved her hands up and gripped his hips. "There is something I would like you to do for me, before you go, you know you are the only man for me, and you know how much I want you, especially when you are angry. That strutting fool will never take your place."

As Cartimandua's pressing on the tops of his legs became more urgent, Vellocatus thrust his doubts and anger away, and standing, lifted Cartimandua to her feet. She smiled and looked at him from under darkened eyelashes, then lingeringly put her hand between his legs. Vellocatus knew his duty and quickly led his Queen to her private chambers. He slowly pulled her dress from her shoulders, letting it slip to the ground and pushed her down on the bed. As she lay there watching him undress, she briefly thought how easy it was to manipulate men, as he leaned over and kissed her violently. As she eagerly responded, Vellocatus raised his head: "I'll teach you who is running this place," he said in quick gasps. "You might be the queen, but I am the power."

Her eyes opened wide. "Of course you are...and always will be. Now be quick, I have a lot to do today."

Aeron had his doubts but decided to keep them to himself. A banquet was the ideal place for an ambush, he thought, when the whole band would be together, feasting and drinking, with their guard down. And what was this errand that Vellocatus was running? The new Roman garrison was still building the first earthwork at Eboracum, but they could soon put their shovels down and pick up spears, and it was not much more than a day's ride away.

He put these worrying thoughts to one side as a servant bowed to Caratacus and offered to show them to their quarters. They followed the servant, leading their horses through the narrow streets. The few tribespeople they encountered flattened themselves against the walls as they passed. Strangers were a source of danger.

Caratacus was in high spirits and eagerly anticipating the evening's entertainment. Even the sight of their sleeping quarters above a stable failed to curb his enthusiasm. There was straw to sleep on and the roof at least looked watertight. "We've had worse," he told his men, "It won't be for long, with a bit of luck we will be riding south to raise the Catuvellauni very soon."

I'll believe that when it happens, thought Aeron.

"What a pity I had to abandon my finery," mused Caratacus. "Still never mind, I shall win Cartimandua over with my wit and charm, and by the end of the evening she'll be desperate to get my clothes off me." He turned to Aeron. "Don't be surprised if I don't return with you tonight; I fancy the Queen has somewhere much nicer for me to sleep tonight. If I get any sleep, that is."

All Aeron could do was smile weakly. "Good luck, lord," he managed.

"Believe you me, Aeron, luck doesn't come into it. Everything about her said she was dying for me to jump her. I don't know how she managed to restrain herself, but I shall make a show of gallantry and, for form's sake, treat her like a real lady rather than the wanton hussy I believe her to be."

And with that confident opinion on the morals of the Queen of the Brigantes, Caratacus went off in search of ale.

CHAPTER XXI

Caratacus stood preening with brushed hair and beard and thinking to himself he was every woman's dream. He had managed to scrape off most of the mud his clothes had gathered in the long ride to Brigantum and he told himself that one day soon he would be wearing fine clothes befitting his position in life. He spun round: "How do I look?" he demanded.

There was a general round of applause from his men, who had also tried to make an effort to look presentable in front of Queen Cartimandua. They were all conscious that they still looked like what they actually were, a band of desperadoes.

"Yes, well," said Caratacus, "afraid they'll have to take us as we are. Come on then, let's see what Brigantian food is like."

The Queen's lodge had been transformed in their honour. The walls were hung with drapes and long tables set up, loaded with candles dispelling the gloom of the afternoon.

As they entered, the room went silent as Queen Cartimandua rose from her couch and came forward to welcome them. She was richly dressed in a long multi-coloured gown, pinned at one shoulder with a heavy silver brooch. The other shoulder was bare, accentuating her size and strength. She appraised Caratacus frankly and welcomed him by grasping his forearm. As she moved closer to him, he could see she was about the same height as him and, despite himself, was impressed with her physique.

"Welcome to you and your men. My people here are looking forward to talking to you all and hearing about your adventures," she said in that low, smoky voice. Then, looking past Caratacus, but still holding his arm: "Gentlemen, please sit anywhere you like, but spread yourselves out. We don't get many strangers here."

The warriors whispered together, they had just realised there were far more women than men at the tables. Aeron nudged the man next to him, "Come on then, let's get stuck in," and boldly walked towards two young ladies who obligingly moved aside so he could sit between them. At this the others were eager to do the same and made a dash to find a seat.

Cartimandua smiled at the scramble as the warriors found places. She turned again to Caratacus. "You will sit with me so we can continue our conversation." She led him to her couch where servants had placed a table with horn beakers and intricately patterned plates. She noticed him looking at the plates and smiled. "Not everything the Romans bring us is bad. They have some quite good ideas. I am having a bath-house built behind the lodge. I will show it to you tomorrow, and who knows - if you are here long enough, we may be able to share the first bath together."

Caratacus swallowed. "I would like that very much," he managed.

She motioned him to his seat, still with a secret smile on her face.

"Why so many women here - are your men all away?" asked Caratacus.

"Not really," replied Cartimandua. "I especially asked these young ladies to attend because I felt sure your warriors would appreciate some female companionship."

Caratacus was impressed. "If the food and drink are up to the standards of hospitality we have seen so far, this will be a night to remember."

"That it will, that it will," murmured Cartimandua.

The evening passed in an increasingly noisy and abandoned slide into drunken revelry. Caratacus was dimly aware that, what with the ale he had consumed that afternoon and what he was drinking at the table, he was taking far more on board than he'd intended. Got to keep my wits about me, he kept saying to himself as he took another slurp of ale.

His men were no better; they attacked the food and drink with gusto, then turned to their young lady escorts who also seemed in the mood for sport. Aeron was the first to leave the hall with a young lady on his arm, generating raucous comments from the others. Cartimandua watched the couple leave by the main door, then gestured to one of her guards, pulling him down by his jerkin so she could whisper in his ear.

"I did not want any of our guests to leave before the final toast," she whispered. "Go and stand by the door and make sure nobody else leaves before I am ready."

The guard straightened and nodded impassively then walked round the room to the door and stood with his back to it, arms folded.

Cartimandua watched the drunken proceedings still with that amused expression on her face. She only took small sips from her beaker but was sure to keep Caratacus topped up. Inevitably one of the other warriors eventually stood, and tried to make his female companion stand with him. Clearly he wanted to follow Aeron's lead. The girl looked up the table and caught Cartimandua's eye who slowly shook her head, discreetly raised one hand and used her fingers to indicate 'stay seated'.

The girl smiled up at the warrior and patted the seat he had vacated. He obviously wanted to follow Aeron but the girl put on an imploring face, then reached up to whisper in his ear. He smiled and looked round with a proud smirk.

The promise of what was to come soon was better than a quick fumble in the wet grass now, thought Cartimandua with satisfaction. She turned back to Caratacus to give him her full attention, but was disappointed to see that by now he had clearly taken too much ale on board, and was swaying slightly with a glazed look in his eye. She smiled at him, then breathed in his ear: "Since you arrived at my village, I have wanted to rip your clothes off and jump on you. If you drink too much I think I will have to wait till the morning to take my pleasure with you."

Caratacus started, and focussed blearily on her. "Don't you worry about me, I've been drunker than this and still acquitted myself handsomely. I can assure you, my lady, that drunk or sober I always do my duty." With that Caratacus sat back with a triumphant smile. Then pulled himself to his feet and raised his beaker. "A toast to your Queen," he roared. "And may she enjoy the pleasure of the future King of Britannia."

The diners all cheered enthusiastically and drank their toast, with several ribald comments about Caratacus's abilities.

Caratacus flopped back down, not really sure he had said the right thing, but looking across at Cartimandua saw she still had that enigmatic smile on her face.

Must have got away with it, he thought.

When the food and most of the debris on the tables were finally cleared away, at the Queen's signal a steward stepped forward and rapped three times on the wooden floor with his stave. In a loud voice he bellowed: "Pray silence for our sovereign lady, Queen Cartimandua."

At this, sweating servants bustled into the room bearing fresh horn beakers, which were passed to everyone in the room. When everyone had the new drink in front of them, Cartimandua stood and looked imperiously round at the gathering. She nodded at a few of the women, who then put a hand on the arm of the warrior guests who wanted to try the new drink straight away.

"We shall drink to the good fortune of the Brigantes and also of the Catuvellauni, and especially of Caratacus and his band, who have such an exciting proposal for us. The drink before you is a special honey mead which is only drunk to celebrate great occasions, so I would ask you to stand and drink with me to our prosperity and freedom."

With a great rustle, and with some help from the servants, everyone finally stood. One of the warriors blearily looked at the mead beaker in his hand and then at the beaker held by the charming girl who had laughed at all his jokes and coyly hinted at greater pleasure to come and observed, "My beaker has a cross on it and I can't see one on yours - why's that?"

The girl simpered: "That's simple, lord. You men are used to much stronger drink than we girls, so ours are watered down."

The warrior focussed on this and nodded sagely. "Of course, that would be it."

At the top of the table Cartimandua raised her beaker, the signal for everyone to do the same.

"Brigantes and Catuvellauni," she shouted and raised her beaker to her lips, taking a long draught.

The room repeated the toast and raised their beakers for a long drink.

As everyone slumped back in their seats, Caratacus once again raised his beaker in appreciation.

"Madam, your toast is well made. May I begin to hope that as well as an alliance between our two great tribes, I could hope for a more intimate alliance between us two?"

"Nothing would give me greater pleasure," she replied, looking at him with heavily lidded eyes.

He leaned in towards her and put his hand on her knee. She looked down at the hand and smiled. Then a pink tongue came out and licked her lips as she put her hand on his. "Why don't we make ourselves scarce for a while, no one will notice we are gone."

Caratacus looked at her, his eyes bright. I knew she would fall for me, he thought exultantly.

"Lead on, my dear, I'm right behind you."

She smiled again and stood, gathering her dress around her, before heading for a doorway behind them. Caratacus hastily stood and followed the queen, hurrying to catch up. She went through the door and down a corridor as he almost trotted behind. At another door with a curtain of a cloth of different colours, she paused and swept the curtain aside. Caratacus looked into the room, lit by candles set into the walls, and his eyes widened when he saw a large bed in the centre of the room, covered in furs.

"That bed is certainly fit for a queen," he said appreciatively as he groped for a handful of buttock.

Again, the Queen smiled and led him to the bed, turning him and pushing him down as he sat on the edge. She reached up to the brooch at her shoulder and unclasped it, freeing her long gown, which slipped down her body to the floor. She was completely naked. Caratacus smiled in anticipation.

"If I remember nothing else, I shall remember this moment," he gasped, leaning over for her.

He tried to look her in the face but found he couldn't focus. Too much to drink, he thought. Hope it doesn't affect my performance. He sat back and tried to concentrate. The room seemed to be getting dimmer. He wiped his sweating brow and blinked to try and see properly. Cartimandua was looking at him with interest, observing every move. He tried again and she moved nearer.

"Why don't you take those clothes off?" she asked, "I can't wait to see the future King of Britannia in all his glory."

By the gods, I have to give her a proper seeing to, thought Caratacus feverishly. The honour of the tribe is at stake. Besides, I want her to come back begging for more. Hastily he bent down and tried to pull off one of his boots but eventually gave up and lay back on the bed. He realised he was sweating. Must be the excitement, he thought.

Cartimandua made a concerned ooh-like noise, then reached down and pulled off his boots. She knelt on the bed, and unstrapped his wide belt, then hauled down his wool trousers. He could only lie there watching this magnificent woman tearing his clothes off. By now, his tunic had been removed and apart from a braided gold chain around his neck he was completely naked. He looked up and tried to focus on Cartimandua, who seemed to be somewhat blurred in the gloom of the candlelight.

She was still smiling as her hands caressed his body, then found his uninterested member.

Caratacus was aware of her taking it tenderly in her hands, but could do nothing to make it stand up proud. He felt in turn nauseous, then dizzy, and couldn't clear his brain. Then it hit him: he'd been drugged. The bitch had slipped something into that mead. No wonder the sweet taste of honey was so strong - it was used to hide the smell of whatever concoction had been added to it.

As Cartimandua busily pumped at Caratacus's limp member, she sighed and thought, the servants have overdone the poison again. He's not going to be any use to me tonight.

Regretfully she dropped the hold she had on him and stepped off the bed, reaching down to replace her gown. Once dressed she looked out into the corridor and shouted for her guards

Dimly as Caratacus fought to stay conscious, he was aware of a crashing sound as he involuntarily jerked and fell onto the stone-flagged floor.

He was aware that Cartimandua was looking down at him as his eyes opened and closed.

"You bitch, you've drugged me! I hope you get the death you deserve."

She shrugged then smiled down at him. "On the contrary, I fancy it's you who will get what you deserve, while I also will get what I deserve as Queen of Brigantia. Why would I want more, you stupid conceited man? Did you really think I would support your ridiculous plan? Did you think I couldn't see that as soon as I raised a Brigantian army, you would have had me killed?"

Caratacus struggled to protest but his world was slipping away.

"The Romans will pay handsomely for ten young, fit and healthy slaves and will pay a fortune for the great Caratacus." She smiled. "I wouldn't have minded finding out if you are as virile as you think you are. But never mind, I'll get over it."

She signalled to the guards waiting outside the bed-chamber, trying not to take an interest in what was going on inside. "Take him away and throw him in one of the cages. You can take his clothes as well. I want him alive."

She stood back as the guards hurried into the room and grabbed the unconscious Caratacus under the arms and by the ankles and unceremoniously dragged him out into the corridor. As they passed through the banqueting hall, the guards looked at each other and tutted at the scene of carnage.

The would-be king's bodyguards had, one by one, either slumped head first onto the table or fallen sideways from their chairs, crashing to the floor. Their female companions gossiped and laughed at the way they had dealt with so many big strong men, just by getting them into such a state of desire and lust that they completely forgot about the possibility they were being tricked.

Caratacus opened his eyes wide, tried to shake his head, then slumped unconscious. As his body finally shut down, his last thought was: What a pity, I bet she would have been a great ride.

Outside, on a grassy bank still in sight of the council chamber, Aeron had his hands underneath the long gown of his new and seemingly willing partner. Suddenly he heard a commotion coming from the direction of the chamber. He looked round quickly as the girl moaned and pulled at him impatiently. He shrugged her off and stood up, anxiously wondering what was going on. Startled, it dawned on him: It's an ambush - we've been duped after all.

He reached for the girl and grabbed her by her long hair, twisting the strands tightly, forcing her to kneel. Her eyes screwed tight shut with the pain as he relentlessly twisted the bunch of hair. "Were you in on this, bitch?" he demanded.

She tried to shake her head, then squealed in fright at the force of a stinging slap to the side of her face. "It was the Queen's orders," she said finally, through her tears. "We had to entertain you and distract you, then make sure you drank the mixture – it was only to put you to sleep."

Aeron suddenly felt afraid. "Have I taken the potion?" he asked slowly.

"No, no," she replied tearfully. "We left too soon. It was to be delivered for a special toast."

The short feeling of relief soon vanished as Aeron realised he was still in a precarious position. The Brigantians had seen him leave with the girl and would soon be looking for him. He had to escape.

He flogged his brain trying to think what to do, and in his anxious state failed to notice the girl beneath him stealthily reaching down to a concealed opening at the hip of her skirt. She closed her fingers on a short dagger, strapped to her leg, while staring at the big warrior. She fumbled with the hilt, then firmed her grip, stealthily drawing it from its hiding place.

Aeron looked down but was too late to stop her plunging the knife into his side. She was trying to pull it out to stab him again, when through the sudden, shocking pain, he grabbed her hand and wrenched the blade from his body. He gasped and convulsed as the pain hit him but twisted her hand, forcing her to let go of the knife. Quickly he found the blade glinting in the long grass as the girl tried to crawl backwards away from him.

He watched grimly as she desperately tried to pull herself away, then with one hand attempting to stem the blood pulsing out of his side, he changed his grip on the knife, took two steps forward and plunged the blade into her neck, twisting it for maximum effect, then stepped back as she sagged and died.

I'm done here, was his frantic thought as he dropped the knife and stumbled back to the stable. His side was in agony and each step seemed to tear at his insides. He rolled the long tail of his shirt into a pad and tried to keep it over the wound, but it was still seeping blood. He looked round carefully when he arrived at the stable; there didn't seem to be anyone there yet, but he knew that would change very soon. It would be the first place they would look. He had to get his horse saddled and ride hard. What he would do then, he had no idea. Survival instinct took over and all he could think of was to get away.

He leaned against the stone wall and tried to summon the strength to find his horse.

He never saw or heard the two women who crept up behind him until one shrieked out a series of profanities. He looked round blearily and gulped as he registered that one was raising a big stone above her head. He tried to hold out his hand in supplication but dropped it again as the woman stepped towards him, bringing the stone down in a crushing blow to the side of his face.

He fell, mortally wounded, and the woman gave a grunt of triumph. She picked up the stone again and smiled as she once again tried to raise it above her head. She struggled, but had to accept shoulder height was good enough. She grunted again and brought the stone smashing down on his forehead.

As his life left him, Aeron could only regret his less than proud death unbefitting of a warrior.

CHAPTER XXII

When Caratacus came to, he had no idea where he was or what had happened. He was in pitch-blackness, lying on a cold stone floor. His head thumped as a big drum banged away just behind his eyes. He raised a hand to his forehead and groaned as he propped himself up on one elbow. He tried to move but couldn't, something was holding his legs. He reached down with nervous fingers, tentatively feeling, till he found cold iron, shackling his ankles. He lay back, trying to digest what was happening through the pulsing pain in his brain.

Through the waves of nausea he remembered his last sight of Cartimandua, magnificently naked, hands on hips and a contemptuous sneer on her face, standing over him just before he collapsed. Then chaos in the banqueting hall as his warriors fell victim to the drugged mead, one by one. No wonder that snivelling bastard Vellocatus was absent. No doubt he'd been sent off to warn the garrison at Eboracum.

He supposed he was in some kind of dungeon, certainly underground, given the cold and damp. He wondered what would happen next. Would they kill him, probably ransom him? What had happened to his men - were they all dead? Then he remembered Cartimandua revealing that all ten were captured. What happened to the eleventh? Was he even now galloping south to get help from the Catuvellauni? Probably pointless, he thought dejectedly.

He lay back on the cold hard floor and decided his life was over, or at least it would be soon. That cold-hearted bitch

Cartimandua was going to sell him to the Romans, of that he was sure. It was just a matter of time before they arrived. Or maybe she was going to put him on display like a performing dog, to show how clever she was.

His thumping headache did not help his abject depression as he lay and shivered, trying not to think of his fate and all his grand plans now utterly ruined.

In a complete contrast, Lenc and Brianna led their small band along a winding path high in the clean air of the windswept mountains above the town. The view from the higher ground was spectacular, and fell away to a patchwork of forest and green meadow. Brianna pointed towards the middle distance where Lenc could see the smoke from a town's fires. "Brigantum," she confirmed. Lenc convinced himself he could see the sea in the far distance.

The rescued Brigantian girl was taking them on a higher path to avoid Rigodunum. For some reason it seemed best, thought Lenc to by-pass the town completely, rather than allow loose tongues to flap about their quest. He looked with interest at their destination, lying quietly peaceful in the morning sun.

"Should get there by midday," Brianna suggested. "Cartimandua has her lodge in the centre of town, next to the river. This time I think it might be best if I go in by myself. There will be people there I know, and I should be able to find out what's happening for you."

Lenc agreed, letting the local girl spy out the lie of the land was a sound idea. After all their adventures he trusted her implicitly. "We'll find a place to hole up while you are gone, then we can decide what we are going to do. Can you think of somewhere?"

Brianna nodded. "If we follow the river through the town, downstream is a copper works, run by Marcus, an old friend of my husband's. He will shelter us all and, more importantly, keep his mouth shut. He may even know something of what's going on."

They arrived at the copper works by late afternoon. Brianna went forward, and after a joyous welcome from her late husband's friend, was directed to a series of caves cut into the hill above the river, where malachite, the raw material for making copper was mined. "If you stay near the entrances, it won't be damp, but it'll keep the rain off and probably ensure you some privacy," said Marcus.

Lenc was introduced to Marcus simply as a Gaul who had been travelling when he fell in with the Ordovicians and Veldicca, before rescuing the Brigantian women. Marcus seemed to accept the story, probably because Brianna was fulsome in her praise for her rescuers.

"Have you seen anything of a tall blond man with a party of Catuvellauni warriors?" Lenc asked.

Marcus looked quizzically at him. "You mean Caratacus? Our Queen, Cartimandua has him in chains in her dungeon."

Lenc was thunderstruck. He had been half expecting this news but even so, it was still a bombshell. "When did this happen?"

"In the last day or so," replied Marcus. "They had only just arrived in Brigantum, when Cartimandua proclaimed that there would be a banquet for him and his men. They all got pissed, then they were given a powerful potion that knocked them all out till they woke up the next day in our dungeon. One of the warriors took a girl outside and unfortunately missed the potion; when he realised they had been duped, he killed the girl, then had his brains bashed out when the women caught him."

What does this all mean? thought Lenc feverishly. Obviously Cartimandua had not fallen under Caratacus's spell, which was surely a good thing. Almost certainly she must have sent a message to the garrison at Eboracum that she had Rome's most wanted man under lock and key. Just as certainly she would no doubt demand quite a ransom for him.

That moved his train of thought on a bit. By the gods, if the legion finds me here I'll be arrested as a deserter, he thought.

Best get to see Cartimandua as soon as possible, find out what she proposes and then work out what to do about it.

As the day was lengthening, Lenc decided that there was nothing he could usefully do until the morning and decided he would walk upstream and find a place for a splash to get rid of some of the mud from his body and clothes. Summer was drawing to a close, but the weather was still pleasant enough even in the high country.

Before long he found a secluded strip of sand hollowed out by the river, and pretty much surrounded by bushes. He stripped off and waded into the icy water and, at waist depth, took a quick breath and belly-flopped in over his head. The water was cold but energising as he swam as hard as possible against the surge of the river. He made little headway against the current and eventually allowed himself to be carried back to where he had dropped his clothes. He pulled them into the water and, one garment after another, pummelled them and rubbed sand into them, then after rinsing them thoroughly, hung them over a bush to dry off a bit before he put them back on.

This was the first moment of peace in a long time, he reflected. Wonder what the next horror is going to be. Suddenly there was a scratching sound from a nearby bush. By the gods, he thought, that was quick. He stood uncertainly, mentally cursing that not only was he stark naked but his sword was some steps away, hanging over a fallen tree and still in its scabbard. As he dived for his weapon, a figure stepped out from behind the bush.

"Agrippa," exclaimed Lenc in relief. "Creeping up on people as usual. Where in Hades did you spring from?"

Agrippa showed his pleasure at the meeting and hurried forward to grasp Lenc's arm. "We've been trailing you and Caratacus for a few days," he said, "and I am so glad we have caught up with you. Tell me everything."

Agrippa threw a cloak to Lenc which he gratefully pulled around his shoulders and sat on the fallen tree. Smiling, Agrippa tossed him a leather flask containing a cool, tangy cider. Lenc showed his appreciation with a long, thirsty pull.

Looking back, his hasty departure from the battlefield seemed like an age away, so much had happened since. He galloped through the events of the pursuit; his meeting with the Ordovicians who promised to kill him once Caratacus was dealt with, the mountain path covered in snow, finding the Druids on Mona, finding Veldicca, and no, she hasn't forgiven me, he added. Then the death of the priest, fending off an ambush from Caratacus's men, and his pursuit of them to Brigantum.

"And we found out when we got here a short time ago, that Caratacus and his men are all in chains in Cartimandua's dungeon."

"Knowing the lady's reputation, I half expected that," conceded Agrippa. "The question is, what do we do now? No doubt she has sent a messenger to Eboracum and will be looking forward to a very big reward. Whatever happens, the cunning bugger must never slip through our fingers again."

"Agreed," replied Lenc. "I thought I would try and get an audience with the Queen tomorrow, if only to confirm her plans. I suppose she is quite capable of going to the Catuvellauni to try and screw a ransom out of them for their errant son, but they won't be able to pay as much as Rome, that's for sure." Lenc stared down at his cider for a second then looked up at Agrippa. "This has given me a personal problem, which I hope you can help me with. You recall I told you that the four Ordovicians agreed to accompany me to kill Caratacus, then they would kill me? With Caratacus firmly shackled until he is taken to Rome, where he will undoubtedly meet his fate, they can only think he is as good as dead. That leaves them free to carry on with the second part of their oath, which is to kill me before heading back to their tribe.

"I could just stay here with you in safety but I also have made two promises. The first to kill Caratacus, and the second to get Veldicca back to her people. I know that the Ordovice could escort her back to their border with the Silures, but it is still my responsibility. Truth of the matter is that there is a faint chance she still has feelings for me, but I fear the feelings for her tribe are stronger. She certainly wants to go back; besides, as a deserter, I have nowhere else to go," he finished bitterly.

Agrippa nodded and looked sympathetic. "Maybe I do have one grain of comfort for you. After you left the battlefield, I had a long conversation with our commander, Quintus Equitius and among other things, your name was mentioned.

"I told the legate that under my orders you set off in pursuit of Caratacus and were tracking him and his gang across the mountains. As far as he is concerned, you are still on the payroll."

This took a bit of digesting by Lenc. It was welcome news, but didn't really help his present predicament. He had to go back to Veldicca, which meant facing Alun and his men, and odds of four to one did seem a bit suicidal.

"The back pay will be welcome," conceded Lenc.

Agrippa thought for a moment. "I have men watching the Eboracum road, waiting for the return of the messenger, or a patrol out of the fort to pick up Caratacus, but I bet the Queen won't release him into their custody till she has seen a big box of gold aurei delivered to her door." He paused to think over the problem. "This could take a bit of time," he said eventually. "Eboracum is little more than a marching camp at the moment, so there will only be as much gold as they need to get by. If Cartimandua holds out for more money than the commandant at Eboracum feels he can give, or even has, the decision may well be passed up to Camulodunum or maybe even all the way back to Rome. In which case we could be waiting here forever, twiddling our fingers, and of course during that time Caratacus could get help and break out."

Agrippa thought again for a second, then leaned forward. "Here's what we'll do. I'll head back and meet my scouts on the Eboracum road; I wouldn't mind intercepting whoever will be sent to verify that the Queen has Caratacus. You go for your audience with Cartimandua, then you can report in to our camp in a copse of oaks further along the riverbank. You won't see us, but we'll be watching for you. "Why don't you take Veldicca? She is a princess after all, and it could help you to get in to the Queen."

Lenc could see the sense in that, although he wasn't sure whether Veldicca would go along with it.

"I can ask her," he agreed dubiously.

In fact, Veldicca was enthusiastic when the proposal was put to her. "What a pity I only have these travelling rags to wear. I'll see if Brianna has any bright ideas."

The next morning Lenc waited with the horses for Veldicca to arrive. He had brushed down and oiled their saddles, even scraped the mud off their hooves. The horses didn't look too bad, but he was aware he still looked scruffy. At least he was clean, he thought.

When Veldicca finally put in an appearance, Lenc could only gape. She had a gold-coloured braid through her hair and wore a shimmering green gown, tied at the waist with an ornate silver belt. Over that was her brushed riding cloak.

"Your mouth is hanging open - are you catching flies?" Lenc hurriedly closed his mouth at the rebuke. He was about to make an equally tart reply when he saw she had an impish grin on her face.

He gave a deep bow. "Apologies my princess, I had forgotten just how you looked as royalty rather than a warrior. I know which I prefer."

He held her horse steady as she climbed up and arranged her skirts either side of the saddle, then, after quickly mounting himself, led her up the track from the river to the road into town.

Into the lion's den, he thought.

A sentry watched them from the top of the outer wall, but one unarmed man and a woman seemed to pose no threat and let them pass.

People stared at the strangers curiously as they threaded their way through the streets of the town to the Queen's lodge. On their horses, they were higher than the walls of the houses, which pressed in on either side. There was hardly room for those on foot to flatten themselves in against the walls, as the two horses ambled by in single file.

The Queen's lodge at least had the benefit of having some space around it and a small square at the front. A stream ran round one side of the stone wall. Two guards with spears stood at the entrance, both sporting beards, long droopy moustaches and metal caps over their long hair. Their uniform was a long wool shirt over wool trousers, tethered with straps. They stepped forward, with their spears at the ready.

"Who comes here, what is your business?" one demanded.

The two riders checked their horses. In his haughtiest voice Lenc responded: "This is the Princess Veldicca of the Silures tribe, who wishes to speak to Queen Cartimandua."

"What about?" came the surly response.

"That is between the princess and your queen, and if you don't go and tell her we are here, I shall ride over you as I ride into her lodge. Now do as you're told."

This was not how a queen's lodge guard was usually addressed, especially by an itinerant who looked as if he had been pulled through a bramble bush backwards. He chewed his lower lip nervously, then telling his comrade to keep an eye on the riders, he went into the lodge.

Veldicca and Lenc dismounted. "So far so good," he whispered. They tied their horses to a rail and affected disinterest, staring into the middle distance as they waited for something to happen. Which it did, almost immediately.

Lenc had been watching some children play in the square and turned when he heard a bustling commotion behind him. There was unmistakably Queen Cartimandua, arms outstretched as she bore down on Veldicca like an unstoppable whirlwind. Her hair was loose and flying and she wore a long dress of intricate coloured patterns, set off by gold bracelets and a gold tiara inset with coloured stones.

Lenc bowed from the waist up as the Queen embraced the princess, who was quite startled at being swept into the bosom of the bigger lady.

"Apologies, Princess, I didn't know you were coming or I would have had a welcoming party greet you. But I am so pleased you are visiting my humble home. Please come in and tell me why you are here. I'm bursting to know."

Cartimandua still held onto Veldicca firmly as the two went into the lodge, dutifully followed by Lenc.

"And who are you, young man?" demanded Cartimandua appraisingly, once the two women were seated with several large dogs at the open fire. Lenc did not know whether he should sit with them, so thought it best to remain standing.

He bowed from the neck up and answered stiffly, "I am Immunis Lenculus of Alesia, of the Twentieth Valeria Victrix and I have been chasing Caratacus and his band, since my legion defeated him and he ran from the field. The princess here saw her father killed by the legion in that battle, and then her betrothed murdered by Caratacus, before she was taken prisoner and forced to ride north away from her tribe. She was set free by the Arch Druid on the Isle of Mona and we have been tracking Caratacus ever since."

Cartimandua looked carefully at Lenc. "I presume you know I have him under lock and key?"

"I do, lady. I was told this only yesterday. In normal circumstances, the princess would have made a courtesy call on you, but not if you were hosting Caratacus."

"If I had been hosting him and his band, what would you have done?"

"It would have been an abuse of your hospitality to have harmed Caratacus while under your patronage, so we would have waited till he left Brigantum and only then would we have taken him."

Cartimandua seemed amused as she questioned Lenc. "You know I intend to hand him and his men over to the Romans? I am awaiting an envoy from Eboracum any time now."

"Both the princess and I would feel great satisfaction in personally killing Caratacus, but as long as he stays in legion custody until you hand him over, I will be content. He may have to travel to Rome in chains, but will assuredly end up on a cross."

"That's between the Senate and their gods," replied Cartimandua. "As long as I get paid handsomely and further cement my friendship with Rome, I will be happy."

At this, Lenc felt obliged to say something. "May I ask, lady, where are you keeping your prisoners - I hope they are secure?"

"Oh yes, well guarded." Cartimandua looked at him with a proud grin. "Would you like to see them?"

Lenc hadn't been prepared for this; he started and then said quickly, "Yes, please."

Cartimandua nodded and clapped her hands; almost immediately a female servant bustled in from a side door.

"Take these two guests to the guard commander. They wish to see the prisoners; then escort them back here - I don't want them locked up as well." She was the only one to laugh at her joke.

Lenc and Veldicca followed the young servant girl back out into the sunshine to another roundhouse, which appeared to serve as the centre of all the realm's military operations. She asked for the guard commander and, when he appeared, told him of Cartimandua's request.

The guard commander, a rangy, muscled man with a drooping moustache and shaved head, called for his sword, then indicated with a twitch of his head for the two visitors to follow him as he buckled his weapon round his waist.

"Do you know the prisoner?" he enquired as they walked.

Lenc replied that, yes, they were acquainted.

The commander grunted. "He's got a very high opinion of

himself. Don't know how long that'll last in our dungeon, only seeing daylight for one hour a day."

Veldicca shot him a warning glance as Lenc said happily, "I always found him to be an optimistic sort; perhaps he thinks this ignominy will come to an end soon."

"It will soon enough when the Romans crucify him," grunted the commander.

By now they had circled the military roundhouse and were confronted by a stone wall protecting a round tower. A sentry opened the gate for the guard commander and saluted as he led Lenc and Veldicca past the heavy door. They paused in an empty, dusty courtyard. "This is where the prisoners get their short period of daylight," grunted the commander. Lenc noted there were no windows on the ground floor of the tower, but there were arrow slits at intervals up the building. Facing them was a heavily armoured door, firmly shut. He estimated four floors before the tower opened out to a ramparted flat roof from where archers could easily shoot over the stone wall. The commander banged hard on the iron-bound door. A muffled voice shouted a question from within and the commander shouted back with a password. Slowly the door creaked open and a face, with a metal cap on top, peered out. He snapped to attention as his commander pushed past him: "I am taking these two people to see our special prisoner." He said brusquely. "It's at the request of Queen Cartimandua."

The guard merely nodded and stood back for the visitors to enter. The round room was bare of decoration and seemed to be used for storage, probably of supplies of food and weaponry in case of a siege. Couldn't last long though, thought Lenc.

On the other side of the round room, through the gloom, Lenc could just pick out a straight wall with a door at either end. The guard commander saw him looking round in the sparse light provided by rush torches set into the walls. "That door is to the upper floors, while this one leads downstairs which is where we are going." He snapped back two large bolts in the right-hand door.

"What do you use the levels above for?" asked Lenc.

The guard commander hesitated. "I suppose there is no harm in telling you; we have quartered here, the brothers of Venutius and their families. They are hostages to keep Venutius docile. He would dearly like to attack us and overthrow the Queen, but knows he will lose his family in the process."

All they could see from the ground floor were the stairs to a cellar tunnel, which turned on itself and followed the foundations of the tower down into the ground. The guard commander lifted one of the rush torches and confidently went down the steps. Lenc looked at Veldicca and shrugged, and followed behind. He could feel Veldicca holding the back of his wool tunic as they carefully felt their way down the uneven steps. At the bottom, the guard commander was standing in front of yet another wooden door about six paces into the tunnel. A voice from inside demanded identification and the commander bellowed back, "Guard Captain Macro and visitors."

Lenc found he could stand upright but noticed a definite change of temperature as they stepped into the gloom of the tunnel. The guard on the gate slammed it shut, blocking out any daylight that had penetrated so far. He handed the commander a guttering tallow lamp, one of three in wall brackets.

Macro gave his torch to Lenc then set off along the tunnel, holding his new lamp up high. Lenc could feel that they were still going downhill. The walls were lined with close-fitting rock, the floor was hammered mud, and the wooden roof supported by rough props. Lenc shuddered; it was a dank and sinister place.

They slowly filed onwards into the dark and were stopped by another door, which again Macro the guard captain banged. When he identified himself, this time a small shutter opened in the door and a pair of eyes peered out.

"Who are these people with you?" the disembodied voice demanded.

"They are guests of our queen who wish to meet her prisoner."

Slowly the big door was opened to a large chamber. The room had lamps around the wall, which gave meagre light to what Lenc thought was a horrifying sight. He had seen how slaves were penned in his various postings with the legion but was not prepared for this cruelty. In one corner was a wooden hut, which was obviously for the gaolers, but the prisoners were all kept in individual iron cages just big enough for them to stand and lie down. The floor was made of large cobblestones, which the cages were set into. Lenc noticed a channel cut in the stones, from all the cells which met at a round hole in the middle of the chamber.

Macro looked at Lenc and guessed his unasked question. "Their food and water goes through a gap in the door; they are fed once a day and can fill their water containers when they are allowed out for an hour. During that time the cells are swilled out and their shit goes down that hole and out to the river. If they want to clean themselves with their water, that's up to them," he said with indifference.

"This is Caratacus on the end."

Lenc looked towards the line of cells, dimly making out that each one contained a body. An occasional stirring showed they were still alive, but the tattered and dejected bodies showed no interest in the visitors, just lay there in their own filth. Looks like the would-be king's bodyguard survived as well, he thought.

At the end of the line, Lenc saw a figure, dressed in rags with his head on his chest, sitting on the dank cobbles, leaning back against the wall.

He looked up as he saw his visitors approaching, his hair filthy, his clothes in tatters, and barefoot. At first, he showed no sign of recognising the man and woman in front of him, then suddenly recognition dawned. "Well, well, you've found me. Come to gloat, have you?" The downtrodden figure who, with a different throw of the dice could be the first King of Britannia, laid his head down on his arms, resting on his knees.

Veldicca stepped forward. "No, not to gloat, just to make sure it's really you. Now that I have confirmed it, I never want to see you again." She turned and swept past Lenc and made for the door. When the guard refused to open the door until his commander said so, she swept round again and folded her arms in frustration tapping her foot.

Caratacus looked up again, eyeing Veldicca, and wondered out loud to no-one in particular: "She doesn't change much does she?"

Lenc raised his eyebrows and then asked Macro if he could get nearer to the prisoner. The guard commander nodded indifferently. Hesitantly Lenc approached the cell and its ragged inmate.

"Caratacus, I have sworn to kill you, but I am still sorry to see you in this situation. All I can tell you is that here you will stay until the negotiations between Cartimandua and the legion are complete, then you will be taken to Camulodunum, where you will be reunited with your family, then onto Rome, where your fate will be decided."

The prisoner snorted. "That's something to look forward to, I suppose."

Lenc swallowed. "I will talk to Cartimandua and ask if there's any possibility of better conditions. If you promise not to escape, perhaps she can find somewhere else to keep you and get you out of those filthy clothes. More than that I cannot do."

Caratacus looked up wearily. "For Cartimandua to get me out of my clothes was my biggest ambition," he said bitterly. "I thought once she had a piece of me, she would be jelly in my hands. Instead, she played me like a fool, the bitch."

Lenc sighed. "I can only try."

Back up in the sunshine, Lenc breathed in the clean air. He had never seen such a change in a person. He tried not to feel sorry for the man who had done so much harm, but he couldn't help it. He would try and get better conditions for Caratacus.

Back in the royal lodge, Cartimandua sat behind a table set

for three. "Come," she said, "have some food. I always think that dungeon-visiting gives the appetite an edge."

By the gods, thought Lenc.

Dutifully he and Veldicca sat down at the table, and Cartimandua motioned for wine to be poured. "The Romans tell me this wine is made in Britannia," she said, "but I'm not sure. It took me a long time to get used to wine, but now I like it. Come, try some."

Lenc held out his beaker and the servant carefully filled it, then filled Veldicca's.

"What did you think of the prisoner?" asked Cartimandua jovially. "He's not the fine nobleman he was when he first came here, I expect you agree."

"I certainly do," said Lenc tentatively. "I have to say, he is in a shocking state. When he travels to Rome, people will want to come out and see the man who very nearly toppled the Roman Empire in Britannia. I just wonder how it would look to those Britons to see the would-be saviour and scourge of the legions looking like an emaciated tramp. Wouldn't it reflect well on your kindness and sense of compassion to at least treat him honourably? After all, when he gets to Rome, he will speak before the Senate even if he is then crucified or strangled at the end of the triumphal parade. A complaint about his treatment by his fellow countrymen might not go down too well."

Cartimandua leaned back in her chair; her eyes narrowed. "What are you suggesting?" she asked slowly.

"I imagine you are looking forward to a generous reward for capturing such a dangerous man, plus a handsome amount for young and fit slaves. If the garrison commander at Eboracum has neither the authority to grant you what you feel Caratacus is worth, or even that he does not hold that amount of gold, then I fancy that the negotiations will be drawn out for quite a long time. Riders will have to take terms to and from Camulodunum, maybe even Rome. It could take many moons, and in that time, Caratacus could succumb in that damp, dark hellhole.

"I am really only thinking that if he promises not to try and escape, you could find him somewhere decent but secure to live and be fed properly. When he gets to Rome, he will be a much more impressive prisoner, which would reflect better on everyone, especially you. I am sure this would filter back to Eboracum and would almost certainly affect the way the garrison commander engages with you."

Cartimandua reflected. "You make a compelling argument, I will put it to Caratacus, and if he gives me a solemn oath, I will improve his conditions, but he will still be under guard. His men, on the other hand, will stay where they are; it will be good training for their new lives as slaves."

Lenc bowed his head in acknowledgement. He had done what he could.

Meanwhile Veldicca had recovered from her shock in the dungeon and seethed that Lenc thought that her enemy should be given better treatment.

Halfway through their meal, Lenc excused himself and left the room to find somewhere to relieve his full bladder. Veldicca took the opportunity to lean into Cartimandua and say quietly, "I do hope that you are not going to be giving that murdering swine preferential treatment, are you?"

Cartimandua smiled knowingly. "It did occur to me that he should be cleaned and fattened up. Besides I felt a touch of regret that I missed the chance of some sport when I tricked him into my bed. I still am quite taken with the idea, but I can resist the temptation." She leaned over and put her large hand on Veldicca's arm. "Fear not, he will stay where he is until I know the Romans are coming for him. Then and only then, will I have him cleaned up and presentable enough to be a gift from the Queen of Brigantia."

Veldicca was quiet for the first half of the ride back to the copper works, and Lenc wasn't saying anything because he didn't want to give her an excuse to snap at him. Then to his surprise she tentatively spoke.

"You do realise that this news about Caratacus puts you in a dangerous position?" she said quietly.

"How so?" replied a puzzled Lenc.

"When we get back, you will describe the way that Caratacus is being held, that there is no chance of escape, and he will rot in that dungeon until the legion comes for him and takes him off to Rome where he will no doubt be crucified or strangled."

"Yes, but how does that affect me?"

Veldicca threw her arms up in exasperation. "You are a spy, but I don't think you are a stupid spy. What are the Ordovicians going to think when they hear this news? Caratacus is as good as dead. What was the second part of their sworn oath?"

This had been a recurring worry, but with Agrippa's welcome intervention, Lenc felt sure they could deal with the Ordovicians. He nodded in agreement. "Of course I know what you mean; it's something I'm going to have to deal with, sooner rather than later. I know that Alun and his men will want to kill me - only then can they return to their tribe. I need to give this more thought, so I'll escort you back to near the copper works, then I will ride up to the hills, where I can work out what to say and do about the Ordovicians. If their work is done here, then so is mine, apart from getting you back to Gobannion of course, so I may just keep on riding and hope you catch up with me."

Veldicca bridled at this. "I don't need an escort; I can take care of myself. Maybe I could ask Brianna and some of her comrades to come with me; they would be as much protection as you."

Lenc smiled at this fresh outburst. "Lady, I have no doubt Brianna and her friends would guard you well, but I have sworn to deliver you back safely, if that's what you want, and my oath is as binding as an Ordovician's. Now I will take my leave of you, and will see you a bit later. If you could just say that you have spoken to Caratacus, he is alive and in the custody of Cartimandua, and I will explain everything on my return.

Better that than give the Ordovicians a chance to plot while I am away."

Veldicca could see the sense of this and nodded assent. She bit her lip, then added quietly: "Take care."

Lenc was surprised and gratified. Maybe she does still care; maybe there is hope for me yet. He smiled and touched his forehead in salute, then turned his horse onto a side trail away from the river, seemingly towards the glowering hills in the distance.

She watched him go with an uneasy sense of foreboding.

Lenc allowed his horse to pick her own way along the path, looking behind several times, and when he was sure that Veldicca was out of sight and heading for the copper works, he concentrated on finding a way to skirt their camp without being seen.

He could see the river, flowing away through the trees, so knew he was going in the right direction. Once he was sure he was past the camp, he headed back to the river and followed it at a steady pace. After about a Roman mile, he saw up ahead a copse of oaks. This must be the place, he thought. Sure enough, as he approached, a rangy-looking short-haired man stepped out onto the track. He was dressed as a local in rough-spun wool and barefoot, but Lenc could see he was fit and confident, a pathfinder for sure.

"Greetings," said the man amiably. Lenc raised his hand in salute, then slid from the saddle. The man beckoned him into the cool shade of the trees. "Keep going about forty paces, with the river to your right, till you come to the camp."

"Is Agrippa in camp?" Lenc asked anxiously. "I need to speak to him."

"He is expected back anytime soon," came the reply. "He went out to check on the lookouts on the Eboracum road and said he would be back straight away."

Lenc nodded and holding his horse's reins walked into the copse. He kept the river on his right shoulder and soon caught the tang of woodsmoke. A few more paces found him in a rough camp, with several men, cleaning and sharpening weapons, their horses close to hand. One stood as he approached.

"Lenc, isn't it?" he asked. "We were told to expect you, but I don't think Agrippa thought you would be here this soon. I expect you have been told; he has gone to check the look-outs and will be back soon. We have some local cider if that's of any interest?"

All Lenc could do was spread his arms in an expansive manner. "I haven't anything else to do, until the boss returns."

The pathfinder nodded and reached into a small stream, which ran through the camp, down to the bigger river, and fished out a pot container. He found two horn beakers and poured the cool amber liquid into them, handing one to Lenc and motioning to him to sit on a fallen tree.

"It's actually quite amazing how much time we spend just sitting and waiting," said the man companionably. "My name is Cornelius Flavius, by the way."

Lenc looked at him sharply. He was a tall, blond lad who had the look of the Praetorian Guard - the Emperor's personal bodyguard in Rome, better paid and less likely to face a barbarian horde than the rank-and-file legions. Lenc creased his brow, he couldn't actually put his finger on it, but the man exuded aristocracy, his accent like cut glass, a sure sign he was high-class, a strange thing to find in a wood in central Britannia.

Cornelius saw Lenc looking and smiled. "I expect you're wondering what I am doing here," he said. "I joined the Guard because my father thought it would stand me in good stead before I went to the Senate. I would only have to serve three years then return to civilian life having done my duty. Unfortunately, they were just a bunch of posing bullies, with nothing better to do than annoy people. The uniform impressed the girls of course, but the thought of spending three years of my life marching up and down, drinking and beating up shopkeepers who wouldn't pay protection just bored me rigid. I met Agrippa in a tavern in Rome on one of his infrequent visits, and I thought, that's the kind of soldiering for me. I begged him to let me join and eventually he gave in. Do you think I would make a good Britannic peasant?" he asked earnestly.

Lenc nearly laughed out loud. Cornelius could never pass himself off as a peasant, he was every inch an aristocrat.

Cornelius saw the look on Lenc's face, disbelief but not wanting to be rude.

"Sorry, you misunderstand," he said. "Right now, I am in camp, but when we ride out, I have to go into character, much like an actor. If the boys I'm with thought I would let them down by acting like a bath-house dandy, they wouldn't go, simple as that. I taught myself the language and can get by in half a dozen of the dialects."

Lenc smiled. "I hope I never have to see you go into character, but if I do, I shall observe with interest."

Cornelius nodded. "Who knows what's going to happen before Caratacus is executed."

Lenc sat back thoughtfully, sipping his cider. He wondered if he could be a pathfinder; there was certainly none of the bullshit to be endured in the regular legion, and Agrippa had said he was pathfinder material - perhaps he was joking. Anyway, after this was all over, he would more than likely end up on one of the Emperor's crosses.

His train of thought was broken when two men, one of them Agrippa, walked their horses into the clearing. Agrippa saw Lenc wave and raised his arm in recognition. He tethered his horse and joined Lenc and Cornelius on the fallen tree.

"You have news of Caratacus?" he asked eagerly.

"Yes, I have spoken to him," replied Lenc. "He's caged like a wild animal and, I would say, is about as pissed off as a would-be king can be. Cartimandua is looking for a handsome reward for snaring him."

"Hmm, that's a bit of a problem," replied Agrippa uneasily. "The powers that be are pleased that he is taken, but not too keen on giving a large ransom. As usual they seem to think we are miracle workers and can spirit ourselves into his dungeon and kill him, so the ransom demand disappears. Having said that, our boss, Quintus Equitius, has been appointed temporary governor, and he wants Caratacus to be paraded in front of the Senate in Rome. He is currently trying to scrape up enough gold and silver to satisfy Cartimandua; we just have to hope that he can find enough." He looked keenly at Lenc. "Tell me about your meeting with Cartimandua, how did it go? What is she like?"

Lenc collected his thoughts. "You were right about taking the princess," he conceded. "I don't know whether I would have got an audience without her, but Cartimandua fed us and then arranged for us to see her trophy, much like a prize bull."

Lenc described the dark journey to the cells in as much detail as he could, and the dispiriting conversation with Caratacus. He mentioned that he had asked Cartimandua if the prisoner could have better conditions so he would look like a fitting opponent when he arrived in Rome, rather than a mud-streaked vagrant.

"But I don't think she cares," he added. "Once she has her payment, he could die on the journey and she wouldn't shed a tear. But do you have any suggestions how I deal with my biggest concern right now, the Ordovicians?"

Agrippa sat back and pondered the problem. "Why don't you say you've made contact with us, and because the governor is not prepared to pay what Cartimandua wants, we have been ordered to get into the dungeon and kill him, thus saving a lot of gold and the nightmare of guarding him on the long road back to Rome. The other alternative is to slip into your camp this evening and kill them."

Lenc pondered. "What if I go back to the copper works, explain that Caratacus is in a dungeon and will some day, when Cartimandua and the Romans have finished arguing about money, be taken in chains to Rome. I could explain that Caratacus would become a real hero to the tribes, which is the last thing we want. Wouldn't it be better all round if I and the

Ordovicians make a plan to break into the dungeon and kill him? They could have a fatal accident on the way out - that's if they get past Cartimandua's guards. I am positive the Ordovicians would like to be able to boast that it was they who killed the madman."

Agrippa looked dubious. "It's a bit thin," he said. "Why would they want to risk it when all they have to do is wait? If they still wanted to kill him themselves, it would be a lot easier to do it on the road."

"You are forgetting these are tribal warriors," said Lenc. "Their honour is at stake; they need to do this to satisfy the oath they made. It's not a case of whether they are crazy enough to do it, but whether they feel obliged to do it. Knowing their victim is going to die anyway at the hands of the Romans isn't the point. They have sworn to do it, and do it they must."

Agrippa still looked dubious. "If you think it's possible, then go ahead, but somehow or other you must leave evidence that it was the tribes that did the deed. If they think it's us, it could start another war."

CHAPTER XXIII

The first person Lenc saw when he finally returned to their copper mine camp was Brianna, washing clothes in the river. "Where are the Ordovicians?" he asked.

Brianna looked blank. "I don't know," she said. "Although they did ask me to find out where the hostages are being held."

"And did you?" asked Lenc, although he already knew where Venutius's family was being held.

"Yes, they are in that stone tower behind the military building, some brothers of Venutius and their families."

Lenc pondered on this for a while and wondered what mischief the Ordovicians were up to now.

At that moment, the Ordovicians were riding hard along poorly defined drovers' tracks, first south-east, then due south, to avoid Eboracum and the new Roman fort, then south-west to Rigodunum. When the sun was high, they stopped by a stream to rest the horses, and Alun decided it was time to take his men into his confidence and outline the new thoughts that would not leave his mind.

"Sit here with me; I have something to discuss," he said gravely.

Madawc, Iestyn and Darren dutifully sat on the grassy bank, after filling their water skins from the clear mountain stream.

Alun looked at each of them in turn. "Something has been on my mind for some time," he said finally, "and the more I think about it, the more attractive it becomes. I have sworn to kill Caratacus because he led us badly and killed so many of our people. Because I have made this oath, you, as Ordovicians have also accepted the responsibility, and I know you all agree with that."

All three nodded. They were wondering what was coming next.

"Caratacus planned to persuade the Brigantes to rise against the Romans, join up with the Catuvellauni, and with the mountain tribes of the west sweep the Romans from power. It was a good plan and could still work, but without Caratacus. What if we suggest to Venutius that with Caratacus in chains, we can free his family from Cartimandua, removing the reason for his fear of overthrowing the mad bitch? We know where the hostages are being kept; we can free them and at the same time kill Caratacus then Cartimandua. Then we tell the Catuvellauni we killed Cartimandua after she executed Caratacus. When they hear that Venutius, who hates the Romans, is now the leader of the Brigantes they will want to rise up with the Brigantes and of course the Ordovices and Silures and fall on the Romans."

Alun sat back in triumph, his eyes shining. "It's a great plan," he said earnestly. "Try as I might, I can't see any fault with it. Whatever happens, the Ordovices will come out of this well; we might even be the kingmakers of Britannia."

His three men looked at him in joint confusion. Eventually Iestyn spoke after looking at the two others. "It's quite a plan, lord, and a bit difficult to grasp, but if you think it will work, then we will support it."

"Good man," replied Alun with satisfaction. "I expected nothing less, and believe me, with Caratacus and the Roman dead, there will be nothing to stop us leading the army of Britannia against Rome. All we have to do is persuade Venutius to take on Cartimandua."

Alun was slightly surprised that his men accepted his grand plan with such equanimity. He expected at the very least there would be some objective reason why it couldn't be done, but nothing, no discussion at all. He had told them what they were going to do and they just accepted it. Makes life easier, he thought.

After a long ride, they camped out overnight, with the prospect of a steep climb up into the Penninus for the final stage of their journey to Isurion.

The next morning, shivering and breathing out great clouds of frosty breath, they arrived at the mountain settlement. It took some time to persuade the guards that they merited an audience with Venutius, and finally it was the hint that they knew where his siblings and their families were being held in Brigantum that gained them entry.

They were escorted to the council lodge and after waiting for what seemed like an eternity, Venutius finally arrived, flanked by two bodyguards. The four Ordovicians stood as Venutius swept in, his cloak barely hiding the sword strapped to his waist.

"I am busy and have a lot to do," said an impatient Venutius. "This better be good."

Alun introduced himself and his three companions, then tumbled his words out: "Lord, I won't waste your time, we have a proposal that will not only restore your exalted place in the tribe, but will make you one of the most famous and revered men in Britannia."

Venutius settled himself on a cushioned high-backed chair and swung a booted leg over the arm. "How so?" Was all he allowed himself.

Alun stepped nearer, then hurriedly stepped back as the two bodyguards half-drew their swords.

"Lord in the last few days you have seen Caratacus, the would-be king of Britannia arrive here, quite confident he could sweep the Queen Cartimandua off her feet, to then join him in sweeping the legions from this country. "You, we - all said he was speaking out of his backside. Cartimandua was never going to give up her position with the Romans - why should she? She has it all. If she threw in her lot with Caratacus, she would never be sure when he would get rid of her. But what if we could free your family and get rid of Cartimandua? You could retake the tribe, and from what I have seen so far, there is more than enough stomach in your people to rise against Rome. Am I making sense so far?"

Venutius leaned forward, intrigued despite himself. "Do you know where my family is being held?" he asked softly.

"Yes lord," said Alun confidently, "and I am sure we can free them. If we could do that and kill Cartimandua and Caratacus would you rise with us against Rome?"

Venutius pondered hard. "What you say has merit, but I couldn't raise the tribe overnight, and Rome will almost certainly come to that mad bitch's rescue."

Alun smiled. "You misunderstand me. Obviously this is not going to happen overnight, but it can be done in stages. You have enough men already to help us overthrow Cartimandua. The legions are about to winter; they are staying close to their forts and won't come out till early spring. By then, Cartimandua will be dead, and they will be looking to a new Brigantian ruler to take her place. During that time, we can raise the other tribes. To the west the Ordovices, I can say from personal experience will be behind you. We have the Princess Veldicca of the Silures with us, and she is no lover of Rome. To the south are the Catuvellauni, who will wish to revenge their son Caratacus. He may be a self-important fool but he is of their royalty.

"The Brigantes are the biggest tribe in Britannia, so when you arm yourself for battle, why of course the country will follow you." Alun leaned forward in his intensity, his eyes blazing. "This is our chance, don't you see?"

Venutius was tempted. "You are saying that if you can free my family and kill Cartimandua, I would take the Brigantian throne with the troops I already have?"

"Exactly, lord. How can you lose?" replied Alun in a tremulous voice. "If we fail, you can say it was nothing to do with you, and you will have lost nothing, but if we win, you have everything to play for. We take it one step at a time, after Cartimandua and Caratacus are eliminated ..."

"And Vellocatus," interrupted Venutius.

"And Vellocatus," agreed an exultant Alun. Got him, he thought, but said: "Then you have time to build your army while appearing docile to the Romans. Then when they come out of their forts in the spring, to steal your animals and produce, we'll be ready for them. Strike hard and melt away - that's the way to deal with them, make them look over their shoulders wondering where the next attack is coming from. We will involve the Druids, who will spread the word around the whole country, and the Romans will see an insurrection like they have never encountered before, led by the great Venutius."

Venutius smiled, he couldn't believe this talk of conquering the Romans; that had been tried before and always failed. But to defeat Cartimandua, now that was something else. With Cartimandua dead, the Romans would have to deal with him. And then if anything came of this grandiose plan to defeat the Romans, he could say he'd supported it all along and take the glory, but if it went wrong – which he suspected it would – well, at least he would have Brigantia.

"Your plan has merit," he conceded slowly. "I will secretly raise an army big enough to defeat Cartimandua, train them and equip them properly. But I will only unleash them when she is dead. The bitch has a bodyguard of about a hundred men; they are fit and highly trained. The gods know, she's been through most of them," he added, bitterly, then continued: "The real test will be the legion's retaliation, which will be swift and merciless, unless I can persuade them that I'll be a better, more malleable vassal than she was. That will give us the breathing space for you to start raiding them, while I put on a great show of being their lapdog.

"Tell me, where does the Princess Veldicca fit in all of this? Surely it is her duty to throw in her lot with us - that would mean the whole of western Britannia, pretty much, would be in open conflict with Rome."

Alun noted the 'us' from Venutius. He is obviously with us, but at the first sign of a set-back he'll drop us like a stone.

"Normally I would agree with you," replied Alun smoothly, "but the princess has a conflict. Amazingly, despite all the wrongs that Lenc, the Roman spy, has done her, she still feels for him. I have seen her look at him and, despite her hot words in public there is still something there. When we take Cartimandua, we will also kill Caratacus. When we decided to make this journey, we made two oaths: one to kill Caratacus, and the second to kill the Roman. Up to now, and until Caratacus is dead, the Roman has been useful to us, but with Caratacus dealt with, Lenc will be eliminated. When he is dead, Veldicca will support us, of that, I am sure."

CHAPTER XXIV

Lenc and Agrippa rode together on the wide track that ran from Eboracum, the fledgling Roman fort to the south, all the way to the Caledonian border. Agrippa's suspicion that a deputation would ride from the fort to meet Cartimandua and try to get the cheapest terms for handing over Caratacus appeared to be confirmed when they met a Pathfinder scout on the road. The scout tried to catch his breath as he announced that had seen a large Roman infantry patrol from Eboracum which seemed to be heading for Brigantum.

At its head, reported the scout, were a tribal warrior - from his description, Vellocatus, the Queen's current bed-warmer - and a magnificent-looking if rather large young officer - a tribunus laticlavius judging by the narrow purple stripe just visible on his toga, beneath his glittering breast plate.

"Good," said Agrippa with satisfaction. "We will ride on at a more dignified pace and see what they have to say for themselves. Should be interesting."

The scout fell in behind them and they continued their journey, sure in the knowledge that they would eventually cross the path of the Eboracum patrol.

With the sun high in the sky, Agrippa called a halt when the scout confirmed that the patrol would be up with them very soon.

"This is as good a place as any," remarked Agrippa. "Let's dismount and water the horses and let the patrol come to us. We don't want to frighten them."

After a frugal lunch of dried meat, bread and spring water, Lenc was dozing in the sun when he first felt the vibration of horses' hooves coming through the ground. He sat up and looked round. Agrippa and the scout had noticed it too and were also feeling for their equipment. They stood just as the patrol came into sight. And sure enough, there were the warrior tribesman and the magnificent tribunus laticlavius, every inch the imperious Roman officer. There were usually five of these young gentlemen on the strength of a legion. They were political appointments and only tended to stay with the army for three years before leaving to join the Senate in Rome with the credentials of a seemingly hardened military man. The reality was that because they were only going to be in the unit for three years and then replaced by another one much the same, they were largely ignored and spent most of their time trying to find out what they should be doing. The drawback was that if their immediate superior fell in battle, they would have to very quickly step in to take command of a cohort.

Behind the tribune was a marching column of sixteen men led by a centurion, who halted the patrol by raising his vine stick when he saw the three scruffy individuals lounging by their horses. He motioned four men to run forward, up the track past the travellers in case of ambush. As they ran past the tribune, he leaned forward on his saddle pommel to peer down his large aquiline nose at the dishevelled-looking creatures in front of him. He clearly wasn't impressed.

"Good morning," said Agrippa pleasantly in Latin. This surprised the tribune who was clearly expecting the tribal warrior riding with him to have to act as interpreter.

"Who in Hades are you?" he demanded, also in Latin.

"I am the senior centurion in charge of the Pathfinder Squadron of the Twentieth Valeria Victrix, on special assignment on the orders of Legate and Commander of the Twentieth, Quintus Equitius now temporarily elevated to Governor of Britannia," replied a smiling Agrippa. "And who are you?"

It never occurred to the tribune to query Agrippa's stated title. He was beginning to regret his early rudeness. He drew himself up in the saddle and tried a simpering smile. "I have the honour to be Tribunus Laticlavius Marcus Paterculus, on special assignment to the court of Queen Cartimandua. This is her envoy, the lord Vellocatus."

Agrippa nodded pleasantly at Vellocatus, who affected indifference as if meeting Rome's special forces was an everyday occurrence.

"Perhaps you would care to step down from your horses and sit with us," Agrippa suggested and turned to the centurion who was leaning on his vine stick and following the conversation with fascinated attention. "You may wish to give your men a short rest. I would put out sentries, but I can assure you there is no danger of ambush."

The centurion nodded and barked out orders, while his men sank gratefully to the ground.

Agrippa nodded with approval that none reached for their water bottles. Water was something to use sparingly on the march. "Would you like to join us?" he asked the centurion who nodded thanks.

Agrippa, the centurion and the tribune all knew who was running the patrol, but it was also important that the higher-ranking tribune received the deference due to his rank. Even if it was an irritation.

"Marcus, I know you are escorting Vellocatus back to Brigantum and you are hoping to take charge of Caratacus and take him first to Eboracum in chains. May I ask, have you agreed on a price for him?"

"I'm afraid I am not at liberty to discuss that," replied the tribune pompously. "It's a highly sensitive subject between Queen Cartimandua and myself."

Vellocatus snorted as he interrupted the tribune. In the local dialect he quickly asked Agrippa if he understood what he was saying.

Agrippa nodded.

"This is a fool's errand," Vellocatus gushed as the tribune looked from one to another, at a stroke ruling him out of taking part in the conversation. "This idiot has come all this way with instructions that the Romans cannot afford her extravagant demands, but if she hands Caratacus over, as a gesture of goodwill, the legion will arrest Venutius, thus removing the only threat to her reign."

The tribune was gasping as he feebly protested. "I must insist that you speak in latin," he said lamely. "It is important that I know what is being said."

"Don't worry Marcus - I can call you Marcus, can't I?" soothed Agrippa. "What Vellocatus has said is what I rather thought would be the garrison commander's opening gambit. I don't suppose there is enough gold in the legion's coffers to satisfy Cartimandua's desires. Mind you, she does have a point; Caratacus arriving in Rome in chains would be an enormous step up for whoever brings him in."

"I'm sure I don't know what you mean," replied the tribune stiffly.

Agrippa allowed himself a half-smile. "If Caratacus was to be taken to Rome in chains, who would command the escort party? Tribune Laticlavius Marcus Paterculus would be making damn sure he was at the head of the triumphal procession marching to the Senate and graciously acknowledging the adulation of the adoring crowd."

The tribune made a "not at all" gesture and modestly bowed his head.

"You are quite right," conceded Agrippa. "Someone will have to be in charge of what could be a thankless and dangerous task."

Despite himself, the tribune was bemused. "How so?" he asked finally.

"Caratacus may have been a shit general, a murdering bastard, and a man who left his troops in the lurch as he fled the field, but he has caught the imagination of the people. They look on him as their potential saviour and the scourge of the legions. Every building, every woodland will be a potential ambush point as the locals try to free him. And don't forget that most of the journey to Camulodunum will be through Catuvellauni country. They may have cast him out of the tribe, but seeing him chained up in a cage, sitting in his own filth, will not go down well with his family. It's quite conceivable that there will be attempts to free him, and if just one succeeds it could be the spark that touches off a full-scale rebellion. Imagine that, the man leading the escort of a prisoner back to Rome could be the person who lost Britannia to the empire."

The tribune balked at this. Suddenly his plan to gain honours and an early place in the Senate, not to mention shaking the dust of this godforsaken dump Britannia from his elegant riding boots was not looking such a great idea.

Agrippa squatted on the ground with a quizzical look on his face. He looked up, first at the centurion, leaning on his vine stick, then at Vellocatus and finally back to the Tribune. He very nearly laughed out loud at the expression on the Tribune's face; he looked as if he had just swallowed a shit pasty. The centurion was earnestly studying the horizon, as if uninterested in the whole business, while Vellocatus was clearly having difficulty in understanding what the problem was.

"Come gentlemen, time to go," said Agrippa as he hauled himself upright. "You can't keep the great Cartimandua waiting, even if you are going to give her news she doesn't want to hear. My men will stay on the trail where you can pass on her reaction to your ultimatum and what she expects you to do about it. Let's hope you can find enough gold to satisfy her, or she may even separate Caratacus's head from his shoulders herself."

He turned to the tribune and fixed him with an intense stare. "Do I have to remind you that a great deal depends on how you handle this negotiation? If you fuck it up, it could set us back years and cause the death of many good soldiers. It could even lose us Britannia. So you take care to get in her good books and assure her that you are doing what you can to raise enough gold to satisfy her. Then you must impress the governor - my boss - that the money has to be raised."

The tribune gulped and swallowed. He wished he was back in Eboracum. "Rest assured, I will do my best."

Agrippa nodded. "I'm sure you will. I will meet you on the road out of Brigantum and take you to Governor Quintus Equitius. We must impress on him that, if necessary, we must gather all of the gold in Britannia if we are to be sure of securing Caratacus. The alternative could be that he orders me to kill Cartimandua and break Caratacus out of his dungeon." He turned to Vellocatus, and said softly, "and we don't want that do we?"

"You can fucking try, Roman," said Vellocatus through gritted teeth with a hand on his sword.

CHAPTER XXV

Alun waited until Veldicca was alone before approaching her about the agreement with Venutius. He found her sitting on a fallen tree, staring out at the river. He paused to look at her, drinking in her beauty, thinking what a wife she would be. Casting these thoughts aside, he approached her, making enough noise so as not to startle her.

"Alun, what brings you here?"

"I have been looking for you, because I have some information you may be interested in."

Intrigued, Veldicca moved up her log, making room for him to sit.

"Thank you, lady. As you know, we have been absent for a few days. We actually went to Rigodunum and had a long chat with Venutius, the deposed consort of the Queen. What I am about to tell you, must go no further; it is vital this information doesn't get out, especially to that bastard Roman. I know you care for him, but you must bear in mind he is the enemy, and his first loyalty is to the legion, not you. By the same token, may I say, that your first loyalty is to your tribe, not to a Roman spy who helped to kill a lot of both our peoples."

Veldicca lowered her eyes, staring at her hands, immobile in her lap. "I know this," she said quietly. "I am resigned to going back to my people and a life of service to them. Since the death of my father, they may well have selected a new leader, and that would be well and good, but if not, I shall take my rightful place at the head of the tribe. Whatever I do from now on will be for the good of the tribe."

"Well said, lady," replied Alun. "As to my news, Venutius has agreed that if we kill Cartimandua and free his hostage relatives, he will seize the throne and declare himself King of Brigantia to the Romans. They are bound to agree because they want to maintain the buffer against Caledonia. Venutius will quietly raise an army and start raiding the Romans.

"At the same time as we kill Cartimandua, we will kill Caratacus and tell the Catuvellauni that the Romans did it. Even though they cast him out, that will be enough to raise the tribe, so with the Brigantes, Ordovices and Catuvellauni, we will have the biggest army this country has ever seen. You and the Silures could be a part of this if you decide to join us in taking our land back."

She looked at him in confusion. "But that's exactly what Caratacus proposed - you will be doing exactly what he wanted to do."

"So it is, lady," agreed Alun. "We joined him because he had a good plan; the fault was in putting our trust in him. Caratacus always fought as a hit-and-run raider, and he had success doing it, but then when our tribes stood behind him, he wanted to take the Romans on at their own game, and once again, despite our superiority of numbers, their discipline and expertise slaughtered us. We don't intend to make that mistake again. We will make the legion fight on our terms, we will raid and burn and then disappear. We will lure the legion out of its strongholds and ambush them.

"At the end of winter, when their food stocks are low and they start to think about venturing out to campaign and steal our food, we will lay siege to their forts and starve them out."

Alun was speaking with an intensity he had never known before. He knew this plan could succeed, with or without the Silures. Better with, but they were still enemies under an uneasy truce. A personal alliance with the Princess Veldicca could well be a fine bonus, he thought.

Snapping his wandering thoughts back to the task in hand, he tried to convince a wavering Veldicca. "There are four legions trying to rule the north, the west and middle Britannia, leaving the rich south pretty much undefended. When campaigning starts again, I believe they will invade Mona and try to destroy the Druids, then I think they will move inland, and north into Caledonia.

"They will get a nasty surprise when we attack Camulodunum then Londinium. Then when the legions are ordered south, they will have tribesmen with them all the way, harrying and destroying men and equipment without being drawn into a set battle. Instead, we will cut supply lines, deny them local food, make them think they made a mistake coming here."

With his fiery speech over, Alun sat back and drew breath.

"Quite a plan. And Lenc, where does he stand in your plan?" asked Veldicca.

Alun looked at her carefully. "You knew that the plan was always to kill the Roman when his usefulness came to an end. That time is now and he is a growing liability. We will finish him tonight before the attack on the dungeon."

Veldicca dropped her head. "I know my duty," she said after a long pause. "I will go back to my people and tell them of your plan, and I think they will agree to it. Do you know how you are going to free the hostages and kill Cartimandua? It won't be easy.

"Not yet," conceded Alun, "but something will come to us. First you must describe your visit to the dungeon below the tower where the hostages are living. Tell me everything, every detail."

"This is a momentous plan," said Veldicca carefully. "I must think it through properly before deciding whether to join you or not. I don't need long, just leave me here for a while. I will come and find you."

Alun bowed his head to her. "I am sure you know where your duty lies," he said softly.

Veldicca was distressed as she wrestled with her conscience. She knew her duty, that much was plain, but did Lenc have to die, especially after all he had done for her? She tried to examine her feelings for him but failed. He was the enemy, she told herself, and they had killed her father. For that alone he should face death, she reasoned, but she couldn't just stand by and see him murdered.

I must wait until there is no chance he can thwart Alun's plan, she thought, then I must warn him to leave Brigantum as quickly as possible. Surely he would take heed of such a dire warning? Perhaps not, she decided sadly.

While she agonised, the four Ordovicians gathered downstream. "Venutius has promised us six men to be outside the tower wall as darkness falls," explained Alun. "He will get a message to the hostages to be ready and overpower the one guard outside their quarters. I don't know how, and didn't ask, but that's their business. From what Veldicca says, there are another six guards in the tower above ground, guarding the doors and another four down in the dungeon.

"We must get Brianna to steal a cart, fill it with dry wood, straw and tallow, then drag it behind the tower, as far away from the guards as possible.

"Then you, Madawc and Iestyn can come back to camp, and deal with the Roman. When you get back, we put a torch to the cart. The front gate is bound to be opened, and we must be ready to stop them slamming it again. We must block it open and kill the guards. We must overpower the guard commander, tie his hands and force him to give us the password. We don't have much time so we can't afford to be gentle with him. We have to frighten the living hell out of him to get that password.

"With his hands tied and a dagger pricking him in the back of the neck we can push his ugly face up tight to the hatch that the guard on the inside of the tower has to open. Then when he gives the password and the door is opened we can push through, kill the guard then onto the next door for a repeat performance."

Alun paused for breath and caught the dubious looks on the faces of his men.

"I know it's risky, but if we don't hesitate and act like we mean it, we will win. Agreed?"

He looked fiercely at his men, who reluctantly nodded. "Good. The hostages are up two flights of stairs, they have been warned that they are going to be rescued and they will deal with their guard. All we have to do is get them out of the building and earn the undying gratitude of Venutius.

"Our first task is to get to Caratacus and kill him. Only then can we take care of the hostages. If we succeed then we know the gods are with us," at this he allowed himself a small smile. "If not, I don't suppose we will be in a position to do anything about it anyway."

Back in the forest, Agrippa called his men together for what he called a prayer meeting. They gathered round expectantly as he started by saying their scout had seen the Legion patrol going back to Eboracum escorting Caratacus's men in chains, "so that's one problem out of the way.

"You will not be surprised that the meeting with her highness went as expected," said Agrippa drily. "That idiot tribune went in, all pomp and bluster, and Cartimandua sent him away with a flea in his ear. She told him she wanted a senior officer, someone who had the power to negotiate. She also gave him a large wooden box, which she expects to be returned before the next full moon, filled with gold, otherwise she may release Caratacus. It's too late for Caratacus's so-called bodyguards though; the tribune had them shackled and the centurion's patrol is marching them back to camp. They'll eventually end up in the slave market and someone will make a tidy profit. That's their problem, and at least they don't pose a threat to us." In his frustration Agrippa paced up and down, stabbing with a finger to make his points.

"The tribune had his tongue hanging out, following Cartimandua like a puppy dog. hoping she would change her mind, but fat chance of that. If the governor can't scrape up enough gold, we could find ourselves in a world of shit. If Caratacus is set free because we can't or won't raise the ransom, when that gets back to the Senate, heads will assuredly roll. Wouldn't like to be in the tribune's shoes.

"The trouble is, I don't think we've got that amount of gold in the whole of Britannia, so I'm inclined to think we are going to have to override Eboracum and take this straight to the stand-in governor, Quintus Equitius. He will have to come up with a solution which will satisfy Cartimandua and give us Caratacus. The governor is currently in Deva and I've sent two riders with a message giving him the news."

"Good," agreed Lenc. "It's probably all you can do. Quintus Equitius is the only person capable of coming up with a solution. In the meantime, Cartimandua is prepared to wait, she knows she has us by the balls."

CHAPTER XXVI

Lenc returned to the copper works, deep in thought. They had done all they could; now people higher up the military chain would have to come up with an answer.

His thoughts were suddenly shattered by Brianna waving frantically at him. He checked his horse and dismounted.

"Come with me," she said urgently. "I must speak to you in private, where no one can hear us." She grabbed him by the arm and hustled him away from the smoking fire pits, down to the riverbank, and upstream until she was sure there were no prying eyes. Lenc could see she was agitated, and as they found somewhere to sit, she poured out her story.

"It's Alun," she said. "You know he asked me where the hostages were being held and I found out for him? Now he wants to free them, which will allow Venutius to rise up. I think they intend to kill Cartimandua too. I asked him if you were in on the plan, and he said no, quite the contrary in fact. On no account was I to let you know what they were doing. I didn't know what to do, because you, more than anyone else saved my life, I owe you that much at least."

"Thank you, Brianna. Do you know when all this is going to happen?"

"No not really, I don't think they have a plan yet, but I think it will probably be tonight. All they asked is whether I and some of the other women could make a diversion by setting a hay cart alight outside the tower wall."

Lenc patted her hand reassuringly. "You did the right thing

in telling me. If you can keep me up to date with their plans, I would be very grateful. Now you'd better go, before people notice you're missing."

She smiled wanly and rose, hesitated and whispered, "Take care and watch your back."

"I will and don't worry."

Lenc watched Brianna hurry back to the camp and thought about everything she had said. There could only be one reason why the Ordovicians wanted the hostages freed, to bring Venutius in on their side to kill Cartimandua. Maybe they had promised to kill the Queen as well. With Cartimandua dead, the Ordovicians could then kill Caratacus and realise their solemn promise. All this to kill Caratacus so their second oath can be realised and they can kill me, he reasoned.

Which puts me in a dangerous position, he thought. Then another thought struck him. If Venutius does manage to take control of the Brigantes, he would potentially command the biggest tribe in the country. It wouldn't take much to persuade the Catuvellauni to avenge Caratacus by joining forces with him. Alun already has the Ordovice on board and Veldicca would see it as her duty to persuade the Silures to join in as well. This could spell the end of Rome in Britannia.

The only thing to do, he decided, was to share these new worries with Agrippa. That evening, he wandered from the camp along the river. It was a peaceful evening; the only sounds the calls of birds and the river chuckling quietly, bubbling over stones. It was hard to imagine the pain and suffering that people were imposing on each other throughout the known world. Most of it done in the name of Rome, or consequences which sprang from it, he thought bitterly.

These melancholy thoughts were swept aside when he confronted a fisherman, line in the water, who nodded pleasantly at him.

"Greetings," offered Lenc. "Catching anything?"

"No luck so far," responded the fisherman. "Have you got

something to report?"

Lenc looked a bit more closely. The fisherman looked for all the world like a local, but he must be a pathfinder. "By the gods, it's Cornelius," said Lenc in surprise. "You said you had to get into the part, but I would never have believed you could change yourself so convincingly. It's amazing."

Cornelius bowed his head in response. "Thank you, kind sir. When I return to Rome, I may try the stage - it apparently pays better than mere soldiering."

"I am sure you will be a great success," replied Lenc, "and if the audience throws things at you, that could well be supper solved as well."

"You see, there's always a silver lining," retorted Cornelius. "But enough of this nonsense. I'm sick of being a fisherman, especially as I haven't caught anything. Let's go and find Agrippa; he is impatient to talk further with you."

He pulled his line out of the water, then plopped the small stone which had been tied to the wet end of the line back into the river and settled his makeshift rod over his shoulder. With one last look round, he made an exaggerated gesture with a sweeping hand for Lenc to follow and strolled upstream.

They found Agrippa sitting by the camp fire, just finishing a gruel of beans, barley and hard bread. The other pathfinders were cleaning equipment and sharpening blades. A line of horses stood placidly near the river, with a pile of hay in easy reach.

Agrippa listened closely as Lenc repeated what Brianna had told him, asking questions at intervals.

At the end he leaned back and thought for a minute.

"Cartimandua is the ally of Rome, and of vital importance in keeping a lid on this particular frontier of the empire, therefore her enemies are our enemies. If holding Venutius's family as hostages keeps him from attempting to overthrow her, then we must ensure they stay safe and secure. As for Caratacus, I would be quite happy to see him die in his dungeon, but the Senate wants to parade him through the streets, so he has to be escorted all the way across the empire just to give the great unwashed of Rome a thrill as he is executed. So be it; reluctantly we will have to look after him as well. The sooner these Ordovicians get their just desserts the better."

Lenc could only agree, although he did have a vested interest. His life hung in the balance, especially as Alun and his men had decided he had outlived his usefulness, and would be better off dead, probably before they killed Cartimandua.

Which proved to be exactly what Agrippa thought as well. "The Ordovicians are going to start killing very soon, so it would be safe to assume they will start with you, Lenc; they need you out of the way before you can raise the alarm. The one advantage you have is that they don't yet know about the pathfinders. I think they are going to find out about us very soon.

"Lenc you must go back to your camp, and make up your bedroll to look like a sleeping body. They'll come looking for you, but stay hidden. We'll be waiting for them."

"Just don't wait too long," Lenc replied, "I don't need you drawing things out so your boys can have fun."

Everything seemed calm as Lenc arrived back at the copper works. That evening, he sat with Brianna and the other women and shared their food.

Brianna seemed tense and whispered, "I think it's going to be tonight."

Later that evening Veldicca came back to the camp and found Lenc, still sitting with Brianna.

"I have news," she said tersely. Lenc shifted along his log to give her space, and Brianna moved as if to leave them in private, but Veldicca motioned to her to stay. "I'd like you to hear this as well," she whispered, then paused before speaking: "Firstly I have been summoned to Cartimandua's lodge, to help entertain her distinguished visiting Roman officer. Why she thinks I would be interested in meeting a Roman however exalted I don't know, but I thought it best to agree. I asked if Brianna could accompany me, the other women can help the Ordovice with their bonfire."

"And your other news?" asked Lenc gently.

"When Alun came to me with his plan to help Venutius take the Brigante throne, he said it would be the start of a proper union of the tribes. With Brigantians leading the attack on the Legions, Ordovice would join with them, then you, Lenc will be blamed for Caratacus's death ensuring the Catuvellauni are sure to join the Brigante. He asked me if I would join him, and I agreed because it seemed my duty to say I would try and persuade the Silures to join as well. I could see that an army that size could sweep the Legions back into the sea.

"I asked him what he was going to do about his promise to kill you, Lenc, and he replied that your usefulness was at an end, and you would be killed before the raid on the dungeon. I thought you should know," she said quietly twisting her fingers together in her lap.

Eventually she sighed and raised her tear-streaked face. "I'm sorry," she said simply.

Lenc was confused. "But why?" he asked.

"Because I still have feelings for you, of course," she replied softly. "I always knew that, but for the good of the tribe I forced those feelings away. My only duty must be to my people, which is why I agreed to Alun's plan in the first place. I never thought it could cost you your life. I'm sorry.

"I still don't know what to do," said an anguished Veldicca, "I have to return to the tribe. If you come with me, they will kill you, and I won't be able to stop them, but the tribe is my destiny."

Lenc tenderly reached for her hands and held them in his. "I understand your feelings, and accept that we can never be together. Our paths crossed, we had some short but good times, and now they are parting. I will escort you to the outskirts of Silurian territory and then say goodbye, but I will never forget you."

Veldicca looked into his eyes and gripped his hands tight in her lap. "Oh, Lenc, this is a terrible mess. Is there no way we can be together?"

Lenc slowly but firmly slid his hands out from hers. "No, it would never work. We both have our duties and our own paths to follow. I am glad I met you, but we live in different worlds. Let's make the best of the journey back to Siluria, and then I will have to return to the legion. If I had a choice, I would take you to Gaul where we could carve out a new life together, but neither of us can escape our destinies."

She sat quietly, looking down at her hands folded in her lap. Then she looked up, with tears in her eyes. "Whatever happens, I will never forget you."

Lenc nodded. He was close to tears and noisily cleared his throat. "If you will excuse me, I have my duties to take care of." He gave a half-smile and stood. For a heartbeat, he gazed at Veldicca's grief-stricken face, nodded and left.

Without saying more, Lenc left the two women and went back to the cave he had taken for his sleeping quarters. He fumbled for his fire-lighting kit and scraped his flint down a small piece of iron over some dry bullrushes. Several strikes later Lenc was rewarded with a spark, which caught the rush and tallow torch giving a meagre light. He opened out his bedroll and laid it on some dry bracken, then found some sacks, which rolled and scrunched up made a passable impression of a sleeping person. When he had done what he could to make the lump look like a sleeping body, he retreated further into the cave, but still close enough to have some dim light from the entrance. He felt sure he would at least see the shape of any intruders as they entered the cave, then he settled down to wait.

Outside, the fires burned down and it was getting decidedly chilly.

Lenc squatted on a small pile of stones, hoping the

uncomfortable position would help to keep him from falling asleep. He could feel his eyelids drooping, but when he heard something metallic scraping just outside, he was alert in an instant. He stared, not at the cave entrance but to one side, using his peripheral vision. His short sword and dagger lay near him in easy reach on the ground, then with a rising feeling of excitement he detected a change in the dark at the entrance to the cave. Through the gloom shapes took form and moved stealthily towards his bedroll. He quietly picked up his sword and dagger, hardly daring to breathe. Two crouching figures were creeping into the cave. The first one put a hand out to steady the second and pointed at the seemingly sleeping body.

The first man took a step forward in the darkness and silently went down on one knee, feeling carefully for his victim. Suddenly he plunged his dagger into the bundle. The blade sliced through the fabric easily – too easily as there was no resistance from a human body. Puzzled, he hurriedly pulled back the blanket and felt nothing but banked-up straw and sacking, and no sign of his victim. His brow furrowed and his eyes widened as it dawned on him; he was now the ambushed, not the ambusher. He turned to his companion and was about to shout a warning when, from the mouth of the cave another intruder appeared and swiftly passed a short wire round the standing man's throat and pulled hard on wooden handles at both ends.

The victim frantically tried to twist away but fell to his knees, desperately clawing at the wire tightening round his neck. His assailant put his knee between the shoulder blades of his victim, giving him more leverage and the end was quick. The dead man slumped onto the straw pile, which was rapidly staining in blood.

The action was fast and furious as at that same moment, Lenc took two paces forward and stood over the kneeling man, who was trying to stand and defend himself. Lenc could just make out the terrified expression on the face of his would-be murderer as he launched himself, stabbing the Ordovice just below the neck. He slumped forward as Lenc frantically tried to pull his sword from the falling body, not knowing whether there were any other would-be assassins.

As his sword thankfully slid from the body with a sickening sucking noise, Lenc whirled round on full alert while the second assailant slumped noiselessly to the ground, the garotte wire still round his neck. Behind him was Cornelius the pathfinder, his grinning mouth lit up by his teeth shining in the half-light. He was still holding the two small wooden handles of the garotte, which he had used so savagely that it had almost severed the head from the body, only jarring on the spine.

"It's just these two," whispered Cornelius. "Have you got more light?"

Lenc took his tallow lamp down from the scraped-out shelf in the wall of the cave and used it to light two more torches. They were an improvement but not much, Lenc held his high as Cornelius dragged the two dead men to the cave wall and arranged them, sitting, and leaning back against the cave wall.

Coming nearer, Lenc could now see the men's faces. "Madawc and Iestyn - Ordovice," he said flatly.

"The other two will be in position by the tower by now, waiting for these two to join them," added Cornelius. "Agrippa should find us on the way into town. It would be churlish to keep everyone waiting."

Cornelius and Lenc kept as close as possible to the sides of buildings as they walked deeper into the sleeping town. There were few people out on the muddy tracks, and the few they did encounter hurried past while averting their eyes.

As they approached the tower, Lenc checked his companion. "Careful now, we don't want to bump into the Ordovicians - they will probably have help. Where's Agrippa?" asked Lenc.

"He's here," came a disembodied voice deep in the shadow of a roundhouse. Agrippa cautiously stepped out of the dark, his longsword in hand. "Are you being followed?" he asked.

Cornelius shook his head. "No boss, quiet as the grave."

"You were lucky; it looks like a butcher's shop at the tower. Would have been worse if we had allowed a band of Venutius's men to join in. Luckily, they agreed with us they would be best served anywhere else but here. They're probably still running," said Agrippa, with a wolfish grin. "You two, follow me and keep quiet."

They hurried past the silent command house, then across the eerily quiet square to the gate in the wall round the tower. The door was ajar, held back by two bodies sprawled in the entrance way.

"The sentries," whispered Agrippa. "Their throats have been cut. Strange that they were surprised, and stranger still that the inside guards were taken care of the same way."

They crept inside, swords at the ready as they approached the tower entrance. Sure enough, the two guards were lying in their own pooling blood slumped against the stone building they were supposed to defend. Agrippa stepped over them and pushed on the door which opened easily into the main hall.

Lenc looked at Agrippa questioningly in the light of the guttering tallow lamps. Agrippa shrugged, as if to say: your guess is as good as mine.

He pointed to the two doors at the other side of the tower. The one to the right was gaping open with the now seemingly inevitable dead sentry spread across the entrance.

"That's the way down to the dungeon," whispered Lenc. He pointed to the other firmly closed door. "That one leads up the tower where the hostages are being kept."

Agrippa nodded. "It looks as though the prime target is still Caratacus. They won't allow the possibility of someone else killing him; they want the satisfaction of doing it themselves. Only then will they see about releasing the hostages."

Lenc had to agree that seemed the likeliest story. "One way to find out," he said nervously.

Agrippa smiled. It wasn't a happy smile.

"With a bit of luck there will only be the two of them; we can sort them out easily enough. Besides we can't let Caratacus miss his chance of a glorious death in front of the Senate."

With one hand holding his torch upright, and the other hefting his long cavalry sword, Agrippa cautiously led the way down the stairs. At the bottom the torch in its wall holder dimly showed the passageway to the final door, which again was hanging open.

They found spare torch holders in the corridor wall then crept slowly forward towards the dim light flickering from the dungeon room. As they crept closer, they could hear several people shouting at once. They started to discern shadows on the wall as people moved about in that sinister, darkened room. Once at the door, Lenc inched his head round until he could see into the room with one eye. Both eyes opened wide at the sight inside.

He stepped back hurriedly and pulled Agrippa to the door to have a look.

"Well, I'll be buggered," Agrippa said eventually.

"What is it boss, what can you see?" said Cornelius, fidgeting impatiently.

Agrippa looked round, teeth bared in a semblance of a grin. "Come on then you two, let's get to work," and launched himself into the astonishing circus inside.

Lenc stepped past Agrippa, who simply stood with a half-smile on his face, mesmerised by what he was staring at. Not to be left out, Cornelius followed Lenc and all three gaped at the scene before them.

The surviving Ordovicians, were trying to break open Caratacus's cage, Alun with a large hammer was trying to knock the pins out of the door to release it while inside, the prisoner was kicking out with his bare feet, if only to persuade either of them to take care and not let their hands get within range.

To one side, the majestic Cartimandua was strung up, her hands tied together above her head, with the rope tied over a hook stuck in an overhead beam. Whether it was because of her angry struggles, or whether her once expensive gown had been cut off, wasn't obvious, but there it was in a pile on the floor at her feet. There she stood in all her naked glory in the flickering lamplight, yet still shouting threats at what she was going to do to the Ordovicians when she got free.

Lenc had to tear his gaze away from the fine supple form of Queen Cartimandua, her breasts jutting out, pulled tight and proud by her arms tied firmly above her head. She had worked herself into a rage and was covered in a sheen of sweat as she called down curses on the Ordovicians. It was then that Lenc noticed the inert and very dishevelled form of Tribunus Laticlavius Marcus Paterculus lying in a heap near to Cartimandua. Behind him was another inert body, Venutius, Cartimandua's new young consort. Lenc wondered whether they were dead, then decided he really couldn't care less either way.

By the gods, behind them were Veldicca and Brianna, not taking part in the drama just looking from one to another, their hands tied and bound round a post.

The immediate concern were the two Ordovicians who were so intent on breaking into Caratacus's cage, that they failed to register the newcomers who had silently arrived. It was Lenc who broke the spell. "Alun why don't you take a rest? You'll wear yourself out."

Alun spun round dropping the big hammer he had ineffectually been using on the cage door to unsheath his longsword. "Who's there?" he demanded, squinting in the poor light, then recoiled when he saw Lenc with sword at the ready.

Lenc stepped forward, flexing his gladius. In his left hand he grasped his dagger, point upwards. "You know who I am, you sorry piece of shit."

Veldicca gasped and shouted his name, "Be careful, Lenc."

Well, well, the Roman returns," said Alun triumphantly. "I thought you would be dead by now, no matter, it just means I have to do the job myself.

"Before I kill you Roman, how did you know my plans, and what have you done with Madawc and Iestyn?"

As he asked the question, an audible gasp came from Veldicca, and a look of understanding flashed across Alun's face as he glanced towards her. "I get it, the Silure bitch couldn't bear to be parted from her Roman and despite everything he did to her tribe, she had to warn him. Just think, for a while there I idly dreamed of an alliance between Silure and Ordovice, cemented by our marriage, but you, you bitch, you're as bad as the rest of them. Typical Silure."

"Madawc and Iestyn won't be joining you," taunted Lenc. "If the Druids are to be believed, I imagine they're looking forward to coming back to this life, probably as sewer rats."

Suddenly Alun let out a frightening yell of rage, and stepping backwards, he swung sideways, letting his longsword carry on the momentum until it cut sickeningly into Veldicca's neck.

As the heavy blade sank into her unprotected throat, Alun quickly jerked it back out and turned to face Lenc, as Veldicca slumped to her knees from the force of the single blow, but still tethered to the post. Her head dropped and she swung, suspended by the ropes around her wrists, but Lenc could see she had taken a mortal cut.

Alun stood on the balls of his feet, with a half-smile on his face and ready to attack. "So dies a traitor," he said triumphantly, "but don't worry, you will be joining her very soon."

Lenc stood his ground, his mind reeling with trying to make sense of the wanton killing of the only person he cared for. Dimly he could hear Agrippa behind him, telling him to concentrate. He nodded and tried to put the horror of Veldicca's death out of his mind, instead filling with an overpowering white-hot rage.

Desperately he forced himself to calm down. Now was not the time for anger he told himself. Concentrate on killing the bastard, then he could grieve. He shook his head, desperate to clear his mind. He looked steadily at Alun who stood with knees flexing, steadily pointing his longsword.

From somewhere deep within his mind, Lenc summoned all his mental strength to put everything to one side except the task in hand. He tried a small smile. "You will be pleased to know that Madawc and Iestyn have paid the price for your selfish deceit," he grated. "One died by my knife and the other virtually had his head cut off with a garotte. They both bled like stuck pigs."

Agrippa and Cornelius looked at each other despairingly. They wanted to give Lenc space, but they were still in a difficult position in the dungeon. As one, they stepped forward, swords at the ready.

Lenc stopped them with a restraining arm. "No, this has been a long time coming. He's mine." And in an aside to Agrippa: "But keep your eye on the other bastard."

Lenc and Alun moved sideways to the centre of the room, their eyes warily on each other, then tensed, knees bent, leaning forward, swords weaving left and right as both looked for any possible weak point. Alun allowed himself a smirk of satisfaction, his longsword was heavier and at least an arm's length longer than the gladius of his opponent, but the weapon was designed for swinging not stabbing. In the close confines of the dark dungeon the shorter, stabbing blade of the gladius could be deadly effective.

Lenc hefted his gladius in one hand and his dagger in the other and carefully looked his opponent up and down. He had to get inside Alun's guard. That's all, he thought, trying to put the image of Veldicca taking the vicious sword swipe out of his mind.

Alun stamped his right foot forward, but stood poised, waiting for Lenc to make a move. He stood immobile, carefully watching his opponent's eyes. Suddenly Alun surged forward, sword raised, ready to deliver a smashing blow. Lenc saw it coming and stepped back onto his left foot, desperately gripping his sword handle, blocking the blow, but forcing him onto one knee. Alun smiled triumphantly and tried to knock Lenc's gladius sideways before raising his weapon for the killer blow, supremely confident that the fight was won.

Desperately Lenc scrabbled backwards then stood and lunged forward under his opponent's longsword, his gladius poised for the killer stroke. Now it was Alun's turn to scramble backwards. The two warily circled each other, both breathing heavily, looking for an opening. Alun gripped his sword in both hands, the long, dull metal of the blade pointing at Lenc's throat. Suddenly, Lenc thrust forward on his right foot and as Alun flinched, took another step and made a powerful slashing cut to the head. As Alun hurriedly raised his heavy longsword to block the cut, Lenc pulled his swing and stabbed out with his dagger, burying it in Alun's thigh.

Alun shrieked and stepped back, trying to pull the blade from his leg then slumped against the wall in pain and blood as Lenc slashed at his sword arm, opening up a deep wound. Alun stepped back, gasping with the pain, then in one final desperate charge, yelled out an ancient war cry and ran at Lenc, sword held left-handed at shoulder height. Lenc crouched, letting him come, then at the last moment, struck out to deflect the long blade and lunged sideways as Alun tried to stop himself. Lenc raised his sword and took two steps forward to bury it underAlun's raised sword arm, feeling ribs breaking as the point finally cut through vital organs , sending a jar up his arm and felling the Ordovice.

Lenc paused, breathing heavily. Alun lay still, no movement. Warily Lenc stood over him and with his foot rolled the body over. Blood was still pumping from the wound, then slowed as the heart finally gave out. Alun's eyes flickered, and he sighed as his life ebbed away.

Suddenly a cry of anguish rang out and Darren, the last of the Ordovice ran forward at Lenc, sword held high in a killing stroke, but before he could land the fatal blow, Cornelius tripped him and sent him sprawling on the dank cobbled floor. Darren struggled desperately to get back on his feet but Cornelius stepped behind him and deftly slipped his garotte over Darren's head then, with a knee in his victim's back, crossed the handles over and pulled back sharply. Darren let out a strangled grunt as his head jerked and his eyes rolled back in death.

Even Cartimandua went silent as the stench of congealing blood circulated round the fetid room that had seen so much pain, suffering and death. Lenc leaned wearily against a damp wall. All he wanted to do was leave this evil place, he desperately yearned for the sun on his back and a fresh wind. Would he ever see and feel them again?

He roused himself and knelt down next to Alun feeling for a pulse, knowing there wouldn't be one. Even though Alun had sworn to kill him, he still felt remorse, they had been through so much in such a short space of time.

Almost reluctantly he stepped over to Veldicca, and tenderly cut her free from her bonds, allowing her to sag onto the floor. He laid her out and put her hands down by her side, then reached down to kiss her cold forehead. He sank down next to the woman he loved and put his hand over hers. His head sank down to his knees oblivious to everything as he sobbed his heart out. Carefully he pulled her collar up to cover the raw red gash across her neck and shoulder.

His black thoughts were abruptly shattered by a strident cry. "Is one of you bastards going to cut me free?" For a moment he had forgotten the other women in the dungeon. Cartimandua had recovered her anger and was still bellowing the dire threats of the revenge she was going to wreak on those people who had violated her royal person. In the gloom, Brianna wept soundlessly, her head bowed.

As Agrippa hurried forward, raising his knife to cut Cartimandua down, Lenc focussed on Veldicca. As he slowly brushed her long hair from her face, Lenc gently touched the livid bruise on her temple, and as the tears ran down his face, he reached forward and again kissed her cold cheek.

His head was bowed as he kneeled, alone in his grief and did not notice Cornelius move past him to cut Brianna's ropes.

Brianna, rubbing her wrists stood behind Lenc, she put her hand out to him then hesitated and withdrew it.

Lenc looked up and half-smiled. "How did you and Veldicca come to be here?" he asked softly.

"You remember Veldicca said we had been invited to the Queen's Lodge? We were supposed to dine with her esteemed guest, that Roman on the floor there," she explained, gesturing at the still inert form of the Tribunus Laticlavius. "I asked the other women to take our place making the diversion and we went to the lodge. Just like when you and Veldicca met the Queen, she wanted to show off her trophy to the Roman and we had to come as well.

"There was much saluting, bowing and scraping, and Cartimandua, the Roman and the rest of us were escorted down into the cells. The Ordovicians must have seen all this and crept up behind us. They overpowered and killed the guards as Cartimandua and her preening monkey walked ahead of us. It was ridiculously easy. We followed a pace or two at the back, and behind us the Ordovice killed the guards as we went.

"Then when we arrived in this filthy place, Alun said he wished that he had managed to kill you, Lenc, the Roman bastard himself, before killing Caratacus. He said it would have been satisfying to kill you both together, but he had to settle for one at a time. The princess called him an Ordovice bastard and tried to stick her dagger in him, but Darren saw it coming and punched her in the face. I tried to stop him and took a clout for my trouble. When I came to, we were tied up and could do nothing as they tried to get into Caratacus's cage. Then you showed up."

He swallowed; he had nothing to say. He just nodded again and carefully laid his cloak over Veldicca's head and body.

Some seconds went by until he was dragged abruptly back to the present by another enraged bellow from Cartimandua. He looked up to see Agrippa leaning into the outraged Queen as he tried to reach the rope holding her hands stretched above her head. "Leave my tits alone, you filthy swine! Just you wait until I get free."

Agrippa stepped back, and with as much dignity as he could manage, said: "In that case, perhaps I'd better leave you where you are."

She was about to shout something else, then thought the better of it. "No, no, please, my hands are numb, please cut me down. I really won't mind if you touch my tits."

Agrippa looked undecided, while Cornelius and Brianna watched with fascination. Lenc still gazed down at the covered body, his hands grasping a small white hand.

"What are you looking at?" demanded Cartimandua glaring at Brianna.

"Nothing, nothing," replied the girl quickly.

Agrippa asked Brianna to pass a stool, then stood it next to the still naked Queen and, with the extra height, easily reached up and sliced through her bonds.

As Agrippa stepped down, Cartimandua looked at him appraisingly as she reached down for her gown and managed to secure it on one shoulder with a brooch. Her eyes went soft and demure as she breathed in a husky voice, "We haven't been introduced."

Agrippa bowed. "Lady I am Agrippa, senior centurion of the Twentieth Valeria Victrix Pathfinders, and I am pleased to see you, er, looking so well." He allowed his gaze to slide over her now respectable, but still voluptuous body.

Cartimandua was on good form as she enjoyed the admiring looks from Agrippa. "Does a senior centurion outrank a tribunus laticlavius?" she asked, looking at Agrippa with a coy expression.

"Very definitely," confirmed Agrippa. Well it was true in practice, he reasoned, especially in this case....

"Then perhaps you can take over the negotiations for the ransom of Caratacus from this idiot; I think it could be quite fun," replied Cartimandua who slowly ran her questing fingers up Agrippa's bare arm.

"That would be my pleasure, I would love to serve you any way I can," replied Agrippa with a slow smile, "but how would this affect Vellocatus? Particularly if I take over some of his more pleasurable duties?"

"Oh him," Cartimandua said dismissively. "That's him, lying on the floor, he stood there looking vacant when the Ordovicians ambushed us, and took a whack on the head for his trouble."

Cartimandua was idly stroking Agrippa's arm. "The urges of a young buck are all very well, but they don't last long, and they rarely care about the feelings of their partner." She sighed, ran her tongue slowly over her lips, and looked steadily into Agrippa's eyes. "The energy of youth is fine for a while, but sometimes you need a real man, if you understand my meaning.

"Besides, he was starting to get a bit tiresome, seemed to think he had a claim on the throne. He was fine for a pleasurable afternoon under the blankets but lately I think he has been getting above himself. Pity but there it is."

Before Agrippa could answer, the tribune, still lying on the cell floor, groaned, stirred, and tried to get up. He groaned again and held his head, where a deep cut just above his ear seeped blood down his neck. He gingerly touched the wound and winced, then looked at his blood-covered hand in horror.

"I'm hurt," he shrieked. He held his hand out to Cartimandua in frightened appeal. "I'm bleeding. For the god's sake, someone help me - they tried to murder me."

"You preening fool, why don't you shut up? You're giving me a headache as well." The disembodied voice came from Caratacus, still crouching in his cage.

Lenc kneeled to get a better look at the prisoner. In what was a relatively short time, he was filthy, with lank, greasy hair spilling past his shoulders in rat's tails. His rags barely covered him and he was so emaciated that he looked like a man without much time left in this world.

For a fleeting moment Lenc felt a touch of outrage.

Cartimandua had promised that Caratacus would be cared for and looked after properly so that when he came into the tender care of the legion, he would be fit and well enough to be executed.

Agrippa decided that action needed to be taken. He turned to Lenc. "Perhaps you could help the tribune up and take him and Queen Cartimandua back to her lodge." He turned to Brianna and bowed, "My men will take the Princess back to the lodge, will you stay with her and ensure that she is treated properly?" Brianna nodded slowly still fighting back her own tears.

Lenc noted the last part with some relief. He was pleased that Agrippa wanted to deal with the Princess as valued royalty rather than an enemy of Rome.

"Cornelius, will you stay here while I rouse a guard detail that can deal with the Ordovicians?" added Agrippa.

"And you better find a dressing for the Tribune's wound, he will probably want to show off the scar he won on active service when he gets back to Rome, then, if you can find a bucket of water, I suggest you throw that over Vellocatus, he can't clutter the place up, lying there for much longer, can't have an untidy dungeon, can we?"

"Right boss, no problems," replied Cornelius.

"What about me? You can't leave me like this," whined a plaintive Caratacus, "especially after these swine got past the guards so easily. My life is in danger - I demand better security."

Caratacus shrank back in his cage as Agrippa stared impassively at him. He spoke thoughtfully: "You must be one of the few people who has been fought over by so many warriors who all want the honour of killing you, and been saved by so many more, just so you can be killed another day. I suggest you consider keeping your damned mouth shut in case I forget you have a date with Roman destiny and run you through myself."

Caratacus seemed to agree it was not the time for further protests and again sank back into his cage, muttering under his breath and plucking at his frayed rags.

With his head down, Lenc stumbled towards the light of the lodge meeting hall, where he encountered Cartimandua and Agrippa in a deep conversation. Before he could back away, they realised he was there and called out jovially.

"Come and have a drink," said Agrippa. "We have some wine, courtesy of the legion, and it isn't half bad."

Cartimandua lay back, looking out from under dark eyelids. By the gods, thought Lenc, she's purring like a fucking cat.

He pulled himself together, thinking furiously; his future would be decided here. "Two things," he said. "One for you," pointing at Cartimandua, then at Agrippa "and one for you."

"I'm yours to command," said Agrippa magnanimously, waving his wine goblet.

Lenc nodded: "To you, Queen Cartimandua, please extract a promise from Caratacus that he won't try and escape then release him from that infernal dungeon, clean him up, fatten him and make him presentable for when you finally release him for transportation to Rome."

He turned to Agrippa and snapped to attention, "Agrippa, you are my superior and I ask just one favour, and that is after I bury the Princess Veldicca I would like to report to Deva to re-join the Twentieth. I will even find you and join your band of cutthroats, should you still want me."

Agrippa looked up sympathetically. "For my part, you can certainly bury the Princess with whatever honours you can manage and if you find your way back to the Pathfinders, I will welcome you. I promise that I shall persuade the Queen Cartimandua, that it is in her best interests to have Caratacus looking his best…for a variety of reasons." He glanced rogueishly at the Queen who merely waved her goblet in agreement.

"Er, thank you both," stuttered Lenc. He managed to walk backwards out of the room, trying not to watch as Agrippa put down his goblet and carefully lay beside the voluptuous Queen.

Caratacus looked up at his visitor. The dungeon had been

cleared of bodies, but it still exuded that spectral aura of death. "How now, Lenc, come back to gloat?"

"No," he replied. "I have arranged a change of scenery for you. Cartimandua has agreed for you to be cleaned up, fed, and provided with better quarters until you start your journey to Rome."

"I suppose I must look my best before the great Senate," Caratacus conceded. "But really, I couldn't care less. They can kill me as a scarecrow, or as a future king and thorn in their side - it's all the same to me.

"One thing though, I was very sorry to watch Veldicca die. If I could I would have run Alun through myself, but all I could do was watch. I know she meant a lot to you."

Lenc looked at him, unsure what to say. He hesitated, then: "Thank you, your sentiments are appreciated. We've not always seen eye to eye," he said, searching for words, "but as I have got to know you as a selfish arrogant bastard, I never thought I would see you as a person who would give in. You are going to Rome, where you will most probably either be crucified or strangled on the steps of the Senate, but don't you see - you will be carrying the hopes and aspirations of all the people of Britannia. You must stand proud, not beg for mercy, but show Rome what a leader from Britannia stands for.

"I'm not saying it will save your life, but if it must be taken, then at least at your passing Rome will say, 'There went a warrior.' And your example, when word gets back to Britannia - as it will - will light a fire here that may be enough to free this land. For Britannia, be proud, be impassioned, be strong, be a king."

Caratacus smiled slowly. "You have become quite the orator, Lenc. I never thought you had it in you. I was sure my destiny was to be King of Britannia." He sighed. "I don't think that is in my stars any more. But your advice is good. I shall be dignified as I face the Senate, and as far as they are concerned, I will be the King of Britannia. And they will marvel at how the King of

Britannia can die."

He paused and smiled again. "Now Lenc, be so good as to get me out of here. I need a bath, clean clothes, something to eat and, of course, drink, and if it's not too much trouble, some female company."

SEPARATING FACT FROM FICTION

When Caratacus was captured, he faced the long journey across Europe to Rome in chains. He was shackled in a specially built cart with strong bars so that the growing crowds of people who turned out to see him had a good view. As a result of his resistance and despite his failures, his fame had spread beyond his own island. People thronged to see the man who had defied Rome for so long.

The legion and Cartimandua, possibly with the help of Agrippa, came to a compromise over the amount of gold that should be handed over as ransom for Caratacus. His long journey, which started high in the Pennines, took him and his escorts first to Camulodunum where he was reunited with his distinctly unimpressed wife Vellibia, then to Portus Dubris for the sea journey to Caletum, then the long trail across the mainland of Europe till finally arriving in Rome.

Along the way, the crowds of people who turned out to see the great Caratacus continued to grow. The great man gracefully acknowledged the adulation of the crowd who cheered him as he trundled past in his mobile cage.

Not even in the great capital of the Roman Empire itself was the name Caratacus lacking in honour. The Emperor Claudius's attempts to enhance his own glory by increasing the renown of his vanquished enemy made Caratacus an unusual celebrity of the time. When he rumbled into the Senate on the barred cart, with his family and entourage following behind, the people of Rome were summoned as though to a splendid spectacle. The stage was set by the cohorts of the Praetorian Guard marshalled under arms on the parade ground in front of their barracks. Then the clients of the king were led past, and the torques, military trappings and spoils of his foreign wars were likewise displayed. Next, Caratacus, his brothers, his wife and daughter, were put on show in front of the Senate. Some of the others, in their fear, made degrading entreaties, but not Caratacus. According to Tacitus, the Roman historian, he was every inch the diplomat and a senior statesman of Britannia. When he stood tall and proud in front of the Senate, he contemptuously brushed aside any suggestion of an appeal for mercy for either himself or his family.

"If I had been blessed with only a moderate measure of prosperity to accompany my noble birth and high rank, I would have entered this city as a friend rather than as a captive, and you would not have thought it beneath your dignity to receive into formal alliance a man sprung from illustrious ancestors, holding sway over many tribes. My present fate confers as much glory on you as shame on me. I possessed horses, men, arms and wealth. Is it surprising if I have been unwilling to give these up? For if it is your desire to rule the whole world, does it follow that all men should readily accept servitude? If I had been dragged here after instant surrender, neither my ill-fortune nor your glorious success would have won such renown. If you were to put me to death, I should be forgotten. But if you preserve my life, I shall be an everlasting witness to your clemency."

Tacitus

In response, Tiberius Claudius Ceasar Augustus Germanicus was so impressed by this stirring speech and, seeing the effect it had on those listening, granted pardon to the would-be king and to his wife and family.

After being released from their chains, Caratacus and his family were taken to their new home, a villa in one of the better parts of the city, where the children were educated and

Caratacus and his forgiving wife Vellibia lived out their lives in comfortable obscurity.

As for Lenc we haven't heard the last of him.....

Douglas McArthur

When I left school in the sixties, jobs were plentiful but I had no idea what I wanted to do. I had a holiday job working in a steel stockholders when I heard there was a job going as a reporter on the local paper, and from that chance beginning, albeit with a few hiccups along the way, I have kept body and soul together.

I was apprenticed to the Grantham Journal in Lincolnshire as a journalist. From there I followed a trail of newspapers from Melton Mowbray to Leicester, London, and Kent, before joining the Ministry of Defence as an Information Officer. A year or so in, I was asked to start a new newspaper for the British Army to run in tandem with the popular Soldier Magazine. This came with promotion and I ran the paper for two years. Then I was posted to Brecon looking after all PR matters for the army in Wales.

When we came to Wales, we created a wine bar in Abergavenny, a strongly held desire of my wife. I worked the bar in the evenings, but shortly after, was posted to RAF Strike Command at High Wycombe. I took the decision to resign and was immediately asked to start a newspaper for the Territorial Army in Wales.

But there was a snag, I had to join the TA, and go through officer training which I naively agreed to do. After a year